THE MILLIONA[

Black Enterprise Books provide useful information on a broad spectrum of business and general-interest topics, including entrepreneurship, personal and business finance, and career development. They are designed to meet the needs of the vital and growing African-American business market and to provide the information and resources that will help African Americans achieve their goals. The books are written by and about African-American professionals and entrepreneurs, and they have been developed with the assistance of the staff of *Black Enterprise*, the premier African-American business magazine.

The series currently includes the following books:

Titans of the B.E. 100s:
Black CEOs Who Redefined and Conquered American Business
by Derek T. Dingle

Black Enterprise Guide to Starting Your Own Business
by Wendy Beech

The Millionaires' Club:
How to Start and Run Your Own Investment Club—and Make Your
Money Grow!
by Carolyn M. Brown

The following books are forthcoming:

The Black Enterprise Straightforward Guide to Investing
by James Anderson

Against the Odds: Ten Inspiring Stories of Successful
African-American Entrepreneurs
by Wendy Beech

Take a Lesson: A Mentoring Guide for African Americans
by Caroline Clarke

THE MILLIONAIRES' CLUB

How to Start and Run Your Own Investment Club—and Make Your Money Grow!

Carolyn M. Brown

John Wiley & Sons, Inc.

New York • Chichester • Weinheim • Brisbane • Singapore • Toronto

To my big sister, Evelyn Kay Parker,
thanks for all your love and support.

Published by John Wiley & Sons, Inc.
Published simultaneously in Canada.

This publication is designed to provide accurate and authoritative information in
regard to the subject matter covered. It is sold with the understanding that the
publisher is not engaged in rendering legal, accounting, or other professional
services. If legal advice or other expert assistance is required, the services of a
competent professional person should be sought.

ISBN: 0-471-36938-1

CONTENTS

Part I: How to Form an Investment Club

Introduction   3

Chapter 1 • Think, Save, and Grow Rich: Getting Started   6

Chapter 2 • All for One, One for All: Recruiting Members   17

Chapter 3 • Great Minds Think Alike: Developing
            an Investment Strategy   29

Chapter 4 • Serious Business: Forming the Club's
            Legal Structure   40

Chapter 5 • Rules to Live By: Designing
            Operating Procedures   69

Chapter 6 • Meeting of the Minds: Running
            Meetings Smoothly and Effectively   81

Chapter 7 • Seven Key Principles to a Profitable Club:
            Following the Right Path to Investing   92

Chapter 8 • Sweat the Small Stuff: Recordkeeping and
            Other Taxing Issues   104

Chapter 9 • Do You Need a Broker? Buying and
            Selling Securities   127

Part II: How to Build a Prosperous Investment Portfolio

Chapter 10 • Grab the Bull by the Horns: Investing in
             the Stock Market   153

Chapter 11 • Invest in What You Know: Researching
             Stocks Like the Pros   176

Chapter 12 • Tools of the Trade: Using the Net and
             News to Find Data   203

Chapter 13 • Thinking Outside the Box: Investing
             beyond the Stock Market   228

Chapter 14 • Never Too Young to Invest: Building
             Youth Investment Clubs   244

Chapter 15 • The Next Frontier: Learning to
             Invest on Your Own   257

Epilogue   275

Notes   277

Index   281

Part I

HOW TO
FORM AN
INVESTMENT CLUB

INTRODUCTION

So you want to be a millionaire? Of course, who doesn't? But let's face it, the chance of Regis Philbin handing you a check for answering some mundane questions or Ed McMahon showing up at your door is one in a million.

If you want to become a millionaire, you have to do it the old-fashioned way—you have to earn it. However, the size of your paycheck has little to do with your ability to accumulate wealth. What counts is your ability to faithfully save and invest your hard-earned dollars, regardless if you make $25,000 or $250,000 a year.

You sweat for money all your working years, but wouldn't it be nice to have money working for you? Whether you are in your teens, early twenties, or mid-life, you can create future riches by constantly educating yourself, accumulating money regularly, and investing in stocks, bonds, mutual funds, and other securities.

The October 1990 issue of *Black Enterprise* magazine featured a cover story on the Evans family of Linden, New Jersey, who had launched an investment club—Family 7 Inc.—in 1985. The 12-member club comprised six couples, tied by blood and marriage to the Evans name, who were full-time professionals, including an insurance sales rep, a marketing director, a doctor, a homemaker, a minister, and a musician. Within five years of "clubbing" their investments, the group parlayed a $700 monthly savings into a portfolio of stocks, bonds, mutual funds, and real estate valued at $2.3 million. *Black Enterprise* readers responded overwhelmingly to the idea of collectively saving and investing money and requests for more information on how to go about it began pouring into the magazine.

The National Association of Investors Corporation, the industry trade organization representing investment clubs, hailed *Black Enterprise*

for its role in increasing investor awareness and club membership. This type of interest led to this how-to book on the subject as part of the *Black Enterprise*'s book series.

The Millionaires' Club: How to Start and Run Your Own Investment Club—and Make Your Money Grow! will tell you what an investment club is and is not. An investment club is a low-cost, low-risk way for a small group of people to pool their money to profit from stocks, mutual funds, and other securities. Clubs educate members on the fundamentals of investing and give sophisticated investors a platform to exchange investment strategies and financial analysis. As a group, club members have more money to invest and more investment choices.

But this book is more than a source of information. It is designed to inspire, showcasing more than 20 investment clubs made up of ordinary people who pooled their money to invest in the stock market—and who have been successful at growing wealth. Their stories are interwoven in each chapter to help you learn by example.

The Millionaires' Club will tell you what an investment club can and cannot do for you. Each chapter of *The Millionaires' Club* helps you devise a systematic, long-term approach to saving and investing as a group and on your own, whether you are a junior-high school student or a senior citizen. By joining an investment club, you will be part of the ranks of more than 700,000 members in the United States, with combined assets that now reach $175 billion. Joining an investment club will not automatically turn you into a millionaire. You have to take a brick-by-brick approach to building wealth. It takes time. And there's no time like the present to get started.

If African Americans are going to begin matching their academic and economic gains of the past few decades with progress on the financial front, it's going to require that more and more of us get down to the business of capital formation in our twenties and thirties. Just think what forty years of investing would mean by the time you enter your nonworking years. You would have more money for retirement—to make new purchases, travel, and live a richer life than the minimum standards that Social Security permits. A person who starts investing $100 per month in his or her twenties will accumulate more than $1 million by retirement age.

After reading this book, you will begin to see investment clubs as a workable formula for accumulating wealth and as a way for you to

provide future generations with the economic boost they need to get started. Learning the ins and outs of the stock market can be intimidating, but you wouldn't have bought this book if you weren't hungry for information about investing. We are hoping that you will find the material covered in these pages easy to digest—so much so that it makes the concept of collective saving and investment clubs the subject of dinner conversation in your home.

1

THINK, SAVE, AND GROW RICH: GETTING STARTED

Success is a journey, not a destination.
—Ben Sweetland

If you think poor, you are poor.
—Wally Amos

Everyone has heard about workplace lottery winners who've gotten rich together. All it took was $10 apiece for the group of machine-shop workers from Ohio to purchase 130 tickets at a local gas station to become winners of the largest Powerball jackpot ever—$165 million. Though the Lucky 13 may have struck it rich overnight, they still were betting on one-in-85-million odds of winning.

Many of those folks who didn't hit it big lost hundreds if not thousands of dollars trying to become millionaires. Week after week millions of people will faithfully buy tickets in hopes of having the "winning number" rather than diligently saving and growing their hard-earned capital by investing in the stock market. You may be one of them.

Let's say you spend a dollar a day (or $7 per week) on lottery tickets. That's $30–$31 per month and $365 per year that you are throwing away if you never win. For many folks, that $365 is a week's pay. Think about it: Would you be willing to go to work for a whole week and not get paid? Well, playing the lottery at that price is the equivalent of

working one week for free. You might as well have torn up your pay-check and tossed it in the trash.

Why take a gamble on your financial future? With the threat of Social Security becoming a minimal (if not obsolete) part of one's re-tirement income, you need to learn how to grow your money, not throw your money away. By putting aside a few dollars every month and giv-ing your money a chance to work for you, you can become a millionaire by the time you retire.

A more practical way for you and your friends to band together and accumulate wealth is to start an investment club. Such clubs have been around since the 1900s, but they have recently attracted great in-terest thanks to a raging bull market (when prices are up). The win-ning ways of an investment club are no mystery. In short, clubs offer a low-cost, low-risk way for novices to learn and profit from the com-plexities of stocks, bonds, mutual funds, and other investments.

Learning to use money wisely is the common thread connecting thousands of clubs in the United States. Furthermore, the concept of investment clubs has taken flight abroad: The World Federation of In-vestors is a European-based organization with membership through-out 17 nations.

Here's how it works: Groups of people pool their money to invest. The club requires members to plunk down a set amount of money each month, which it then uses to buy shares in securities—mostly stocks. Profits and dividends are plowed back into the portfolio until the club reaches its financial goal.

The appeal is simple: As a group, people with small amounts of money can consolidate their financial resources to make larger pur-chases of company shares. This way, investors can better diversify their investments and increase their money than by investing on their own. So, belonging to an investment club gives you more for your money while minimizing risk; it also helps ease the strain and rigor of picking stocks on your own.

The primary purpose of an investment club is to provide invest-ment education. "We want people to use what they learn as a group in terms of finding good stock purchases and then begin to build their own personal stock accounts outside of the club," says Robert Wynn, member of the NAIC Board of Trustees and Federal Reserve Board of Governors' Consumer Advisory Council.

Before you take the plunge into stock-infested waters, you need to shore up your basic knowledge of personal finance and investing.

"I highly recommend that members take classes through adult education programs at their local college," advises Wynn, who called on fellow members of the local Black Lawyers Association as well as his fraternity brothers from Kappa Alpha Psi Inc. to form the Madison Area Investment Club in Madison, Wisconsin. "Members should read fairly simple books on investing, such as Peter Lynch's *One Up On Wall Street* and Calvin Boston's *Smart Money Moves for African Americans*. . . . They should affiliate themselves with trade organizations."

For example, The Coalition of Black Investors (COBI: www .cobinvest.com), headquartered in Winston-Salem, North Carolina, is made up of some 1,400 member investment clubs. This investors' group offers various educational materials and provides lists of African-American brokers and brokerage firms. It also sponsors seminars on money management and investing. The National Association of Investors Corp. (NAIC: www.better-investing.com), a 48-year-old trade group in Madison Heights, Michigan, represents over 700,000 members, including investment clubs, computer groups, and young investors, with combined assets over $175 billion. NAIC has some 115 local chapters or councils throughout the United States. NAIC offers stock study courses, low-cost investment plans, and a series of reading materials, such as *Better Investing* magazine.

NAIC statistics show several clubs have been going strong after 25 years, many of which have amassed portfolios valued over $1 million. However, joining an investment club will not automatically turn you into an armchair millionaire. Even today's millionaires, including talk-show queen Oprah Winfrey, or the richest billionaire in the world, Microsoft's Bill Gates, didn't get where they are overnight. It took long, hard effort, time, and skill. Realistically, it is going to take years of consistent and concerted effort for you and your fellow club members to attain a portfolio worth millions of dollars.

THE GRANDFATHER OF ALL CLUBS

Frederick C. Russell gave birth to the modern investment-club movement in Detroit in 1940.[1] Unable to find a job and wanting to buy a small business, the recent college graduate formed the Mutual Investment Club as a vehicle for accumulating capital. The club had three

objectives: invest every month, reinvest all dividends, and buy stock in growth companies.

More than 50 years later, the club is still active. Membership has grown from six people to 22 (only 15 invest regularly). The value of the club's portfolio is worth more than $6 million, notwithstanding members who have withdrawn over $3 million from the club at one time or another.

Members made withdrawals at various times for such purposes as making downpayments on new homes, financing education for their children, and even funding start-up businesses and other small entrepreneurial ventures. Many of Mutual Investment Club's older members have accumulated $100,000 or more toward their retirement years. Russell's fellow club members have realized a gain of more than $250,000 each from monthly contributions of $10 to $25 during the club's lifetime.

Thousands of clubs have followed in the footsteps of the Mutual Investment Club. What's exceptional about investment clubs is that, over the past decade, two-thirds of all investment clubs have matched or beaten professional money managers at their own game.

Investment clubs have compounded annual earnings at an average rate of 14.96 percent (several individual clubs average a return of 21 percent). If those same members had invested in the Standard & Poor's 500 Index of stocks, their portfolios would have earned 12.25 percent. Such a professional track record puts money managers to shame. Only 19 percent from their ranks have managed to beat the S&P over that same period of time.

Beyond delivering superb performance, an investment club provides a simple and generally cheap way to enter financial markets. Investment-club membership can be a lifelong experience. It only works when members stick with it long term. Those clubs that fold early on usually do because of a get-rich-quick mentality among members.

CULTURAL TRADITIONS FOR POOLING MONEY

Long before Frederick Russell, people had been coming together for decades to pool their finances. Historically, models of group-savings plans can be found in America's immigrant communities: West Indians use *susu*, Africans have *ekoubs*, and Asians have *gaes*. Generally, these are family-run pools, and the money is used to set up business shops, buy homes, pay for weddings, and fund education.

In general, these pools work similarly. A group of 10 to 20 people invest a set amount of money each week or month. One person in the group receives the full amount. The process is repeated on a weekly basis until everyone has a turn. So, if 10 people contribute $100 each week, each person receives his or her $1,000 (minus an agreed-upon token sum paid to the banker, who is a member designated to hold and distribute the money).

It's not unheard of for the banker to skip off with the group's funds. This emphasizes a major down side of these pools—they have no legal status or recourse. Nor are they designed to be long-term arrangements for accumulating savings. A big difference between these dealings and investment clubs is that the former doesn't offer any interest on the pooled money.

Many people, especially African Americans, are familiar with *susus.* Unfortunately, there are scores of folks who are unaware of the advantages of forming an investment club, which is a much safer and more profitable way to save money as a group.

You want to start an investment club for fun, education, and profit. One of the benefits of forming your own club is that you start the learning curve at the same time that everyone else does. To help you get started, test your investment knowledge in Figure 1.1.[2] Given the right resources and steadfast commitment, members will reap the financial rewards of belonging to a formal, legalized investment group.

THE REWARDS OF INVESTING

It is important to understand the difference between saving and investing money. *Saving* refers to putting money aside for a rainy day in a bank account, including that popular Christmas club account that your parents opened for you. Your money draws a little interest and you can get to it whenever you need it.

On the other hand, *investing* is when you put money aside but are not worried about the immediate accessibility of your cash (or *liquidity*). Instead, you are buying stocks, bonds, properties, or anything you think will increase in value over a period of time. Most people have yet to discover this art of using money to make money.

One of the reasons that investing over a long period of time is so profitable is that your earnings compound (Figure 1.2) and, as a result, grow by larger and larger amounts. The concept of compound interest is simple—you earn interest on your initial deposit *and* the interest.

Figure 1.1 Test Your Investment Club IQ

Whether you intend to start your own club or join an existing group, you need to gauge just how much you do (or don't) know about investing. The following test is designed to help you better understand the ins and outs of investment clubs. Your responses to the following questions provide a framework for getting started.

Please check true or false for the statements below:

1. Most clubs are formed by family members, co-workers, and/or friends. True _____ False _____

True. The ties that often bind investment clubs are relatives, friends, and/or co-workers. Clubs also are often organized around people from already established social ties, such as sports teams, church congregations, fraternities/sororities, or civic groups.

2. Many clubs stay together for more than 10 years. True _____ False _____

True. Though most married couples may experience the seven-year itch, a number of clubs have been together long enough to celebrate their silver and golden anniversaries.

3. Many clubs split due to bickering members. True _____ False _____

True. If you think it's tough for you and your mate to decide whether to see an action flick or a romantic comedy, imagine trying to get 20 people to be of like mind when it comes to money. Most clubs get off to a shaky start, because disputes arise over members, dues, and investment picks—choosing the right stocks means discussion and, often, dissension.

4. The average club size is more than 20 people. True _____ False _____

False. Size does matter when it comes to chemistry. Bigger does not necessarily mean better. Investment clubs tend to recruit anywhere between 10 and 25 members. Any club with fewer than 10 members may have trouble raising adequate investment capital, whereas larger clubs may become too unwieldy and divisive.

5. Members must pay an initial ante of $1,000 to join plus monthly dues anywhere from $100 to $500. True _____ False _____

False. Although clubs with deep-pocketed members can afford to shell out that kind of money, most clubs ask up front for $100 dollars per member, and monthly dues anywhere from $25 to $50. Whatever the amount, members must fork up their share each and every month, whether the market is in a boom, recession, depression, or recovery phase.

6. Investment clubs are passive organizations whereby members merely pay monthly dues and show up for a meeting or two during the year. True _____ False _____

False. Slackers need not apply. Everyone is expected to play an active role, including conducting research and handling administrative duties.

(continued)

Figure 1.1 *(Continued)*

7. An investment club is a formal arrangement between partners.
   True _____ False _____

   True. Clubs don't just happen—they must operate within a legal structure. Though some are incorporated, most are formed as partnerships. Also,
   every club has bylaws—a written statement of procedures, processes, and
   officers' roles (e.g., president, vice president, and treasurer).

8. You must have previous knowledge about investing in the stock market in
   order to join or form an investment club. True _____ False _____

   False. Green—or inexperienced—investors form or belong to many
   investment clubs. A club is an ideal way for new investors to learn and understand investing, and a great way for experienced investors to sharpen their
   investment skills, get new ideas from friends, keep up to date on economic
   trends, and find new opportunities. Be patient. The business and administrative part of starting an investment club could take a year before you even
   invest in your first stock.

9. Most clubs actually lose money the first two years in existence.
   True _____ False _____

   True. In the first year or two, many clubs show losses or only small gains.
   As club members gain knowledge and experience, their portfolio grows expo-
   nentially.

10. Clubs rely solely on the stock picks of brokers and money managers.
    True _____ False _____

    False. A professional money manager brings experience and knowledge
    about the stock market, but final investment decisions are made by members,
    who usually end up taking crash courses in the world of securities when they
    join the club.

Add up your score. If your total is between 8 and 10 correct, you're financially savvy. You have more knowledge about investment clubs than most
people. If you answered 5 to 7 questions correctly, you're on the right path but
you need to brush up on your investment knowledge. Less than 5 correct:
don't fret, although you may have your work cut out for you.

Whatever your score, keep in mind that this IQ test is not meant to be a
gauge of your ability or inability to invest. The idea is to use what you learned
about yourself to help organize your club easily and properly and to assist
you along the road to becoming a better investor.

Figure 1.2   The Power of Compound Interest: Annual
Investment Required to Reach $100,000

Interest Rate	Years							
	5	10	15	20	25	30	35	40
5%	$17,236.00	$7,572.00	$4,414.00	$2,880.00	$1,966.00	$1,433.00	$1,054.00	$788.39
6%	16,736.00	7,157.00	4,053.00	2,565.00	1,720.00	1,193.00	846.59	609.58
7%	16,254.00	6,764.00	3,719.00	2,280.00	1,478.00	989.39	676.08	468.14
8%	15,783.00	6,392.00	3,410.00	2,024.00	1,267.00	817.36	537.34	357.42
9%	15,332.00	6,039.00	3,124.00	1793.00	1,083.00	673.06	425.31	271.52
10%	14,890.00	5,704.00	2,661.00	1,587.00	924.37	552.66	335.43	205.40
11%	14,467.00	5,388.00	2,618.00	1,403.00	787.41	452.67	263.74	154.84
12%	14,055.00	5,088.00	2,395.00	1,239.00	669.64	369.97	206.41	116.40
13%	13,658.00	4,805.00	2,190.00	1,070.00	568.67	301.83	168.00	87.29
14%	13,270.00	4,536.00	2,001.00	963.69	482.32	245.86	126.47	65.36
15%	12,898.00	4,283.00	1,828.00	848.82	408.64	200.02	98.68	48.88

Example: By investing $924.37 per year earning an interest rate of 10% in 25 years, you would have a total of $100,000.

Source: The Black Woman's Guide to Financial Independence by Cheryl D. Broussard, Penquin Books, 1996.

To get a better idea, look at some raw figures. Start with investing $100 a month. After compounding 6 percent interest on the initial investment, you would amass $16,470 over 10 years and $46,435 in 20 years. Take that return to the stock market—using the 12 percent annual return posted by the S&P 500 as your benchmark—in 20 years, your treasured savings has grown to $99,915. If you were able to invest $100 a month in a vehicle that produced an average rate of return of 30 percent, you would earn $1.5 million in 20 years.

One of the easiest ways to calculate the effects of compounding, and one which bankers and financial advisers often refer to is the *Rule of 72* (Figure 1.3). This rule states that if an asset grows x percent a year, its value will double in 72 ÷ x years. For example: How long will it take for an investment that is growing by 10 percent a year to double in value? Answer: 72 ÷ 10, or 7.2 years.

Most people save and invest for short-term goals, like buying a car, or long-term goals, such as supplementing their retirement income. There are at least five key reasons why you, your family, and friends should invest:[3]

1. *Earn money.* Too many people think that bringing home a paycheck is the only way to earn money. They may realize business ownership is a source of income, but they rarely consider

Figure 1.3   The Rule of 72 for $1,000

Rate of Return	4%	6%	8%	10%	12%
Years					
6					$2,000
7.2			$2,000		
9		$2,000			
12		$2,000			
14.4				$4,000	
18	$2,000		$2,000		$8,000
21.6				$8,000	
24		$4,000			$16,000
27			$8,000		
28.8				$16,000	
30					$32,000
Final Amount (36 years)	$4,000	$8,000	$16,000	$32,000	$64,000

Example: 12% rate of return, your $1,000 will double in six years.

Source: The Black Woman's Guide to Financial Independence by Cheryl D. Broussard, Penquin Books, 1996.

the possibility that, by owning shares of stock, they themselves are participating in business ownership and business profits.

2. *Build a lifetime of financial success.* Financial success grows out of the assets you build over a period of time. Investing brings the deeper and more lasting rewards of security and the economic power that comes from accumulation of wealth.

3. *Time is on your side.* There are good times on Wall Street (bull market) and bad times (bear market). Stock prices go up and down but, over the long haul, they always go up and patient stockholders profit from that trend.

4. *Own a piece of corporate America.* They money you invest helps companies buy facilities and equipment they need to do business or to turn a creative idea into an exciting new enterprise. If the businesses you have contributed to make money, you have a claim to a share of the profits.

5. *Have a little fun.* Sports fans never seem to tire of trying to predict who is going to win the big game. Investors are trying to pick winners, too. The teams they are rooting for have names like AT&T, Intel, Disney, and Nike. Sometimes investors, like

sports fans, play a hunch. If they are smart, they base their choices on research and reliable information.

LOW-COST, LOW-RISK INVESTING

You don't have to have a lot of money to own a piece of America.[4] Just ask the Dividend Divas and Dons Investment Club of Baltimore, Maryland. Thanks to the support of their local community and NAIC's Maryland Council, eight club members are making a Healthy Start in investing in the stock market.

Members contribute as little as $5 per month; all are participants in Healthy Start, a federally funded program that targets areas with high infant-mortality rates, providing jobs and employment opportunities. Through the investment club, low-income families are learning about managing their personal finances and investing in the stock market.

Some members were initially skeptical of the club's lofty goals and the push to get them to invest in Wall Street. "You don't want to put your money in something that is not there down the road," explains Victoria Ellis, the club's secretary. However, "the club has showed us how to save money as well as build a financial future." Now she's teaching her 12-year-old son. "We read the business pages together every day."

The Divas and Dons were fortunate enough to get assistance from NAIC's Advisory Service to help them deal with the legal issues of organizing and structuring the club. Members also are getting schooled on the fundamentals of investing with the aid of directors from NAIC's local chapter, who teach courses on picking stocks.

The club's vice president, Keysha Goodwin, a 20-year-old business major at Coppin State University, admits that her education has just begun, although she knows how to find the nuts and bolts about companies and why that's important: "There is so much to learn. When do businesses increase their shares? What makes them split? What makes a business go public?" she asks.

The club held its first meeting in May 1997 and purchased their first shares in Baltimore Gas and Electric. Impressed with their efforts, the Women's Investment Growth Club, based in nearby Columbia, donated ten shares of BGE to help the group get started.

The group then added 40 shares using their monthly dues and donations from local businesses, such as the Chapman Company, one of the largest minority-owned brokerages in the country, owned by Nate

Chapman. The Chapman Company is also providing education and brokerage services to the Divas and Dons. In fact, their broker doesn't miss a club meeting.

The club chose to buy BGE stock because the utility was something the women were familiar with, says Ellis. "Everybody needs gas and electric. I pay my bill each month, but being a shareholder means I can go down there and walk up to the building and say I own a little piece of this company, even if it is a little pebble," she adds.

Since the company is located in their own backyard, it made even more sense for the club to invest in the utility company. Members also discussed the fact that BGE paid dividends and had a track record of stability. Their research showed that the company may not grow really quickly, it wasn't going to plummet with the market either.

The Divas and Dons are learning that, short of being an entrepreneur, stock ownership is the most direct way for investors to be part owners in a company. The more money the company makes, the greater the potential for the price of the stock to appreciate and the dividends to increase. At the same time, if the earnings dwindle, the stock's price and possibly dividends are likely to decrease. As that company prospers and grows, so does your club's investment portfolio.

For many new to the stock market, there is fear and concern about the possibility of losing hard-earned cash. The problem is financial ignorance. Money doesn't come with an owner's manual, nor do most folks learn about it in school. Instead, people pick up tidbits from family members, friends, and co-workers. Once people become educated, they soon come to realize there is a greater probability of building larger profits by investing in the stock market.

CONCLUSION

In forming an investment club, you are joining the thousands of other men and women who are following the profitable path of learning how to invest by doing it. Aside from sheer capital growth, you share with them the opportunity to gain experience that you can apply to a wide range of investments. Not only will you learn to enhance the club's till, but to build your own personal-investment portfolio and accumulate wealth to finance your children's education, travel the world, or avoid the money blues during your golden years.

2

ALL FOR ONE, ONE FOR ALL: RECRUITING MEMBERS

There are four rungs on the ladder of success: Plan purposefully, prepare prayerfully, proceed positively, pursue persistently.

—African American folklore

It was a regular social gathering—food, fun, and family games—that spawned the Organization Investment Club in Beaumont, Texas, in 1986. It was the idea of eight young relatives to accrue capital as a family unit by pooling their money and, at the same time, maintaining family ties. The club started out as family only, but has now opened up membership to friends as well—mostly couples.

Once a month, meetings are held at a different member's home. "We have dinner, we talk, we socialize together. But when we meet it is strictly business. We sit down and discuss the stock holdings in our portfolio—what we are going to buy, sell, or hold," says Vay Smith, the club's financial secretary. All together, the club owns shares in 15 stocks, including Maytag, AT&T, IBM, Cifra, Apple Computers, Reliant Energy, and Wal-Mart—one of the first stocks the group purchased and its biggest performer.

There have been squabbles here and there, but members have learned how "to agree to disagree," says the club's president, Eddy Bossette, who, along with his wife, Pat, are the only original members remaining. "Those of us who are in the club now have been together for

ten years," he adds. With the average age of the Organization's members around 55, most are saving for retirement. In an effort to build intergenerational wealth, several members have helped their children organize the Unlimited Investment Club, which comprises 15 youth from eight years of age to 25. Says Bossette, "We want them to have a better life than we had and to pass it on."

Groups like the Organization Investment Club know firsthand that all it takes to get started is for one person to believe that you can make money in the stock market and to convey that conviction to others. While you may have the right attitude about investing, make sure that you recruit like-minded individuals.

Where to get started? It isn't necessary for you to enlist all the members yourself. Just talk to two or three friends. If they are interested, ask each of them to find others who might want to join an investment club.

Bossette and members of the Organization are by no means unique; many clubs are formed by relatives. Even though it may be a comfort to invest with family and friends, this doesn't mean that club members have to be bosom buddies. If you belong to an organization such as a neighborhood social club, a church group, or a service club, you may have a ready-made group of people who'll be interested in forming an investment club. Frat brothers and sorority sisters are all natural candidates. If you belong to a sports league, what about your teammates?

Don't overlook co-workers. Several clubs are formed by people who work together, because it is a lot easier in some ways. The biggest complaint among club members is finding a convenient time and place to meet each month, as people often come up with a lot of excuses at the last minute as to why they can't meet. Well, you can catch up with the people you work with—you see them all the time. You know their schedules. You can talk about club news over the water cooler.

Still, it is best to start a club with co-workers with whom you are friendly and socialize already—whether you eat lunch together or go shopping after work. It's fine to mix staff members and managers as long as everyone gets along.

Also, many clubs are wary of tapping a membership entirely from the office. A little variety in the occupations or interests of members may be useful to setting up and running the club. Ideally, you want to round out your club with various club members' experiences and skills.

For some clubs, age makes little difference, with members ranging from teens to people in their eighties. For others, age plays a major role in how members invest their money. A club formed by Generation Xers just starting their careers may tend to be more aggressive than a club of midlife civil workers. If your club is truly going to work, it requires good working relationships.

BY INVITATION ONLY: A CALL TO MEMBERS

Once you have identified who you want to join your group, send out formal invitations—setting a time two to three weeks in the future—asking select potential members to come to an introductory meeting to discuss the idea of forming a club.

You may decide to have more than one preliminary meeting to assess whether there is strong enough interest to proceed, and to help distinguish between the merely curious and truly serious. You can see if potential members are on the same page by having them fill out an application form (Figure 2.1). There are a number of issues you will want to go over before actually scheduling a meeting:[1]

- How many people to invite and should those invited be encouraged to bring others? You can invite a large group to ensure that enough people attend, since everyone who is called to join the club may not do so.
- Should those who fail to attend the first meeting be invited to subsequent meetings?
- Will the club be for men only, women, or both?
- Should personal income be considered? You may decide you only want to invite those people who can afford to contribute a specific amount.
- What is the time frame for forming the club or abandoning the idea? This will vary with each group and depend, to some degree, on your personal tolerance level. Some clubs take months to get off the ground.

If potential members stop attending preliminary meetings or cannot agree on how to proceed with the club, you may want to start

Figure 2.1 Evaluating Club Candidates

Windy City Investment Club
N.A.I.C. member since 1991

Application for Membership

Personal Data:

Name: (Print and Sign)

Address:

Phone No:

Occupation:

1. Have you ever been a member of an investment club?

2. Why do you want to join an investment club?

3. Can you realistically afford $50.00 dues per month? _____Yes _____No

4. Can you attend regularly scheduled meetings the first Saturday of every month?

5. Do you have time in addition to the monthly meeting to commit to the club?

6. Are you willing to commit to the club for 5 years?   _____Yes _____No

7. What is your personal investment philosophy?

8. What investment experience, if any, do you have?

all over again with a new group. You don't want to risk forming a club with people who can't get along.

You may even end up forming more than one club, as did the Allen Ministries. In the fall of 1997 at the regular men's Bible Study Forum, the brothers of Allen A.M.E. Church began to look at how to involve themselves and their families in the economic development of their community as well as how to participate on Wall Street. As a resolution for the new year, they explored the concept of starting an investment club. In January 1998, the Allen Investment Ministries (AIM) was born, serving both the men and women of the Jamaica, Queens, New York church and surrounding neighborhood.

Under the leadership of former U.S. Representative Rev. Dr. Floyd A. Flake, the congregation of the Allen A.M.E. Church has grown to exceed 12,000 members, requiring four different services each Sunday. Not surprisingly, when an invitation was extended to its members to form AIM, a staggering 336 people rushed to sign up.

Aside from the difficulties of managing such a large number of people in one organization, the Securities Exchange Commission (SEC)—the governing body of the securities industry—restricts the number of individuals who may belong to an investment club that is organized as a partnership to a maximum of 99 members. Therefore, AIM reorganized, forming 11 separate investment clubs, each with its own name and officers.

Each club now has an average of 43 members. Meetings are held in the banquet hall located in the Cathedral (the church's new home), which was dedicated in September of 1997. AIM, which functions as an association of the individual clubs, continues to serve the 11 different groups by coordinating the educational classes and seminars. AIM also schedules guest speakers to address such topics as portfolio management, selecting mutual funds, developing an individual investment portfolio, full service brokers versus discount brokers versus online brokers, and purchasing and financing a home. The objective of AIM is to provide guidance to its members and to teach "Financial Stewardship"—managing your finances from a biblical perspective.

"During the first three months of their membership, each new member of one of the AIM investment clubs is put on a probationary status," says Ewan D. Anderson, Esq., AIM's president. "We want the members to see how much work is involved in running a successful club, and how much work is required of each member. When the probationary period expires, each person is given an opportunity to decide if they want

to continue their membership," Anderson explains. "Furthermore, during this period the probationary member is required to be financially current; however their contributions are not invested, rather they are held in escrow until the end of the probationary period. This avoids having to liquidate the club's investments, should a probationary member decide that he or she does not wish to continue his or her membership."

There are three things you want to keep in mind in the selection of members for the club:

1. *Compatibility.* Club members should enjoy one another's company. Belonging to a club will put a further strain on the working or personal relationships of colleagues or friends who are at odds. Remember, members are embarking on a long-term program that may last the rest of their lives. A club isn't right for anyone who doesn't like to work in a group, especially given that all decisions will be put to a vote.

2. *Shared investment outlook.* Members should share the same investment goals and objectives. The group should adopt an investment philosophy it wishes to follow in order to prevent a fundamental disagreement at a later date. Since the premise of a club is to reap long-term gains, people who want to trade in and out of the market can be a sore spot.

3. *Teamwork.* All prospective club members should be prepared to investigate and analyze securities and to make periodic reports. Keep in mind, people are going to bring their usual poor work habits to the club. You want people who are truly dedicated, which means meeting each month and sharing the workload.

While an investment club can offer a pleasant social opportunity, anyone who regards the monthly activity as simply a night out presents a problem, and may hinder the club's progress. Those individuals who recognize that they are making a commitment that may involve them in a life-long program of investing and financial study are likely to be the best members.

A CALL TO ORDER: THE FIRST MEETING

The invitations are out and the responses are back. Now you are ready to meet. Make it clear to all that the first meeting is for discussion and that attendance is not a commitment to join.[2] This meeting is primarily

for the purpose of explaining why members should join, what will be expected of those who do join, and how the club will operate. The goal is to ensure that all potential members understand what belonging to an investment club involves.

To enhance the discussion, you might want to send out membership surveys along with the invitations (Figure 2.2), a sample partnership

---

Figure 2.2   Membership Survey Questions

---

1. Describe your tolerance for risk concerning the money you have and are willing to invest in the club from month to month.
   a. Very conservative
   b. Moderately conservative
   c. Moderately aggressive
   d. Very aggressive

2. How important is it to you that the club have significant cash on hand or securities that can easily be converted into cash?
   a. Very important
   b. Moderately important
   c. Somewhat important
   d. Not important

3. If having cash readily available is a big deal for you, what percentage of the club's assets should be set aside for this purpose?
   a. 10%
   b. 15%
   c. 25%
   d. 50%
   e. Other _____

4. How important is it that you get back the actual dollars that you put into the club?
   a. Very important
   b. Somewhat important
   c. Not important

5. What is the average annual rate of growth you expect the club's portfolio to achieve?
   a. 10%
   b. 15%
   c. 20%
   d. Other _____

6. What areas are you most interested in pursuing? Rank in order of importance.
   a. Securities (stocks, bonds, and mutual funds)   _____
   b. Real estate   _____

(continued)

Figure 2.2 *(Continued)*

c. Entrepreneurial ventures   _____

d. Other (specify)   _____

7. What investments are you most interested in the club pursuing over the next two to five years?

_____

_____

_____

8. What areas are you personally interested in learning about? Rank in order of preference.

a. Budgeting   _____

b. Financial planning   _____

c. Tax planning   _____

d. Estate planning   _____

e. Retirement planning   _____

f. Insurance   _____

g. Stocks   _____

h. Bonds   _____

i. Mutual funds   _____

j. Treasuries   _____

k. Commodities   _____

l. Art, gold, silver, stamps, and gems   _____

m. Other areas (specify) _____

9. How do you think club members can become better educated about investments and ultimately become more financially savvy?

a. Invite guest speakers   _____

b. Bring in a financial advisor   _____

c. Require certain reading   _____

d. Assign each member particular areas to research   _____

e. Other (specify) _____

10. On average, how much time per month do you think members should devote to research and related activities outside of the club's general monthly meetings?

a. 1–3 hours   _____

b. 3–5 hours   _____

c. 5–10 hours   _____

d. Other _____

Any general comments?

agreement, and articles of incorporation (discussed in more detail in Chapters 4 and 5). Potential members should be asked to review the sample agreement and to be prepared to answer the following questions:

- How serious are you about joining an investment club?
- What did you think of the sample partnership agreement? What ideas do you have about the club's legal structure?
- In what type of securities should the club invest?
- Are you interested in investing solely in securities or would you like the club to invest in other projects, such as real-estate properties?
- What amount would you suggest as a joining fee?
- How often and when can you meet?

You may want to invite a financial advisor or an experienced member of a successful investment club to attend the first meeting to serve as a resource. At the end of this discussion, ask for a show of hands of those who feel they would like to continue with the organization of an investment club.

MEMBERSHIP SURVEYS

Surveys are critical to the survival of the club because they will help clarify the club's goals, what members hope to gain from being in a club, and the amount of time, money, and effort they are willing to collectively contribute to make the club a success. These surveys also will help the club to develop an investment philosophy and to focus on the types of investments that make members enthusiastic about belonging to a club.

Assessing members' attitudes about investing will also help the club to address members' concerns and resolve problems. Keep in mind that members' feelings and notions about investing are likely to change over time, so you use membership surveys on a regular basis.

The survey questions in Figure 2.2 will help you get into the heads of potential members.

THE NEXT STEPS

If at least five people are interested and indicate they want to form a club, you can then proceed with the following steps.

Set a Regular Meeting Date

You will first need to set a date within the next month when all who want to join the club will be invited to return. Initial investment deposits can be collected at that time. Agree on a regular time and place to meet each month. It should be the same day or night of the month, say every third Saturday at 3 P.M. This makes it easier for members to plan, and should boost attendance and dedication to your club. Also decide where you will meet—in the church basement, office conference room, public library, or a member's home? Most clubs rotate meetings among members' homes.

Decide the Amount of Monthly Deposit

Discuss and pass a motion for dues. Your club may require an initial ante of $100 per member to cover certain start-up costs, such as buying accounting software and research materials, and opening a checking account. After that first significant deposit, most clubs decrease the amount for regular dues to between $20 and $50 monthly. It all depends on what members feel comfortable investing. There are some clubs where members pay $200 each month. Others, like the Organization, start out paying $10; dues have since gone up to $40 a month.

While it is not necessary, many club members make equal contributions in the club the first year, after which, some members may wish to vary their deposits—those who can afford it may kick in additional money that month.

During the first 12 months of their membership, the monthly investment of an AIM club member is restricted to $20 per month. Thereafter, each member may continue to invest the $20 minimum or he or she may invest up to a maximum of $100 per month. "New members join the clubs with enthusiasm brought on by the infectious fever created by media hype," says Anderson. "However, the leaders of AIM believe that during a member's initial introduction to investing, that individual must concentrate on developing the skills necessary to be a prudent and successful investor, and he or she must develop the habit of systematic investing and saving, regardless of what the market is doing."

Anderson further explains, "We do not want a new member to be unduly concerned about what is happening to their investment on a

minute-by-minute or day-by-day basis. We teach the basics and later that member can get re-infected with the fever."

Your club must use due diligence concerning recordkeeping procedures to permit the receipt of varying deposits, the acceptance of new recruits, and how their deposits will be handled.

Decide How and Where to Invest Your Funds

This is a scary proposition for any club—especially since many members will be new to the markets when they join. Most investment clubs stash their cash in stocks—and with good reason: Since 1926, stocks have packed an average annual return of 10.9 percent, compared to, say, 5.6 percent for corporate bonds.

The Organization has its $100,000 portfolio invested in *blue chips*—the biggest and brightest of stocks—such as Exxon, AT&T, and IBM, as well as small companies, mutual funds, and such high-risk investments as new stocks issues or IPOs (Initial Public Offerings). The club's somewhat aggressive investment style has averaged the group a 28 percent rate of return.

The stocks held by each of the AIM clubs include Bell Atlantic, AT&T, Oracle, EMC, Compaq, Lucent Technologies, Home Depot, Wal-Mart, Sara Lee, Tommy Hilfiger, Pfizer Pharmaceuticals, Bank of New York, Goldman Sachs, and Waste Management. Collectively, the 11 clubs control roughly $250,000 in assets.

It is important that you ask a series of questions to assess how members feel about particular types of securities. Be specific: Would they like to see the club invest strictly in stocks, bonds, mutual funds, and/or real estate, or even entrepreneurial ventures?

Decide on the Club Name

Come up with a club name that fits your group. Be creative. Pick a first and second choice—just in case another club or entity may be doing business under that name.

Each of the AIM clubs has adopted similar partnership agreements and bylaws. Every club has its own identity and name derived from the Bible, for instance: Solomon, 2 Corinthians, Joseph, Matthew, Genesis, and Revelations.

Discuss the Operation of the Club

Talk over the adoption of the club's operating agreement and bylaws (to be discussed in more detail in Chapter 5). Most clubs operate as partnerships rather than incorporating. Club members must report investment income or losses on their individual tax returns. A written statement of procedures and processes for running the club and addressing members' needs is called the bylaws.

The adopted bylaws require each member to complete all of the training classes that AIM establishes, particularly those conducted by the NAIC. "Because we are able to guarantee sufficient participants, the local chapter of the NAIC agreed to conduct their classes onsite for AIM members," says Anderson. Classes are held on Saturday mornings. He adds that more than 50 percent of the clubs' activities involve education and training.

In selecting a particular company to invest in, the clubs try to select companies that are socially conscious. In other words, companies like the Philip Morris Company, which manufactures Marlboro brand cigarettes and owns Miller Brewing Company, bottler of Miller Beer brands, are off limits. Anderson notes that sometimes problems may not come to light until after the investment has been made, at which point, the clubs may choose to voice their concerns to management via shareholders meetings.

CONCLUSION

Just keep in mind, if you cast a wide a net, you will have a better chance of bringing into your club people with diverse interests and areas of expertise. For instance, one group has an engineer for a member who follows the club's high-tech holdings. Your club might recruit a doctor who could offer some inside knowledge about companies in the pharmaceutical, medical supplies, or health services industry. Indeed, the company you keep could influence your club's potential.

3

GREAT MINDS THINK ALIKE: DEVELOPING AN INVESTMENT STRATEGY

Economics do not dictate a level of intelligence. However, economics do dictate opportunity.

—Bill Cosby

Husband and wife André and Medina Jett, along with fellow colleague Greg Smith, formed Enterprising Minority Investors (EMI) in 1991. The founding partners drafted the operating agreement and devised the by-laws. The club was open to everyone living in the greater Hartford, Connecticut area—as long as he or she was a young, African-American professional who was willing to invest in the stock market.

After the first meeting, 13 people joined. It was the first sign of bad luck for the group. The new club was beset with problems, namely infighting among members, who couldn't agree on how the club should be run and how the money should be invested.

For instance, there was one doctor in the club who liked to invest in penny stocks (small company stocks that sell for under $1 and have no track record). "He would buy something one day and sell it the next," explains Medina, who disagreed with his mentality of speculative trading. The Jetts and Smith wanted the club to stick with a more traditional buy-and-hold or wait-and-see approach to the market.

"We said from the very beginning that the term of the club would be at least 20 years, so everyone who joined could expect to stay with

the club until the year 2011," she adds. "With that in mind, we thought a long-term investment strategy was the way to go. But that turned out to be the thinking of Greg, André, and myself. As we brought new members into the club, they didn't necessarily agree with the investment strategy we already had in place."

Members argued about how much risk they were willing to take on. There were those who, instead of voicing their concerns, simply wouldn't show up at the meetings. As a result, EMI lost six members within the first year. That's okay with the Jetts, Smith, and remaining members who share the same level of commitment and investment philosophy.

EMI learned from the school of hard knocks that coming up with an investment strategy is one of the most important decisions that a club will make. It will guide your club's selection of investments, determine the overall direction of the group, and define the club's short-, intermediate-, and long-term goals.

Some clubs use surveys to help guide the development of their investment strategy and to assess changes in that philosophy over time. Other clubs rely on a process of elimination to arrive at the most appropriate strategy for investing their funds.

In answering the question of how to invest the club's money, members need to take into account several considerations: How much time will they devote to the club? What is the investment objective of the group? What rate of return do members expect on investments? What level of risk is tolerable for the group?

- *Time.* Honesty is the best policy when it comes to assessing if members have the necessary time and energy for managing the club's portfolio. The amount of time each member has to contribute to the activities of the club will vary, but everyone has a responsibility to attend meetings, research and vote on securities, and undertake special assignments when called on.

- *Investment objective.* The group's investment goal is to achieve capital appreciation over time, but individuals will have their own agendas. The group needs to know up front what members plan do with their percentage of the pot. How soon are they looking to get at the funds? Are they more concerned about long-term investment goals, such as supplementing their retirement income, or shorter-term goals like footing the bill for their children's college tuition?

- *Rate of return.* NAIC states a club's investment goal ought to be to attain an average growth in prices and dividend income of 14.9 percent compounded annually. At this rate of return, the club will double the value of its holdings every five years. A 15-member club in which members fork over $150 each month should amass a portfolio worth about $100,000 in five years, $400,000 in 15 years, and $1.6 million in 20 years. Equally, the club should realize a 4 percent to 6 percent yield (rate of return) over time on an investment from dividend income. So, if a stock sells for $20 and pays an annual dividend of $2 per share, it has a yield of 10 percent.

- *Risk tolerance.* A key factor in developing an investment strategy is the relationship between risk and potential return. Everyone wants to get whopping returns on their money, but few people are willing to lose a dime. However, investments in which there is very little risk of losing money generally generate a relatively low rate of return. Ventures where there is a considerable risk of losing money have the potential to generate high returns, mainly because they have to pay a lot more in order to persuade people to invest in them. Experienced investors understand that there are times for avoiding risk and times when a calculated degree of risk is in order.

RISKY BUSINESS: INVESTING THE CLUB'S FUNDS

We all take risks every day, whether it's driving on the freeway each morning to work or meeting someone on a blind date. There are folks who may love the same thing yet experience different levels of risk. Take, for instance, a Caribbean vacation. A group of people could travel to the same destination all with the purpose of having fun. Some folks will go to the beach and lay on the sand while they read a book and soak up a few rays of sun. Others will take a swim in the crystal-blue ocean. Still more adventurous people will jet ski or parasail, while the do-or-die folks will go deep-sea scuba diving hoping to avoid an encounter with sharks.

As a group of vacationers, it doesn't matter who enjoys doing what—to each his or her own. When it comes to investing as a group, everyone has to be on the same plane. Otherwise, your club will be pulled in too many different directions and your portfolio will take a nosedive.

It is important that members understand that every investment has some degree of risk. One kind of investment is not necessarily better than another. The goal is to develop a mix of investments that will help your club achieve a balance of risk and potential return.

There are four basic categories of investments and risk:

1. *Safety of principal.* The main objective is preservation of capital. This category includes money-market accounts and certificates of deposit (CDs), available at your local bank or savings and loan. CDs are issued for a period of three months to five years or longer. They usually pay interest on a monthly or quarterly basis, with a penalty if you cash them in before *maturity* (the date when you will get paid back). Other safe investments include *treasuries,* issued at a discount by the U.S. Treasury and guaranteed by the government. Treasury notes and bonds require a $1,000 minimum investment and pay interest semiannually at maturities from as short as one year to as long as 30 years. Treasury bills are available in $10,000 minimum amounts and pay interest at maturity in three-month, six-month, or one-year terms.

2. *Income.* The goal is to get safe investments that generate income—dividends and interest. This category includes income-producing stocks (e.g., electric, gas, and telephone companies, and some banks), and municipal (munis) and corporate bonds. *Munis* are debt instruments issued by cities, states, and counties and are federally tax-free. If you buy these bonds within the state where you live, they may be exempt from local taxes. Corporate bonds are IOUs that a particular company issues, typically in increments of $1,000, $5,000, or $10,000, with maturities up to 30 years and from 5 percent to 10 percent interest. Literally, you are lending money to the issuer who specifies when you will be paid back and how much interest you will be paid.

3. *Growth.* The objective is *capital appreciation* (increase in the value of an asset). Growth stocks are shares in companies that are industry leaders and have demonstrated consistent growth rates in both earnings and revenues in excess of 12 percent. These companies usually pay low dividends, but offer investors opportunities to profit from rising stock prices.

4. *Aggressive growth.* The objective is maximum capital appreciation. This category includes emerging growth companies (e.g., tech stocks), speculative penny stocks, options, and futures.

Options are contracts to buy or sell a stock at a certain price during a specified period of time. Investors are betting on the future direction of the price of that stock. Commodity futures are contracts to buy and sell items that are mined or grown—soybeans, coffee, cattle, crude oil, and so on. Again, investors are betting on the future movement of prices.

The members of EMI adopted a moderately risky investment strategy. In 1999, they invested 15 percent of their $104,000 portfolio in Ball Girl Inc., a minority-owned woman's sports-apparel company in New York City. André had a working relationship with the management of the firm, so he was comfortable taking a position via a private offering—shares sold to a small group of investors. Still, he acknowledges that the club's stake in Ball Girl is a departure from its more measured approach of the stock market.

EMI has positions in nine companies and one mutual fund, with an average rate of return of 36 percent on their portfolio. The club has a big position in Citigroup, with 27 percent of its portfolio invested in the New York City financial services powerhouse. The club bought its first shares when the company was Travelers Group, at an initial investment of roughly $3,000, before Travelers Group merged with the former Citicorp. The club now owns 600 shares worth $26,000. EMI's next largest holdings are Santa Clara, California-based semiconductor maker Intel, representing 11.4 percent, and San Francisco-based retail apparel chain The Gap, at 9 percent.

The club's policy requires each member to research a stock and recommend it to the group based on specific pieces of information (e.g., price, risk, and growth rates). "We look to see where that company fits within our investment strategy," Medina explains. "Is it conservative or risky? From there we look to see if we are already heavily weighted in that industry. We analyze our portfolio each month, looking at each stock on a case by case basis."

THE PYRAMID: BALANCING YOUR INVESTMENTS

One technique used to help spread risk is the pyramid model. The pyramid (see Figure 3.1) is built on the idea that an investment portfolio should have the right balance of safe, income, and growth investments. The higher up the pyramid, the more risky it becomes.

Figure 3.1   Investment Risk Pyramid

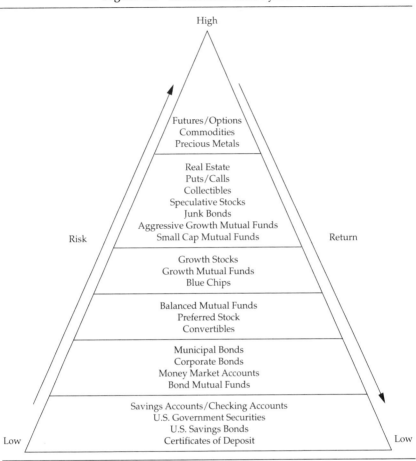

There are six basic tiers:

First Tier. This is the base of the pyramid, which is the foundation of your portfolio and designed to preserve capital. This level consists of the lowest risk and lowest return, such as CDs, treasury securities (bills, notes, and bonds), U.S. savings bonds, and federally insured bank accounts (checking and savings). In case of a financial crisis—when a member suddenly has to leave the group—your club has cash on hand that is easily accessible.

Second Tier. This level offers low risk and low return, and includes such investments as money-market accounts, bond mutual funds, high-grade corporate bonds, and high-quality municipal bonds.

Third Tier. This level includes relatively low risk investments, such as high-quality convertible bonds. A *convertible* is a corporate bond that pays a fixed rate of interest, but can be swapped for shares of common stock at a future date. Other third-tier vehicles are *balanced mutual funds* (invest in both bonds and stocks), and *preferred stock* (fixed income security, much like a bond).

Fourth Tier. This level offers intermediate risk and includes quality growth stocks or mutual funds and *large-cap stocks* (blue chip common stock).

Fifth Tier. The higher up, the more risk. The investments in this category include *mid-cap mutual fund or stocks* (companies with market capitalizations ranging from $1 billion to $5 billion), *small-cap mutual funds or stocks* (companies with market capitalizations under $1 billion), real-estate investment properties, puts and calls, and speculative common stocks and bonds (e.g., junk bonds). Another fifth-tier item is collectibles, such as those autographed baseball cards or art you have tucked away in a safe place, or items such as rare coins and historical memorabilia.

Sixth Tier. This level is only for the experienced investor who wants to speculate and take on large amounts of risk. These investments consist of futures/commodities, options, and gold, silver, or other precious metals.

Whether your club invests in low-risk, intermediate-, or high-risk investments goes back to how much risk members can tolerate. The answer will determine your club's investment style, and it is an answer that will almost certainly change in time.

Most people fall within three classes of risk-takers:

1. *Staunch conservative.* Many of us know some relative or family member—maybe a great-aunt or grandparent—who hid their money under a mattress. Afraid to take any chances, even with a bank, this diehard conservative failed to increase his or her money. Some investment clubs adopt a conservative philosophy in that they limit their investing to purchasing only one type of security, mostly blue-chip stocks.

2. *Moderate.* Some people adopt a middle-of-the road attitude. They are willing to put their money in different kinds of investments, namely blue-chip stocks, growth and income mutual funds, and bond funds. These folks are willing to take moderate risk, seeking the average rate of return on their investments—anywhere between 10 percent and 15 percent.

3. *High roller.* No pain, no gain is the attitude of the risk-taker—an investor who seeks a high rate of return—20 percent and above. Many clubs, especially those with younger members, adopt an aggressive investment philosophy. Generally, these clubs purchase shares in fast-growing, up-and-coming companies (e.g., Internet stocks). Often members are not satisfied with investing solely in securities; and look to other ventures, such as real estate.

INVESTOR PROFILE: TESTING MEMBERS' ATTITUDES

It's important that you assess members' attitudes about investing. Gail Perry-Mason, past vice president of investments at First of Michigan in Detroit, works with 15 local investment clubs. The first thing she does is give members a risk-profile personality test. "This way, you know up front where everyone stands—whether an individual likes to take a lot of risks."

Maybe you are not trying to weed out Hannibal Lechter-like personalities, but you do want to tell lamb-like members apart from the more aggressive ones. Club members who are extremely risk averse are more likely to bail out at the slightest hint of market volatility.

A risk-assessment test or investor's profile (see Figure 3.2) will help members to better understand their investment personality and to shape the club's investment strategies to reflect members views. Financial adviser Gail Perry-Mason suggests that you want to find out three things: how much money members are willing to lose in any given period, whether it's quarterly, semi-annually, or annually; how much risk are they comfortable with; and what is each member's investment objectives. Be honest. If a member says he or she is an aggressive investor and can stand to part with 20 percent of his or her portfolio, that means he or she is willing to lose $2,000 on a $10,000 investment portfolio.

Figure 3.2   Investor Profile

INVESTOR PROFILE QUESTIONNAIRE

The purpose of this worksheet is to provide you with a rule of thumb to determine your investment profile. We ask that you follow the instructions and add up points along the way that will help you best decide your tolerance for risk.

There are two things we'd like to stress. The numerical values posted by each question are not value judgments, neither should they be looked upon as absolute. If you feel you fall somewhere in-between, feel free to fudge your point figure to better reflect your nature. The same goes for your final tally. If you think it just doesn't reflect your personality, feel free to tinker—after all, it's your personal profile we're after.

1. How much money do you currently have to invest?
 (a) Less than $2,000
 —add 0
 (b) Between $2,000 and $50,000
 —add 5
 (c) More than $50,000
 —add 10

2. How long do you have to invest before you will need money to fund your most important financial goals?
 (a) Less than 2 years
 —add 0
 (b) Between 2 and 7 years
 —add 5
 (c) Beyond 7 years
 —add 10

3. What rate of return do you expect to earn on your investments?
 (a) 6%–8% per year
 —add 0
 (b) 9%–11% per year
 —add 5
 (c) above 12% per year
 —add 10

4. What is most important to you?
 (a) How much monthly income you can generate.
 —add 0
 (b) The safety of your savings.
 —add 5
 (c) How fast you can increase your wealth.
 —add 10

5. You turn on the news and hear that your favorite stock investment has just lost 10% of its value. What do you do?
 (a) Sell immediately.
 —add 0
 (b) Wait until it drops further.
 —add 5
 (c) Call your broker and place an order to buy more shares because you think that it's cheap.
 —add 10

6. Do you think your income over the next five years will
 (a) Decrease
 —add 0
 (b) Stay roughly the same
 —add 5
 (c) Increase
 —add 10

7. How would you describe your appetite for risk?
 (a) Low—add 0
 (b) Moderate—add 5

 (c) High—add 10

8. How secure do you feel about your job, your future?
 (a) Worried
 —add 0
 (b) Reasonably confident
 —add 5
 (c) Secure and improving
 —add 10

9. What's your feeling on the economy?
 (a) You're either not very confident about the direction of things or you're feeling that it's impossible to pinpoint where it's going.
 —add 0
 (b) Your impressions are that the economy is stable; it'll keep moving steadily along, neither tanking nor rocketing upward.
 —add 5
 (c) Things look positive, very strong for the years ahead, and growth should continue.
 —add 10

10. What's your impression on new financial products you might've learned about, whether they're options, derivatives, commodities or futures?
 (a) You're scared to death of anything you haven't heard and avoid anything that smacks of a get-rich-quick scheme.
 —add 0
 (b) You'd like to learn more, but probably wouldn't risk your money on anything of the sort.
 —add 5
 (c) You're eager to find out more just to see if you can get in on a new way to create wealth.
 —add 10

DISCUSSION OF THE RESULTS:

After totaling your results, you'll get a figure that indicates your appetite for risk:

A score anywhere from 0 to 30 qualifies you as a relatively conservative investor. You're not eager to take risks with your money and are willing to sacrifice a little in the way of gains to protect your savings. Look at growth and income funds first, and perhaps growth funds if you're feeling a bit frisky. When you dive into stocks, you'll be happiest with blue chips. You'd like to learn more about bonds.

35 to 60 places you among moderate risk takers. You're conscious of the fact that you have to stick your neck out a little to boost gains, but you're not willing to do anything foolish. Growth funds are for you. Should your total be nearer to 35, we'd suggest looking at growth and income as a side investment. Should it be closer to 60, we'd suggest international and aggressive growth funds. Blue chip stocks seem like a good bet, although you'd be willing to get into technology and high-growth companies.

65 and up, your score has you clearly labeled as a risk taker. Aggressive and international funds seem to be to your liking, and high-flying tech and biotech stocks are your ticket.

Source: Black Enterprise Magazine, October 1997.

Having members fill out an investor's profile also will help determine the diversification (or allocation) of assets in the club's portfolio. Independent studies have shown that a portfolio's returns stem from the decision of the myriad investments that you can target. Starting out, your club may invest moderately and stick with the generic asset classes—cash, stocks, and bonds.

Putting together an asset allocation plan is like buying a custommade suit—it has to fit your club. The Organization Investment Club of Beaumont, Texas, divided its portfolio into 10 percent cash, 85 percent stocks, and 5 percent mutual funds.

During the first four years, the club needed cash on hand to pay out fleeing family members. The group also uses a small percentage of its funds to cover their annual retreat. Previous excursions have been out of state, such as the club's Las Vegas trip. A more recent club retreat was to the Bahamas.

Whatever the mix of the different asset classes, clubs like the Organization realize it's important that their portfolio stays fully invested in good and bad times. Asset allocation is not a market-timing device but a tool for building long-term wealth. Your club should monitor its portfolio's performance on a monthly, quarterly, and annual basis. You may have to adjust or reallocate your assets as the club—and its members—mature.

INK TO PAPER: WRITING YOUR CLUB'S MISSION STATEMENT

Once you have assessed and discussed members' investment profiles and attitudes about risk and asset classes, your club needs to write a *mission statement* that outlines the group's investment strategy or policy. The mission statement may be as simple as one paragraph stating that the Investor 2000 Investment Club of Richmond, Virginia, will invest in growth stocks and companies with a five-year history and a projected growth rate of 15 percent. A more detailed outline of the club's investment goals should be spelled out in the operating or partnership agreement.

Keep in mind, the main thing that keeps clubs together is a shared focus on what the club is about—its goals. The investment strategy is a must in meeting these goals. By establishing your policy for investing upfront before any money is actually shelled out, you also establish what the club is *not* about.

This investment strategy will be the driving force of the group; it will also help to circumvent many arguments. A major cause of clubs breaking up is that members fail to stick with their investment strategy, says Walter L. Clark, president of Clark Capital Investments L.L.C. in Baltimore.

For instance, some members may want to invest in commercial real estate or fast-growing small-cap enterprises, yet that may not be the club's policy. Or, in another case, members set on growth stocks may go one way and start their own club, while aggressive members who want to invest in emerging small company stocks—say the latest wave in tech stocks—may head out on their own to form a second club.

One club fell apart because several members wanted to invest in IPOs. "Some members get caught up in the buy/sell frenzy on Wall Street," says Clark. "They have the mindset that they want to con-stantly trade stocks to garner higher returns quickly." He stresses that besides being a highly developed skill, "short-term trading doesn't work with a long-term growth objective. What tends to hap-pen is that the group splits up and members cash out, depleting the club's reserves."

Whenever your club buys or sells a stock it has to take into ac-count how that decision will impact the club's overall portfolio, Clark advises. The first two years are the crucial building blocks. Your club can't afford to have such setbacks as wavering and departing members. Think about it: Each time someone leaves, the club loses money in two ways. First, there's that member's share of the cash bin. Second, there's that member's contribution, which means there is less money coming into the group each month.

CONCLUSION

As the amount of money invested grows, so will the club's understand-ing of investing. In later years, both the knowledge and the money will grow substantially if sound investment rules are followed. Members who survive the two-year hump tend to hang on for the long haul—20 years or more. Ideally, the club's progress should began to show after five years. Your club's success and longevity will depend on how well it keeps members active and in accord.

4

SERIOUS BUSINESS: FORMING THE CLUB'S LEGAL STRUCTURE

Two birds disputed about a kernel when a third swooped down and carried it off.

—Anonymous

Preparation is hard work, running is the easy part.

—Edwin Moses

B.BIG is not just the acronym but the goal of the Black Business Investment Group, LLC in Oakland, California. Initially, it was six Bay Area African-American businessmen and women who started the club in the spring of 1997 that required a monthly offering a bit more hefty than most clubs require—$500. "We wanted not just to save but to save 'big,' thus the reason for having members pay such a large sum money," explains Rod Carter, the club's president and CEO of his own construction company, with more than 20 years of experience under his hard hat.

"We decided early on that if we reached full membership participation (the club has 30 members) we would be taking in about $180,000 a year in dues," he adds. "And we wanted to look into more than investing in stocks." The industrious six decided that one-third of their investment portfolio would be reserved for buying stock, another third for granting small-business loans, and the final third for investing in community-related ventures (e.g., real-estate holdings or franchises).

Given such lofty objectives, members wanted to personally protect themselves and their assets from any financial or legal obligations of a club. As a result, the Black Business Investment Group was formed as an LLC or limited liability company, which consists of several owners or members all of whom have authority over the affairs of the business, but members are not held personally responsible for debts incurred by the business.

To run a legal and legitimate investment club, you must set up a legal form of operation. The typical business has eight to choose from: sole proprietorship, general partnership, limited partnership, corporation, subchapter S-corporation, limited liability company, closely held corporation, and professional corporation.

Since a sole proprietorship is just that—an individual venture—your club can't go that route. Neither will it want to form a closely held corporation, which is traditionally associated with family-owned businesses. Every state allows groups of professionals or firms that have a sole principal and associates to set up a *professional corporation* (PC), which is designed especially for doctors and lawyers who don't want to get zapped with malpractice due to each other's negligence. So, this form isn't right for the group either.

In choosing among the five remaining legal forms under which to operate, your club needs to address five areas:

1. *Taxes.* Under which type of organization would members pay the least taxes from the time the money was first earned until it was received by individual members?
2. *Personal liability.* Which type would minimize members' financial risk? Meaning, when and if can members be sued? Will members be held liable for the personal debts of other partners?
3. *Transfer of securities.* With which form can securities be transferred with the least need for extraneous paperwork or supporting resolutions?
4. *Organizational costs.* Which type would minimize the cost of setting up the club? For instance, licensing and registration fees.
5. *Maintenance costs.* From the standpoint of both time and money, which type would be more economical over the life of the club? This relates to paperwork, tax filings, administrative duties, and legal and accounting fees.

Administrative and set-up costs are the key considerations. Personal liability protection will factor in as well, meaning that forming a corporation may be more appropriate if the club decides to invest in entrepreneurial ventures or real-estate properties and individual members want to limit their liability.

OPERATING AS A PARTNERSHIP

There are no hard, fast rules as to how your club will operate. But most likely, your club will go with the easiest, cheapest, and most common legal form found among investment clubs: the partnership.

Under a general partnership, each partner has the authority to make decisions unless the partnership agreement stipulates otherwise. When it comes to running a partnership, every partner is personally accountable for all debts.

The primary advantage of using a partnership structure is that the club does not incur taxes. Rather, federal and state governments assess any taxes against members' proportionate share of the earnings. Each member must report the club's earnings—including dividend and interest payments, capital gains and losses—on his or her individual tax return. The partnership files a separate income tax return (Form 1065) that states profits or losses, and how the money was appropriated.

The first step is to draw up a partnership agreement (see Figure 4.1) which establishes some ground rules for running the club and spells out the responsibilities of each partner as well as the distribution of profits. Ideally, the partnership agreement should be reviewed by an attorney and signed by all parties.

A typical partnership agreement includes the following items:

1. Name of the partnership, business address.
2. Date partnership was formed.
3. Each partner's name.
4. Specific duties and responsibilities of each partner.
5. Officers and their duties.
6. Purpose of the partnership.
7. Meeting date, time, and place.
8. Candidacy for membership.
9. Monetary contribution of each partner.

Figure 4.1 Sample Partnership Agreement

The parties hereto do hereby agree to form a general partnership in, and in accordance with the laws of ___(State)___, as follows:

ARTICLE ONE
NAME, CHARACTER OF BUSINESS AND
TERM OF PARTNERSHIP

1. The name of the partnership shall be the ___(Name)___ Investment Club.
2. The business of the partnership shall be the investment of funds received by the partnership.
3. The term of the partnership shall commence as of ___(Date)___. The parties hereto agree the partnership shall not be terminated by the death or withdrawal of any partner but shall continue until terminated by the vote of three-fourths of the partners. In the event of the death or withdrawal of any partner, the remaining partners agree to elect to reconstitute and continue the partnership.

ARTICLE TWO
BANK OF THE PARTNERSHIP

1. The bank of the partnership shall be such bank or banks as the partnership shall from time to time agree upon.
2. All partnership monies shall, as and when received, be paid into or deposited in the bank to the credit of the partnership account. Such funds shall, at the direction of the partnership be invested by the Treasurer in interest-bearing or dividend-bearing accounts maintained by a bank or other financial institution to the extent that such funds are not currently required for the operations of the partnership.
3. All checks on any partnership account shall be drawn in the partnership name and manually signed by the President or the Chairman of the Investment Committee of the partnership and the Treasurer or such other individual or individuals as may be designated from time to time by a majority vote of the partnership, except that the withdrawal of petty cash will require the signature of only one officer of the Club.

ARTICLE THREE
MEMBERSHIP

A candidate for membership shall be sponsored by at least two (2) partners and shall be admitted upon receiving the approval of three-fourths ($\frac{3}{4}$) of the partners attending any regular meeting of the partnership. The number of partners shall not exceed twenty-five (25).

(continued)

Figure 4.1 *(Continued)*

ARTICLE FOUR
MEETINGS

1. A regular meeting of the partners shall be held bi-monthly, at a day, hour and place agreed upon by the partnership. The partnership may designate another day for a meeting in case it is impractical or generally inconvenient to hold a meeting as herein provided.
2. Except as set forth in Article Five, Section 4, the presence of a majority of the partners at a meeting shall constitute a quorum for the transaction of any business. A partner may be present at a meeting either in person or by proxy, provided that no proxy shall be effective unless it is in writing and in a form previously approved by the partnership for that purpose. All proper proxies shall be included in the count of the quorum.
3. A regular monthly meeting may be passed by a majority vote at the prior monthly meeting.
4. In an emergency, the President of the partnership, designated in Article Six, may call a special meeting, provided at least three day's notice in writing is sent to all partners. The President shall also endeavor to give at least three days' personal notice of such special meeting to each partner. Notwithstanding the foregoing, on twenty-four (24) hours notice, a telephone conference may be held as a special meeting.

ARTICLE FIVE
VOTING

1. Each partner is entitled to one vote.
2. Except as otherwise specifically provided in these Articles, a simple majority vote of the members of the partnership present at a regular or special meeting shall be required to authorize the taking of any action by or for the partnership provided, however, that a matter may be deferred to the next regular meeting if the number of partners voting in favor of deferment equals one less than a simple majority.
3. No partner or group of partners shall have the authority to take any action by or for the partnership unless such action has been authorized by a majority vote of the partners in accordance with this Article, except as otherwise specifically provided in these Articles.
4. No partner shall, without the written consent of at least three-fourths of the other partners, do any of the following:
   (a) Assign partnership property in trust for creditors or on the assignee's promise to pay the debts of the partnership.
   (b) Dispose of the good will of the business.
   (c) Confess a judgment.
   (d) Submit a partnership claim or liability to arbitration or legal action.

Figure 4.1 *(Continued)*

(e) Make, execute, or deliver for the partnership any bond, mortgage, deed of trust, guarantee, indemnity bond, surety bond or accommodation paper or accommodation endorsement.

(f) Borrow money in the partnership name or use partnership property as collateral except as set forth in Article Nine.

(g) Assign, transfer, pledge, compromise or release any claim of or debt owing to the partnership except upon payment in full.

(h) Pledge or transfer in any manner her interest in the partnership or its assets or profits except to another partner.

(i) Do any other act which would make it impossible to carry on the business of the partnership.

ARTICLE SIX
MANAGEMENT

1. The officers shall be: President, Vice President, Secretary and Treasurer.
2. Officers shall be elected at the Annual Meeting, shall take office on the day of election, and, with the exception of the Secretary, shall serve for one year, or until their successors have been elected. The Secretary shall serve for six (6) months. After that period, the position will be assumed by the next person on the alphabetical list of partners. Partners who have previously served as officers may be excluded from the list until all partners have served as officers.
3. It shall be the duty of the President to preside at meetings, appoint committees, and oversee all partnership activities.

The term of the first class shall expire one year after its election, and the term of the second class shall expire two years after its election. Thereafter, at each election, at least two partners shall be elected to replace the two partners whose terms expire at the time of such election, to serve for one year. A quorum of the Investment Committee shall consist of a minimum of four partners, and the transaction of business shall be by majority vote.

ARTICLE SEVEN
CAPITAL CONTRIBUTIONS

1. Each partner shall pay __(Amount)__ to the partnership at the __(Date)__ monthly meeting. By the meeting in __(Date)__, each partner shall pay an additional __(Amount)__ to the partnership.
2. Beginning in __(Date)__, each partner shall pay to the partnership at or before each monthly meeting a sum agreed upon by the partnership by a three-fourths ($\frac{3}{4}$) vote of all the partners.
3. A single monthly payment may be waived in accordance with a majority vote at the meeting before the meeting at which the payment is due.

(continued)

Figure 4.1 *(Continued)*

4. Each new partner admitted in accordance with Article Three shall pay, in addition to her first monthly payment a special initial contribution in an amount determined by dividing the fair market value of all partnership assets by the number of partners, excluding the new partner. For purposes of this paragraph and paragraph 2 of Article Fifteen, the fair market value of the partnership assets shall be determined by the Investment Committee, and the Committee's decision shall be conclusive. For purposes of determining the total capital contributions to be made by such new partner for purposes of Article Twelve, such new partner's special initial contribution shall be deemed equal to __(Amount)__ plus the monthly dues amount multiplied by the number of regular monthly payments made by the original partners since the beginning of the partnership.

5. If a partner fails to make her monthly payment to the partnership before the end of the month, regardless of whether a monthly meeting was held, she shall be fined the sum of __(Amount)__. This fine should be sent to the Treasurer with the monthly payment.

ARTICLE EIGHT
INVESTMENTS

1. The purchase and sale of securities investments shall be made by the partnership upon the recommendation of the Investment Committee.

2. Each partner shall have an affirmative obligation to disclose to the partnership any interest that she, or any individual or entity with which she is or has been associated or related in any way, has in any investment proposed to the partnership, without regard to whether she believes that such investment will create a conflict of interest for herself. No investments shall be authorized if a partner, having reason to believe that such investment will create a conflict of interest for herself, so states and casts a dissenting vote.

3. In an emergency, a quorum of the Investment Committee, excluding the Chairman of the Investment Committee, and the President may take whatever action they agree is necessary to protect the assets of the partnership, provided however, that the partners shall be notified of the action taken within 72 hours, and any four partners may call a special meeting to consider the action taken.

ARTICLE NINE
LOANS

1. If at any time, in the opinion of the partnership, additional capital shall be desirable to carry out the partnership's investment program, the President may secure such additional capital from banks or other sources, or from any partner. The President shall not, however, have the authority to obligate

Figure 4.1 *(Continued)*

the partnership with respect thereto unless such action has been specifically authorized by an affirmative vote of not less than seventy-five percent (75%) of the members of the partnership voting in person or by proxy at a regular or special meeting of the partnership. Evidence of such authorization shall be in the form of a writing containing the date and location of the meeting at which the authorization was so voted and the signature of each member of the Investment Committee. No partner shall be liable for the repayment of such borrowed additional capital beyond her proportionate share of partnership liabilities, and the partnership and each of the partners shall indemnify and hold each partner harmless from and against any liability in connection therewith that exceeds that partner's proportionate share of partnership liabilities. In the event of any borrowing for the purpose of acquiring real property, such financing shall be on a non-recourse basis secured by the assets of the partnership and no partner shall have any obligation for the repayment of such loan.

ARTICLE TEN
COMPENSATION

The partnership may, by a vote of a majority of the partners present at any regular meeting, authorize the payment of reasonable compensation to any person who performs legal, accounting, or other services for the partnership.

ARTICLE ELEVEN
TITLE TO PARTNERSHIP PROPERTY

All property purchased with partnership funds shall be carried in the name of the partnership or in the name of the President as trustee for the partnership.

ARTICLE TWELVE
PROFITS AND LOSSES

1. Subject to the provisions of Articles Fifteen and Sixteen, the net profits of the partnership shall be divided among the partners and the net losses shall be borne by them in proportion to their partnership interests.
2. All or part of the assets of the partnership may be apportioned and distributed among the partners equally upon a three-fourths ($\frac{3}{4}$) vote at a regular meeting of the partnership.
3. For purposes of the federal Internal Revenue Code and any similar tax law of any state or jurisdiction, the determination of each partner's distributive share of all items of income, expense, tax deduction and depreciation, if any, shall be allocated to the partners in proportion to their partnership interests and in accordance with the regulations under section 704 of the Internal Revenue Code.

(continued)

Figure 4.1 *(Continued)*

ARTICLE THIRTEEN
ACCOUNTING AND AUDITS

1. The partnership books shall be kept on a calendar year basis.
2. The partnership books shall be kept on a cash basis.
3. The Treasurer shall submit a report in writing to each of the partners at least bi-annually, in which she shall set forth the partnership's balance sheet and the quarterly and year-to-date results of operations for the partnership.
4. The partnership may, once a year, designate a committee, consisting of three partners not members of the Investment Committee, to make an audit of the partnership's books and to submit a report of their audit at a regular meeting of the partnership.

ARTICLE FOURTEEN
LIABILITY OF PARTNERS

1. It is the intention of the partnership that no partner shall be requested to contribute more than the capital contribution which is specified in Article Seven.
2. The partnership agrees to indemnify any partner with respect to any claim, including the expense of defending against such claim, made against such partner for actions taken by her as an agent or representative of the partnership, provided that (i) the defense of such claim is tendered to the partnership as soon as is practicable and, in any event, within 20 days of the notice of the institution of any suit or administrative proceeding; and (ii) such claim is not premised on willful acts of misfeasance or malfeasance by the partner and does not arise from a breach of the partner's obligations to the partnership.
3. In the event that (i) a judgment is entered against a partner with respect to a claim as to which the foregoing indemnity is applicable and (ii) the assets of the partnership are not sufficient to satisfy the judgment, each partner agrees to pay her pro rata share of the remaining part of the judgment, to be determined by dividing that amount by the number of partners, who were partners at the time the claim arose. To the extent that the judgment is not in excess of the partnership assets, all amounts which a partner is obligated to pay which are not in excess of their capital contribution shall be reflected in a readjustment of each partner's capital account. To the extent that the judgment is in excess of the value of the partnership assets, each partner agrees that such liability shall be borne equally. Accordingly, each partner agrees to pay to her pro rata share of the remaining part of the judgment that is in excess of each partner's capital contribution.

Figure 4.1 *(Continued)*

ARTICLE FIFTEEN
WITHDRAWAL OF A PARTNER

1. A partner may withdraw from the partnership by giving notice in writing to the President, and her withdrawal shall be effective thirty (30) days after the receipt of such notice. Thereafter, such partner shall not be liable for any dues of the partnership, nor shall she be entitled to attend any meetings or to vote on any partnership business.
2. A member whose withdrawal from the partnership has been effected in accordance with paragraph 1 of this Article is entitled to receive in full satisfaction of her partnership interest, an amount equal to the fair market value, as of the effective date of withdrawal, of the net assets of the partnership divided by the number of partners, less any expenses arising out of the liquidation of assets or borrowing done by the partnership, if such liquidation or borrowing is required to pay the withdrawing partner.
3. The interest of a withdrawing partner, determined in accordance with paragraph 2 of this Article, shall be paid to such withdrawing partner as soon as practicable and to the extent practicable, but in any event shall be paid in its entirety within 24 months after the effective date of her withdrawal. If the amount to be paid to such withdrawing partner is not paid in full within 60 days of the effective date of her withdrawal, the unpaid amount shall bear interest, at the statutory rate paid on judgments, from the date her withdrawal is effective. The Investment Committee shall determine the manner and timing of the payment or payments, and its decision shall be conclusive.
4. If a new partner is admitted into the partnership at any time within 60 days from the date of a partner's withdrawal, the withdrawing partner shall be entitled to receive the initial contribution of the new partner in lieu of her share of the partnership assets determined in accordance with paragraph 2 of this Article.

ARTICLE SIXTEEN
TERMINATION OF PARTNER'S
INTEREST, OR PARTNER'S DEATH

1. The membership of a partner may be terminated without her consent by a majority vote of the partners for (a) failure to pay one monthly payment plus her fine for a period of 60 days following the date the payment is due, or (b) failure to attend at least three meetings during a calendar year.
2. A partner whose membership is terminated under paragraph 1 of this Article shall be deemed to have waived any right to any of the assets of the partnership or any right to any profits or obligation for losses of the partnership that are thereafter apportioned or distributed.

(continued)

Figure 4.1   *(Continued)*

3. If a partner dies, her membership shall be terminated as of the last business day of the month in which her death occurs. The value of the proportionate share of the deceased member shall be determined in accordance with the provisions of Article Fifteen; provided, however, that if a new member is admitted into the partnership at any time within sixty days of the death of the deceased partner, such deceased partner's heirs shall be entitled to receive the initial contribution of the new partner in lieu of a share determined under Paragraph 2 of Article Fifteen.

4. Any partner may elect to have the proceeds of her partnership interest paid directly to any individual or entity designated by her in the event of her death. If no such election has been made, such proceeds shall be paid to the executor or administrator of the deceased partner's estate.

ARTICLE SEVENTEEN
DISSOLUTION

The partnership may be dissolved and terminated upon (i) the vote or agreement of three-fourths of the partners or (ii) upon the failure of the remaining partners to purchase a withdrawing partner's interest in accordance with this Agreement. Upon any such dissolution and termination, the partners shall promptly liquidate the affairs of the partnership and by distributing all remaining assets, in cash or in kind or partly in cash and partly in kind, to the partners or their representatives in the ratios of their respective capital accounts on the date of dissolution and termination.

ARTICLE EIGHTEEN
AMENDMENT

These Articles may be amended or revoked, or new Articles may be adopted, upon a vote of three-fourths ($^3/_4$) of all the members of the partnership. All prior partnership agreements are superseded and replaced by the provisions of this partnership agreement.

ARTICLE NINETEEN
ARBITRATION

Any dispute which cannot be settled among the partners involved shall, upon request of any partner involved, be settled by arbitration in accordance with the rules of the American Arbitration Association then in effect.

Figure 4.1 *(Continued)*

ARTICLE TWENTY
NOTICES

All notices provided for in this agreement shall be directed to the partners at the address set forth below and to the partnership at the office of the President, or some other address designated in writing by the President.

IN WITNESS WHEREOF, the following Partners hereunto set their hands and signatures as of the day and year indicated.

_____   _____

Date   Partner's Signature
                   Address

_____   _____

Date   Partner's Signature
                   Address

---

10. Banking and check signing privileges.
11. Voting rights.
12. Admission of new partners.
13. Procedures for sale and purchase of securities.
14. Rules for borrowing money.
15. Accounting and recordkeeping procedures.
16. Distribution of assets at the time the club is dissolved.
17. Provisions for the partial or full withdrawal of any partner's interest.
18. Liability of partners.
19. Arbitration of disputes.
20. Termination of a partner's interest.

Even though B.BIG is an LLC, "When we first started out, we had a partnership agreement," says Carter. "This way we were able to hammer out what we wanted and what we didn't want. The lawyer we hired (who specialized in LLCs) was able to incorporate much of that information into the papers he prepared to form the club's legal structure."

For instance, B.BIG decided that only 2 percent of the club's funds could be spent on administrative costs, and registration fees for any financial conferences or workshops members wished to attend. Anything beyond that amount, the members—who have now risen to 20—would have to pony up additional funds. There also were some stipulations made to deter members from leaving the club. Anyone who bailed out would be hit with a 5 percent penalty fee, meaning that the member would walk away with only 95 percent of his or her investment. If the person was terminated by the club, the penalty would be higher.

In terms of the small-business loans, the group ruled that any member could borrow up to 85 percent of his or her share of the pot for a period of three months. After which time, that member could pay the interest and ask for a three-month extension. At the end of the second three-month term, the total amount is due plus interest. There were no stipulations on the loan, although most members used the money for buying equipment or making payroll.

Although B.BIG has its eye on self-sustaining real estate properties and one commercial building, to date the club's $250,000-plus portfolio is invested only in securities—four growth mutual funds and some 20 stock holdings, mostly high tech, including Cisco Systems; Intel; Unicom, Compuwear, Microsoft; Worldcom; Pfizer; Home Depot; Bed, Bath, and Beyond; Stride Rite; and Telabs.

Once you have written your partnership agreement, you need to register the club with the IRS (800-TAX-FORM) and get a tax identification number (Form SS-4, application for employer identification number; see Figure 4.2). More than likely, you will operate under a fictitious business name (e.g., Ebony Investors). So, you need to file a "Certificate of Conducting Business as Partners" form. A fictitious-name affidavit can be obtained from the local county clerk's office. Filing requirements vary according to jurisdiction, so contact your state secretary's office and local county clerk to find out about proper filing procedures.

The NAIC, in conjunction with the Securities Transfer Association, established Rule 3.0610, which permits investment clubs operating as partnerships to transfer securities directly into and out of the club's name with the signature of only one partner. To reduce the risk of any one member misusing the club's funds, the treasurer should circulate at every meeting a copy of the club's brokerage account statement.

Professor Perry Wallace of the American University School of Law, in Washington, DC, notes that, for the average club, the partnership is

Figure 4.2 Form SS-4, Application for Employer Identification Number

Form **SS-4**	**Application for Employer Identification Number**	EIN	
(Rev. February 1998) Department of the Treasury Internal Revenue Service	(For use by employers, corporations, partnerships, trusts, estates, churches, government agencies, certain individuals, and others. See instructions.) ▶ **Keep a copy for your records.**	OMB No. 1545-0003	

Please type or print clearly.

1 Name of applicant (legal name) (see instructions)

2 Trade name of business (if different from name on line 1) | **3** Executor, trustee, "care of" name

4a Mailing address (street address) (room, apt., or suite no.) | **5a** Business address (if different from address on lines 4a and 4b)

4b City, state, and ZIP code | **5b** City, state, and ZIP code

6 County and state where principal business is located

7 Name of principal officer, general partner, grantor, owner, or trustor—SSN or ITIN may be required (see instructions) ▶

8a Type of entity (Check only one box.) (see instructions)
Caution: *If applicant is a limited liability company, see the instructions for line 8a.*

☐ Sole proprietor (SSN) _____ ☐ Estate (SSN of decedent) _____
☐ Partnership ☐ Personal service corp. ☐ Plan administrator (SSN) _____
☐ REMIC ☐ National Guard ☐ Other corporation (specify) ▶ _____
☐ State/local government ☐ Farmers' cooperative ☐ Trust
☐ Church or church-controlled organization ☐ Federal government/military
☐ Other nonprofit organization (specify) ▶ _____ (enter GEN if applicable) _____
☐ Other (specify) ▶

8b If a corporation, name the state or foreign country (if applicable) where incorporated | State | Foreign country

9 Reason for applying (Check only one box.) (see instructions) ☐ Banking purpose (specify purpose) ▶ _____
☐ Started new business (specify type) ▶ _____ ☐ Changed type of organization (specify new type) ▶ _____
☐ Purchased going business
☐ Hired employees (Check the box and see line 12.) ☐ Created a trust (specify type) ▶ _____
☐ Created a pension plan (specify type) ▶ _____ ☐ Other (specify) ▶

10 Date business started or acquired (month, day, year) (see instructions) | **11** Closing month of accounting year (see instructions)

12 First date wages or annuities were paid or will be paid (month, day, year). **Note:** *If applicant is a withholding agent, enter date income will first be paid to nonresident alien. (month, day, year)* ▶

13 Highest number of employees expected in the next 12 months. **Note:** *If the applicant does not expect to have any employees during the period, enter -0-. (see instructions)* ▶ | Nonagricultural | Agricultural | Household

14 Principal activity (see instructions) ▶

15 Is the principal business activity manufacturing? ☐ Yes ☐ No
If "Yes," principal product and raw material used ▶

16 To whom are most of the products or services sold? Please check one box. ☐ Business (wholesale)
☐ Public (retail) ☐ Other (specify) ▶ ☐ N/A

17a Has the applicant ever applied for an employer identification number for this or any other business? ☐ Yes ☐ No
Note: *If "Yes," please complete lines 17b and 17c.*

17b If you checked "Yes" on line 17a, give applicant's legal name and trade name shown on prior application, if different from line 1 or 2 above.
Legal name ▶ Trade name ▶

17c Approximate date when and city and state where the application was filed. Enter previous employer identification number if known.
Approximate date when filed (mo., day, year) | City and state where filed | Previous EIN

Under penalties of perjury, I declare that I have examined this application, and to the best of my knowledge and belief, it is true, correct, and complete. | Business telephone number (include area code)
| Fax telephone number (include area code)

Name and title (Please type or print clearly.) ▶

Signature ▶ Date ▶

Note: *Do not write below this line. For official use only.*

Please leave blank ▶	Geo.	Ind.	Class	Size	Reason for applying

For Paperwork Reduction Act Notice, see page 4. | Cat. No. 16055N | Form **SS-4** (Rev. 2-98)

customary since the members basically will be investing in mutual funds, bonds, and stocks; they aren't doing anything speculative or highly creative to generate any liabilities. Wallace, who specializes in corporate law, finance, and economic development, says once a club moves into an arena where investments may be a little more risky or speculative, or it gets involved in activities that are likely to generate liabilities or debts, members will then want to protect themselves by setting up some type of limited-liability vehicle. An example would be those clubs interested in financing minority businesses.

Or, as the club's structure gets more complex, members may seek liability protection. Let's say a club decides to purchase commercial real estate. There are 25 members, but not all members can be the managing partners. So, you may end up with five people overseeing this aspect of the club's portfolio. Cautions Wallace: "What happens if one of those five managing partners goes out and signs a deal to buy some property without the other members' knowledge or authorization? That one person has the power to bind into contract the whole group which now has an obligation that they have to fill or they could be sued and they could lose."

In that situation, the last legal form you want to have is a partnership in which any of the members could be held liable and made to pay, says Wallace. "But if your club is formed as a limited-liability entity, should somebody in your group go out and conduct a transaction that causes debt or liability, then basically that individual person is the only one whose assets can be taken, not those of the innocent club members or investors," he adds.

Wallace cautions that it's admirable that many black clubs are pushing and adding in economic-development vehicles to the whole picture of investing. Unfortunately, many of these clubs end up operating illegally, as they attempt to do more creative deals to generate wealth. Their big mistake: failure to realize that they are being regulated by the Securities and Exchange Commission (SEC), the government agency empowered to supervise the selling of securities.

FORMING A CORPORATION

To incorporate or not to incorporate? That is the question. Among entrepreneurs, a corporation is a commonly used business form, but it is also the most complex and more expensive entity to set up, compared to a

general partnership. Should your club decide it wants to invest in community economic development projects or purchase real-estate properties, then the best route to follow may be to operate as a *corporation*.

When you incorporate, you create a separate legal entity that is owned by one or more shareholders. In forming a corporation, stock is issued to shareholders—the number of which is unlimited—in exchange for cash or other assets.

Typically, individual shareholders do have control over the operations of the business. This is left in the hands of a board of directors who are the major policymakers. The board usually consists of the club's officers—president, vice president, treasurer, and secretary—and then general directors.

Back when Ma Bell was still the matriarch of the telecommunications family and Lucent Technology was still a member of AT&T, the Alliance of Black Telecommunications Employees (ABTE) was born to provide employees career and professional development on a national and chapter-by-chapter basis. One of the various committees within ABTE focused on economic development, a part of which involved helping employees improve their wealth.

ABTE's New Jersey Chapter voted to form an investment club at one of its general meetings in August 1994. The idea was to get more African Americans involved in investing.

There were 34 members present, who elected four officers to develop and submit a proposal on how to form the club (currently, Alliance averages about 90 members). "Because we were extending an invitation to join to the entire universe of African-American employees at AT&T, we knew we could not be a successful club with all of those people sitting at the table trying to make investment decisions," explains Alliance President Nathaniel "Nate" Watson. "So, we decided to form the club as a legal corporation with a nine-member board of directors that would be responsible for making all of the buy and sell decisions."

Indeed, the SEC limits the size of a partnership to 99 members, and an S-corporation allows for no more than 75 shareholders (prior to 1997, that number was only 35) and limited liability companies have only recently become all the rage in business circles.

Not only was a corporation a better structure because Alliance was catering to a large group of people, it also protected individuals from any personal liability. In other words, the corporation could buy, sell, enter contracts, sue, and be sued. Thus, the business entity was responsible for its activities. The stockholders or owners could only lose their

financial interests and investments, not their personal assets—you could not be sued for more than the value of your shares.

The bylaws were accepted by 23 members, who then wrote out the initial checks to get the club started. The Alliance was fortunate to have members from various disciplines within the AT&T corporation, one of them a corporate lawyer who handled all the paperwork at minimum cost.

It comes as no surprise that Alliance's portfolio is heavily weighted in technology stocks. EMC, a data storage company, has been the club's greatest performer, followed by Microsoft and Lucent. The group also owns shares in mutual funds: One specializes in technology, another focuses on financial services, and still another invests in Internet companies.

The Alliance Investment Group (AIG) is starting to spread its money across other sectors such as insurance, retail, drugs, and entertainment. The club has 15 holdings, including AFLAC, Wal-Mart, Home Depot, Walgreens, McDonald's, and Disney.

A disadvantage of forming a corporation is the double tax whammy. Since members and the company are two separate entities, both must pay taxes. The company files a separate income tax form and members file personal tax returns. Any income earned by the corporation must be recorded on Form 1120 (see Figure 4.3). The club (or corporation) must pay taxes on profits before dividends—15 percent on the first $50,000 earned, 25 percent on $75,000, and 34 percent on all taxable income over $75,000. Club members (or shareholders) must pay taxes on dividends distributed from profits, thus causing a form of double taxation.

Under the Treasury Department rulings, clubs are taxable as corporations if they have four or more of the following characteristics:

1. A group of associates.
2. A common objective to carry on a business and divide the resulting capital gains.
3. Continuity (how and when the business is dissolved).
4. Centralization of management.
5. Limited liability.
6. Free transfer of interests in the business.

When you are ready to incorporate, register the club's name with the secretary of state's office (most states allow you to reserve a name

Figure 4.3 Form 1120, U.S. Corporation Income Tax Return

Form **1120**
Department of the Treasury
Internal Revenue Service

U.S. Corporation Income Tax Return

For calendar year 1999 or tax year beginning ...., 1999, ending ...., ...
▶ Instructions are separate. See page 1 for Paperwork Reduction Act Notice.

OMB No. 1545-0123

1999

A Check if a:
1 Consolidated return (attach Form 851) ☐
2 Personal holding co. (attach Sch. PH) ☐
3 Personal service corp. (as defined in Temporary Regs. sec. 1.441-4T—see instructions) ☐

Use IRS label. Otherwise, print or type.

Name

Number, street, and room or suite no. (If a P.O. box, see page 5 of instructions.)

City or town, state, and ZIP code

B Employer identification number

C Date incorporated

D Total assets (see page 6 of instructions)
$

E Check applicable boxes: (1) ☐ Initial return (2) ☐ Final return (3) ☐ Change of address

Income

1a	Gross receipts or sales [ ] b Less returns and allowances [ ] c Bal ▶	1c
2	Cost of goods sold (Schedule A, line 8)	2
3	Gross profit. Subtract line 2 from line 1c	3
4	Dividends (Schedule C, line 19)	4
5	Interest	5
6	Gross rents	6
7	Gross royalties	7
8	Capital gain net income (attach Schedule D (Form 1120))	8
9	Net gain or (loss) from Form 4797, Part II, line 18 (attach Form 4797)	9
10	Other income (see page 7 of instructions—attach schedule)	10
11	**Total income.** Add lines 3 through 10 ▶	11

Deductions (See instructions for limitations on deductions.)

12	Compensation of officers (Schedule E, line 4)		12
13	Salaries and wages (less employment credits)		13
14	Repairs and maintenance		14
15	Bad debts		15
16	Rents		16
17	Taxes and licenses		17
18	Interest		18
19	Charitable contributions (see page 9 of instructions for 10% limitation)		19
20	Depreciation (attach Form 4562)	20	
21	Less depreciation claimed on Schedule A and elsewhere on return	21a	21b
22	Depletion		22
23	Advertising		23
24	Pension, profit-sharing, etc., plans		24
25	Employee benefit programs		25
26	Other deductions (attach schedule)		26
27	**Total deductions.** Add lines 12 through 26 ▶		27
28	Taxable income before net operating loss deduction and special deductions. Subtract line 27 from line 11		28
29	**Less:** a Net operating loss (NOL) deduction (see page 11 of instructions)	29a	
	b Special deductions (Schedule C, line 20)	29b	29c

Tax and Payments

30	**Taxable income.** Subtract line 29c from line 28		30
31	**Total tax** (Schedule J, line 12)		31
32	Payments: a 1998 overpayment credited to 1999	32a	
b	1999 estimated tax payments	32b	
c	Less 1999 refund applied for on Form 4466	32c ( ) d Bal ▶	32d
e	Tax deposited with Form 7004		32e
f	Credit for tax paid on undistributed capital gains (attach Form 2439)		32f
g	Credit for Federal tax on fuels (attach Form 4136). See instructions	32g	32h
33	Estimated tax penalty (see page 12 of instructions). Check if Form 2220 is attached ▶ ☐		33
34	**Tax due.** If line 32h is smaller than the total of lines 31 and 33, enter amount owed		34
35	**Overpayment.** If line 32h is larger than the total of lines 31 and 33, enter amount overpaid		35
36	Enter amount of line 35 you want: **Credited to 2000 estimated tax** ▶ Refunded ▶		36

Sign Here

Under penalties of perjury, I declare that I have examined this return, including accompanying schedules and statements, and to the best of my knowledge and belief, it is true, correct, and complete. Declaration of preparer (other than taxpayer) is based on all information of which preparer has any knowledge.

▶ Signature of officer   Date   ▶ Title

Paid Preparer's Use Only

Preparer's signature ▶	Date	Check if self-employed ☐	Preparer's SSN or PTIN
Firm's name (or yours if self-employed) and address ▶		EIN ▶	
		ZIP code ▶	

Cat. No. 11450Q   Form **1120** (1999)

(continued)

57

Figure 4.3 *(Continued)*

Schedule A	**Cost of Goods Sold** (See page 12 of instructions.)		
1	Inventory at beginning of year	1	
2	Purchases	2	
3	Cost of labor	3	
4	Additional section 263A costs (attach schedule)	4	
5	Other costs (attach schedule)	5	
6	**Total.** Add lines 1 through 5	6	
7	Inventory at end of year	7	
8	**Cost of goods sold.** Subtract line 7 from line 6. Enter here and on line 2, page 1	8	

9a Check all methods used for valuing closing inventory:
  (i) ☐ Cost as described in Regulations section 1.471-3
  (ii) ☐ Lower of cost or market as described in Regulations section 1.471-4
  (iii) ☐ Other (Specify method used and attach explanation.) ▶

  b Check if there was a writedown of subnormal goods as described in Regulations section 1.471-2(c) . . . . ▶ ☐
  c Check if the LIFO inventory method was adopted this tax year for any goods (if checked, attach Form 970) . . . . . ▶ ☐
  d If the LIFO inventory method was used for this tax year, enter percentage (or amounts) of closing inventory computed under LIFO |9d|
  e If property is produced or acquired for resale, do the rules of section 263A apply to the corporation? . . . . . ☐ Yes ☐ No
  f Was there any change in determining quantities, cost, or valuations between opening and closing inventory? If "Yes," attach explanation . . . . ☐ Yes ☐ No

Schedule C	**Dividends and Special Deductions** (See page 13 of instructions.)	(a) Dividends received	(b) %	(c) Special deductions (a) × (b)
1	Dividends from less-than-20%-owned domestic corporations that are subject to the 70% deduction (other than debt-financed stock)		70	
2	Dividends from 20%-or-more-owned domestic corporations that are subject to the 80% deduction (other than debt-financed stock)		80 see instructions	
3	Dividends on debt-financed stock of domestic and foreign corporations (section 246A)			
4	Dividends on certain preferred stock of less-than-20%-owned public utilities		42	
5	Dividends on certain preferred stock of 20%-or-more-owned public utilities		48	
6	Dividends from less-than-20%-owned foreign corporations and certain FSCs that are subject to the 70% deduction		70	
7	Dividends from 20%-or-more-owned foreign corporations and certain FSCs that are subject to the 80% deduction		80	
8	Dividends from wholly owned foreign subsidiaries subject to the 100% deduction (section 245(b))		100	
9	**Total.** Add lines 1 through 8. See page 14 of instructions for limitation			
10	Dividends from domestic corporations received by a small business investment company operating under the Small Business Investment Act of 1958		100	
11	Dividends from certain FSCs that are subject to the 100% deduction (section 245(c)(1))		100	
12	Dividends from affiliated group members subject to the 100% deduction (section 243(a)(3))		100	
13	Other dividends from foreign corporations not included on lines 3, 6, 7, 8, or 11			
14	Income from controlled foreign corporations under subpart F (attach Form(s) 5471)			
15	Foreign dividend gross-up (section 78)			
16	IC-DISC and former DISC dividends not included on lines 1, 2, or 3 (section 246(d))			
17	Other dividends			
18	Deduction for dividends paid on certain preferred stock of public utilities			
19	**Total dividends.** Add lines 1 through 17. Enter here and on line 4, page 1 ▶			
20	**Total special deductions.** Add lines 9, 10, 11, 12, and 18. Enter here and on line 29b, page 1 . . . . ▶			

Schedule E	**Compensation of Officers** (See instructions for line 12, page 1.)					

Note: *Complete Schedule E only if total receipts (line 1a plus lines 4 through 10 on page 1, Form 1120) are $500,000 or more.*

				Percent of corporation stock owned		
	(a) Name of officer	(b) Social security number	(c) Percent of time devoted to business	(d) Common	(e) Preferred	(f) Amount of compensation
1			%	%	%	
			%	%	%	
			%	%	%	
			%	%	%	
			%	%	%	
2	Total compensation of officers					
3	Compensation of officers claimed on Schedule A and elsewhere on return					
4	Subtract line 3 from line 2. Enter the result here and on line 12, page 1					

Form **1120** (1999)

Figure 4.3 *(Continued)*

Form 1120 (1999) Page **3**

Schedule J **Tax Computation** (See page 15 of instructions.)

1 Check if the corporation is a member of a controlled group (see sections 1561 and 1563) . . . . ▶ ☐

Important: Members of a controlled group, see instructions on page 15.

2a If the box on line 1 is checked, enter the corporation's share of the $50,000, $25,000, and $9,925,000 taxable income brackets (in that order):

(1) $ **(2)** $ **(3)** $

b Enter the corporation's share of: **(1)** Additional 5% tax (not more than $11,750) $

(2) Additional 3% tax (not more than $100,000) $

3	Income tax. Check if a qualified personal service corporation under section 448(d)(2) (see page 15) . ▶ ☐		3
4a	Foreign tax credit (attach Form 1118)	4a	
b	Possessions tax credit (attach Form 5735)	4b	
c	Check: ☐ Nonconventional source fuel credit ☐ QEV credit (attach Form 8834)	4c	
d	General business credit. Enter here and check which forms are attached: ☐ 3800 ☐ 3468 ☐ 5884 ☐ 6478 ☐ 6765 ☐ 8586 ☐ 8830 ☐ 8826 ☐ 8835 ☐ 8844 ☐ 8845 ☐ 8846 ☐ 8820 ☐ 8847 ☐ 8861	4d	
e	Credit for prior year minimum tax (attach Form 8827)	4e	
5	**Total credits.** Add lines 4a through 4e		5
6	Subtract line 5 from line 3		6
7	Personal holding company tax (attach Schedule PH (Form 1120))		7
8	Recapture taxes. Check if from: ☐ Form 4255 ☐ Form 8611		8
9	Alternative minimum tax (attach Form 4626)		9
10	Add lines 6 through 9		10
11	Qualified zone academy bond credit (attach Form 8860)		11
12	**Total tax.** Subtract line 11 from line 10. Enter here and on line 31, page 1		12

Schedule K **Other Information** (See page 17 of instructions.)

		Yes	No
1	Check method of accounting: **a** ☐ Cash **b** ☐ Accrual **c** ☐ Other (specify) ▶		
2	See page 19 of the instructions and enter the:		
a	Business activity code no. ▶		
b	Business activity ▶		
c	Product or service ▶		
3	At the end of the tax year, did the corporation own, directly or indirectly, 50% or more of the voting stock of a domestic corporation? (For rules of attribution, see section 267(c).) . . . . If "Yes," attach a schedule showing: **(a)** name and employer identification number (EIN), **(b)** percentage owned, and **(c)** taxable income or (loss) before NOL and special deductions of such corporation for the tax year ending with or within your tax year.		
4	Is the corporation a subsidiary in an affiliated group or a parent-subsidiary controlled group? . . . . . . If "Yes," enter name and EIN of the parent corporation ▶		
5	At the end of the tax year, did any individual, partnership, corporation, estate, or trust own, directly or indirectly, 50% or more of the corporation's voting stock? (For rules of attribution, see section 267(c).) . . . . If "Yes," attach a schedule showing name and identifying number. (Do not include any information already entered in **4** above.) Enter percentage owned ▶		
6	During this tax year, did the corporation pay dividends (other than stock dividends and distributions in exchange for stock) in excess of the corporation's current and accumulated earnings and profits? (See sections 301 and 316.) . . . If "Yes," file Form 5452. If this is a consolidated return, answer here for the parent corporation and on **Form 851,** Affiliations Schedule, for each subsidiary.		

		Yes	No
7	Was the corporation a U.S. shareholder of any controlled foreign corporation? (See sections 951 and 957.) . . . If "Yes," attach Form 5471 for each such corporation. Enter number of Forms 5471 attached ▶		
8	At any time during the 1999 calendar year, did the corporation have an interest in or a signature or other authority over a financial account (such as a bank account, securities account, or other financial account) in a foreign country? If "Yes," the corporation may have to file Form TD F 90-22.1. If "Yes," enter name of foreign country ▶		
9	During the tax year, did the corporation receive a distribution from, or was it the grantor of, or transferor to, a foreign trust? If "Yes," the corporation may have to file Form 3520 . .		
10	At any time during the tax year, did one foreign person own, directly or indirectly, at least 25% of: **(a)** the total voting power of all classes of stock of the corporation entitled to vote, or **(b)** the total value of all classes of stock of the corporation? If "Yes,"		
a	Enter percentage owned ▶		
b	Enter owner's country ▶		
c	The corporation may have to file Form 5472. Enter number of Forms 5472 attached ▶		
11	Check this box if the corporation issued publicly offered debt instruments with original issue discount . . ▶ ☐ If checked, the corporation may have to file Form 8281.		
12	Enter the amount of tax-exempt interest received or accrued during the tax year ▶ $		
13	If there were 75 or fewer shareholders at the end of the tax year, enter the number ▶		
14	If the corporation has an NOL for the tax year and is electing to forego the carryback period, check here ▶ ☐		
15	Enter the available NOL carryover from prior tax years (Do not reduce it by any deduction on line 29a.) ▶ $		

Form **1120** (1999)

(continued)

Figure 4.3   *(Continued)*

Form 1120 (1999) Page **4**

Schedule L Balance Sheets per Books	Beginning of tax year		End of tax year	
Assets	(a)	(b)	(c)	(d)
1 Cash				
2a Trade notes and accounts receivable . . .				
b Less allowance for bad debts	( )		( )	
3 Inventories.				
4 U.S. government obligations				
5 Tax-exempt securities (see instructions) . .				
6 Other current assets (attach schedule) . .				
7 Loans to shareholders				
8 Mortgage and real estate loans				
9 Other investments (attach schedule) . . .				
10a Buildings and other depreciable assets . .				
b Less accumulated depreciation	( )		( )	
11a Depletable assets				
b Less accumulated depletion	( )		( )	
12 Land (net of any amortization)				
13a Intangible assets (amortizable only) . . .				
b Less accumulated amortization	( )		( )	
14 Other assets (attach schedule)				
15 Total assets				
Liabilities and Shareholders' Equity				
16 Accounts payable				
17 Mortgages, notes, bonds payable in less than 1 year				
18 Other current liabilities (attach schedule) . .				
19 Loans from shareholders				
20 Mortgages, notes, bonds payable in 1 year or more				
21 Other liabilities (attach schedule)				
22 Capital stock: a Preferred stock . . .				
b Common stock . . .				
23 Additional paid-in capital				
24 Retained earnings—Appropriated (attach schedule)				
25 Retained earnings—Unappropriated . . .				
26 Adjustments to shareholders' equity (attach schedule)				
27 Less cost of treasury stock		( )		( )
28 Total liabilities and shareholders' equity . .				

Note: *The corporation is not required to complete Schedules M-1 and M-2 if the total assets on line 15, col. (d) of Schedule L are less than $25,000.*

Schedule M-1 Reconciliation of Income (Loss) per Books With Income per Return (See page 18 of instructions.)		
1 Net income (loss) per books	7 Income recorded on books this year not	
2 Federal income tax	included on this return (itemize):	
3 Excess of capital losses over capital gains .	Tax-exempt interest $	
4 Income subject to tax not recorded on books this year (itemize):	....	
....	8 Deductions on this return not charged	
5 Expenses recorded on books this year not deducted on this return (itemize):	against book income this year (itemize):	
a Depreciation . . . . $	a Depreciation . . . . $.............	
b Contributions carryover $	b Contributions carryover $	
c Travel and entertainment $	....	
....	....	
	9 Add lines 7 and 8	
6 Add lines 1 through 5	10 Income (line 28, page 1)—line 6 less line 9	

Schedule M-2 Analysis of Unappropriated Retained Earnings per Books (Line 25, Schedule L)		
1 Balance at beginning of year	5 Distributions: a Cash	
2 Net income (loss) per books	b Stock	
3 Other increases (itemize):	c Property	
....	6 Other decreases (itemize):	
	7 Add lines 5 and 6	
4 Add lines 1, 2, and 3	8 Balance at end of year (line 4 less line 7)	

Form **1120** (1999)

60

for up to 100 days). When choosing your club's name, include one of the terms *corp.* (corporation), *inc.* (incorporated), *ltd.* (limited), *co.* (company), or *chartered,* to show that your club is a legitimate corporation. Make sure no one else already has the same name as your club's. You can check with your secretary of state or search the Internet to find out if some other entity is operating under your chosen name.

The next step is to pay the appropriate fees and file an articles of incorporation with the secretary of state. This document is the official record of your club's name and location, business purpose, shares of stock, and capitalization. In addition, it identifies key players, such as the president, vice president, and other officers. Filing fees vary from state to state.

These days you can get a corporation kit online, which would include an articles of incorporation form. Your club may want to consult an accountant and a lawyer about specific tax concerns before forming as a corporation, which could cost you more than $500 and take days or weeks to get off the ground.

In terms of maintenance fees, check with state and local agencies to find out if your club is required to file an annual report and pay any fees for registration renewal. In some states, for instance, a partnership merely has to renew its registration, whereas a corporation must meet certain reporting requirements.

FILING AS AN S CORPORATION

In 1982, a group of frat brothers and graduates from Atlanta's Morehouse College decided to pool their money to create intergenerational wealth for their families. They started Omega Diversified Investment Consortium (the name is taken from Omega Psi Phi Fraternity Inc.). The group of 35 members legally formed a subchapter S corporation, which is incorporated under the same rules as a regular corporation. An S corporation operates like a corporation—it has a board of directors, officers, and shareholders.

"The reason we incorporated when we started out was because we wanted this to be a professional venture. We also wanted to insulate any of the members from liabilities," explains Charles Hicks, chairman of the board of directors. Like a regular corporation, S corporation shareholders have limited personal liability, so they can lose only the amount they have invested.

In addition to investing in individual stocks and mutual funds, the enterprising group owns three urban-music radio stations. Currently, the club has 50 percent of its portfolio invested in venture capital deals and the other half in stock and mutual funds (30 percent in mutual funds and 20 percent in stocks). The average rate of return on their investments is about 25 percent. The club's portfolio, which includes investment market and venture capital projects, has a net worth valued above $500,000.

Omega takes comfort in knowing that they won't be taxed twice on their business income. That's because they enjoy the best of both worlds—the corporate advantage of limited liability but taxation as a partnership—as a subchapter S corporation.

Unlike a corporation, S corporation business income is taxed only once, at the shareholder level. Income, losses, tax credits, and other tax items pass through the company to shareholders. Club members (or shareholders) must declare all earnings and dividends and can benefit from certain tax deductions. However, this applies only to the federal level; states continue to tax S corporations as corporations.

The subchapter S corporation designation is available only if your club meets the following requirements:

1. You can have no more than 75 shareholders.
2. Shareholders are individuals and not members of other partnerships or corporations.
3. All shareholders are residents of the same state, and are legal residents of the United States.
4. You have only one class of stock.
5. Income and losses must be declared and distributed to shareholders in the year in which they were incurred.

As an S corporation, your club must file a special IRS form (Form 2553) to be taxed similarly to a partnership. Also, you will need to file Form 1120S (see Figure 4.4) annually to report earnings or losses to the IRS. To set up your club as an S corporation, you must first incorporate by filing an articles of incorporation with your secretary of state's office. From that point, everything works like a regular corporation, including the free transfer of a member's interest. Again, check with your state or local agencies regarding maintenance and registration renewal fees.

Figure 4.4 Form 1120S U.S. Income Tax Return for an S Corporation

Form **1120S**	**U.S. Income Tax Return for an S Corporation**	OMB No. 1545-0130
Department of the Treasury Internal Revenue Service	▶ Do not file this form unless the corporation has timely filed Form 2553 to elect to be an S corporation. ▶ See separate instructions.	**19 99**

For calendar year 1999, or tax year beginning , 1999, and ending ,

A Effective date of election as an S corporation	**Use IRS label.**	Name		C Employer identification number
	Other- wise,	Number, street, and room or suite no. (If a P.O. box, see page 10 of the instructions.)		D Date incorporated
B Business code no. (see pages 26–28)	**please print or type.**	City or town, state, and ZIP code		E Total assets (see page 10) $

F Check applicable boxes: (1) ☐ Initial return   (2) ☐ Final return   (3) ☐ Change in address   (4) ☐ Amended return

G Enter number of shareholders in the corporation at end of the tax year . . . . ▶

Caution: *Include **only** trade or business income and expenses on lines 1a through 21. See page 10 of the instructions for more information.*

Income

1a	Gross receipts or sales [ ] **b** Less returns and allowances [ ] **c** Bal ▶	1c	
2	Cost of goods sold (Schedule A, line 8)	2	
3	Gross profit. Subtract line 2 from line 1c	3	
4	Net gain (loss) from Form 4797, Part II, line 18 *(attach Form 4797)*	4	
5	Other income (loss) *(attach schedule)*	5	
6	**Total income (loss).** Combine lines 3 through 5 . . . . ▶	6	

Deductions *(see page 11 of the instructions for limitations)*

7	Compensation of officers	7	
8	Salaries and wages (less employment credits)	8	
9	Repairs and maintenance	9	
10	Bad debts	10	
11	Rents	11	
12	Taxes and licenses	12	
13	Interest	13	
14a	Depreciation *(if required, attach Form 4562)*	14a	
b	Depreciation claimed on Schedule A and elsewhere on return . .	14b	
c	Subtract line 14b from line 14a	14c	
15	Depletion **(Do not deduct oil and gas depletion.)**	15	
16	Advertising	16	
17	Pension, profit-sharing, etc., plans	17	
18	Employee benefit programs	18	
19	Other deductions *(attach schedule)*	19	
20	**Total deductions.** Add the amounts shown in the far right column for lines 7 through 19 . ▶	20	
21	Ordinary income (loss) from trade or business activities. Subtract line 20 from line 6	21	

Tax and Payments

22	**Tax: a** Excess net passive income tax *(attach schedule)* . . . 22a		
b	Tax from Schedule D (Form 1120S) 22b		
c	Add lines 22a and 22b (see page 14 of the instructions for additional taxes)	22c	
23	**Payments: a** 1999 estimated tax payments and amount applied from 1998 return 23a		
b	Tax deposited with Form 7004 . . . . 23b		
c	Credit for Federal tax paid on fuels *(attach Form 4136)* . . . 23c		
d	Add lines 23a through 23c	23d	
24	Estimated tax penalty. Check if Form 2220 is attached . . . . ▶ ☐	24	
25	**Tax due.** If the total of lines 22c and 24 is larger than line 23d, enter amount owed. See page 4 of the instructions for depository method of payment	25	
26	**Overpayment.** If line 23d is larger than the total of lines 22c and 24, enter amount overpaid ▶	26	
27	Enter amount of line 26 you want: **Credited to 2000 estimated tax ▶** [ ] **Refunded ▶**	27	

Please Sign Here	Under penalties of perjury, I declare that I have examined this return, including accompanying schedules and statements, and to the best of my knowledge and belief, it is true, correct, and complete. Declaration of preparer (other than taxpayer) is based on all information of which preparer has any knowledge.

	▶	Date	Title
	Signature of officer		

Paid Preparer's Use Only	Preparer's signature ▶		Date		Check if self-employed ▶ ☐	Preparer's SSN or PTIN
	Firm's name (or yours if self-employed) and address	▶			EIN ▶	
					ZIP code ▶	

For Paperwork Reduction Act Notice, see the separate instructions.   Cat. No. 11510H   Form **1120S** (1999)

(continued)

Figure 4.4 *(Continued)*

Schedule A   **Cost of Goods Sold** (see page 15 of the instructions)

1	Inventory at beginning of year	**1**
2	Purchases	**2**
3	Cost of labor	**3**
4	Additional section 263A costs *(attach schedule)*	**4**
5	Other costs *(attach schedule)*	**5**
6	**Total.** Add lines 1 through 5	**6**
7	Inventory at end of year	**7**
8	**Cost of goods sold.** Subtract line 7 from line 6. Enter here and on page 1, line 2	**8**

9a   Check all methods used for valuing closing inventory:
    (i) ☐ Cost as described in Regulations section 1.471-3
    (ii) ☐ Lower of cost or market as described in Regulations section 1.471-4
    (iii) ☐ Other (specify method used and attach explanation) ▶ --
  b Check if there was a writedown of "subnormal" goods as described in Regulations section 1.471-2(c) . . . . . ▶ ☐
  c Check if the LIFO inventory method was adopted this tax year for any goods *(if checked, attach Form 970)*. . . . . ▶ ☐
  d If the LIFO inventory method was used for this tax year, enter percentage (or amounts) of closing
     inventory computed under LIFO . | **9d** |
  e Do the rules of section 263A (for property produced or acquired for resale) apply to the corporation? . . . . ☐ Yes ☐ No
  f Was there any change in determining quantities, cost, or valuations between opening and closing inventory? . . ☐ Yes ☐ No
     If "Yes," attach explanation.

Schedule B   **Other Information**

		Yes	No
1	Check method of accounting: **(a)** ☐ Cash **(b)** ☐ Accrual **(c)** ☐ Other (specify) ▶----------------------		
2	Refer to the list on pages 26 through 28 of the instructions and state the corporation's principal:		
	(a) Business activity ▶ ------------------------------- **(b)** Product or service ▶ --------------------------		
3	Did the corporation at the end of the tax year own, directly or indirectly, 50% or more of the voting stock of a domestic corporation? (For rules of attribution, see section 267(c).) If "Yes," attach a schedule showing: **(a)** name, address, and employer identification number and **(b)** percentage owned.		
4	Was the corporation a member of a controlled group subject to the provisions of section 1561?		
5	At any time during calendar year 1999, did the corporation have an interest in or a signature or other authority over a financial account in a foreign country (such as a bank account, securities account, or other financial account)? (See page 15 of the instructions for exceptions and filing requirements for Form TD F 90-22.1.)		
	If "Yes," enter the name of the foreign country ▶ -------------------------------		
6	During the tax year, did the corporation receive a distribution from, or was it the grantor of, or transferor to, a foreign trust? If "Yes," the corporation may have to file Form 3520. See page 15 of the instructions.		
7	Check this box if the corporation has filed or is required to file **Form 8264**, Application for Registration of a Tax Shelter . . . . ▶ ☐		
8	Check this box if the corporation issued publicly offered debt instruments with original issue discount . . . ▶ ☐		
	If so, the corporation may have to file **Form 8281**, Information Return for Publicly Offered Original Issue Discount Instruments.		
9	If the corporation: **(a)** filed its election to be an S corporation after 1986, **(b)** was a C corporation before it elected to be an S corporation **or** the corporation acquired an asset with a basis determined by reference to its basis (or the basis of any other property) in the hands of a C corporation, and **(c)** has net unrealized built-in gain (defined in section 1374(d)(1)) in excess of the net recognized built-in gain from prior years, enter the net unrealized built-in gain reduced by net recognized built-in gain from prior years (see page 15 of the instructions) . . . . . ▶ $ ----------------		
10	Check this box if the corporation had accumulated earnings and profits at the close of the tax year (see page 16 of the instructions) . . . . ▶ ☐		

Form **1120S** (1999)

Figure 4.4 *(Continued)*

Schedule K	**Shareholders' Shares of Income, Credits, Deductions, etc.**		
	(a) Pro rata share items		(b) Total amount

Income (Loss)	1 Ordinary income (loss) from trade or business activities (page 1, line 21)	1	
	2 Net income (loss) from rental real estate activities (attach Form 8825)	2	
	3a Gross income from other rental activities	3a	
	b Expenses from other rental activities (attach schedule).	3b	
	c Net income (loss) from other rental activities. Subtract line 3b from line 3a	3c	
	4 Portfolio income (loss):		
	a Interest income	4a	
	b Ordinary dividends	4b	
	c Royalty income	4c	
	d Net short-term capital gain (loss) (attach Schedule D (Form 1120S))	4d	
	e Net long-term capital gain (loss) (attach Schedule D (Form 1120S)):		
	(1) 28% rate gain (loss) ▶ .... (2) Total for year ▶	4e(2)	
	f Other portfolio income (loss) (attach schedule)	4f	
	5 Net section 1231 gain (loss) (other than due to casualty or theft) (attach Form 4797)	5	
	6 Other income (loss) (attach schedule)	6	
Deductions	7 Charitable contributions (attach schedule).	7	
	8 Section 179 expense deduction (attach Form 4562).	8	
	9 Deductions related to portfolio income (loss) (itemize)	9	
	10 Other deductions (attach schedule)	10	
Investment Interest	11a Interest expense on investment debts	11a	
	b (1) Investment income included on lines 4a, 4b, 4c, and 4f above . . .	11b(1)	
	(2) Investment expenses included on line 9 above	11b(2)	
Credits	12a Credit for alcohol used as a fuel (attach Form 6478)	12a	
	b Low-income housing credit:		
	(1) From partnerships to which section 42(j)(5) applies for property placed in service before 1990	12b(1)	
	(2) Other than on line 12b(1) for property placed in service before 1990.	12b(2)	
	(3) From partnerships to which section 42(j)(5) applies for property placed in service after 1989	12b(3)	
	(4) Other than on line 12b(3) for property placed in service after 1989	12b(4)	
	c Qualified rehabilitation expenditures related to rental real estate activities (attach Form 3468)	12c	
	d Credits (other than credits shown on lines 12b and 12c) related to rental real estate activities	12d	
	e Credits related to other rental activities	12e	
	13 Other credits	13	
Adjustments and Tax Preference Items	14a Depreciation adjustment on property placed in service after 1986	14a	
	b Adjusted gain or loss	14b	
	c Depletion (other than oil and gas)	14c	
	d (1) Gross income from oil, gas, or geothermal properties	14d(1)	
	(2) Deductions allocable to oil, gas, or geothermal properties	14d(2)	
	e Other adjustments and tax preference items (attach schedule)	14e	
Foreign Taxes	15a Type of income ▶...................................		
	b Name of foreign country or U.S. possession		
	c Total gross income from sources outside the United States (attach schedule)	15c	
	d Total applicable deductions and losses (attach schedule)	15d	
	e Total foreign taxes (check one): ▶ ☐ Paid ☐ Accrued	15e	
	f Reduction in taxes available for credit (attach schedule)	15f	
	g Other foreign tax information (attach schedule)	15g	
Other	16 Section 59(e)(2) expenditures: a Type ▶....................... b Amount ▶	16b	
	17 Tax-exempt interest income	17	
	18 Other tax-exempt income	18	
	19 Nondeductible expenses	19	
	20 Total property distributions (including cash) other than dividends reported on line 22 below	20	
	21 Other items and amounts required to be reported separately to shareholders (attach schedule)		
	22 Total dividend distributions paid from accumulated earnings and profits	22	
	23 Income (loss). (Required only if Schedule M-1 must be completed.) Combine lines 1 through 6 in column (b). From the result, subtract the sum of lines 7 through 11a, 15e, and 16b.	23	

Form **1120S** (1999)

(continued)

Figure 4.4 *(Continued)*

Form 1120S (1999)

Schedule L Balance Sheets per Books		Beginning of tax year		End of tax year	
Assets		(a)	(b)	(c)	(d)
1	Cash				
2a	Trade notes and accounts receivable . .				
b	Less allowance for bad debts				
3	Inventories				
4	U.S. Government obligations				
5	Tax-exempt securities				
6	Other current assets *(attach schedule)*. .				
7	Loans to shareholders				
8	Mortgage and real estate loans				
9	Other investments *(attach schedule)* . .				
10a	Buildings and other depreciable assets .				
b	Less accumulated depreciation				
11a	Depletable assets				
b	Less accumulated depletion				
12	Land (net of any amortization)				
13a	Intangible assets (amortizable only) . . .				
b	Less accumulated amortization				
14	Other assets *(attach schedule)*				
15	Total assets				
Liabilities and Shareholders' Equity					
16	Accounts payable				
17	Mortgages, notes, bonds payable in less than 1 year				
18	Other current liabilities *(attach schedule)*				
19	Loans from shareholders				
20	Mortgages, notes, bonds payable in 1 year or more				
21	Other liabilities *(attach schedule)* . . .				
22	Capital stock				
23	Additional paid-in capital				
24	Retained earnings				
25	Adjustments to shareholders' equity *(attach schedule)* .				
26	Less cost of treasury stock		( )		( )
27	Total liabilities and shareholders' equity . .				

Schedule M-1 Reconciliation of Income (Loss) per Books With Income (Loss) per Return (You are not required to complete this schedule if the total assets on line 15, column (d), of Schedule L are less than $25,000.)			
1 Net income (loss) per books		5 Income recorded on books this year not included on Schedule K, lines 1 through 6 (itemize):	
2 Income included on Schedule K, lines 1 through 6, not recorded on books this year (itemize):		a Tax-exempt interest $	
....		6 Deductions included on Schedule K, lines 1 through 11a, 15e, and 16b, not charged against book income this year (itemize):	
3 Expenses recorded on books this year not included on Schedule K, lines 1 through 11a, 15e, and 16b (itemize):		a Depreciation $	
a Depreciation $		....	
b Travel and entertainment $		7 Add lines 5 and 6	
....		8 Income (loss) (Schedule K, line 23). Line 4 less line 7	
4 Add lines 1 through 3			

Schedule M-2 Analysis of Accumulated Adjustments Account, Other Adjustments Account, and Shareholders' Undistributed Taxable Income Previously Taxed (see page 24 of the instructions)	(a) Accumulated adjustments account	(b) Other adjustments account	(c) Shareholders' undistributed taxable income previously taxed
1 Balance at beginning of tax year . . .			
2 Ordinary income from page 1, line 21 . .			
3 Other additions			
4 Loss from page 1, line 21	( )		
5 Other reductions	( )	( )	
6 Combine lines 1 through 5			
7 Distributions other than dividend distributions .			
8 Balance at end of tax year. Subtract line 7 from line 6			

Form **1120S** (1999)

ESTABLISHING A LIMITED LIABILITY COMPANY

The newest and most closely watched form of legal operation is a *limited liability company* (LLC). Until recently, only 38 states recognized this type of business entity. Now, it is legal in all fifty states, but the laws governing LLCs differ in each state. An investment club seeking tax breaks and liability protection should consider a limited liability company.

Unlike an S corporation, an LLC lets you offer different classes of stock. An unlimited number of individuals, corporations, and partnerships can participate as shareholders.

Like S corporations and partnerships, LLC owners must report any loss or income on their individual tax returns. Income and losses generated in an LLC pass through to personal income and are taxed at the personal tax rate. LLC partners can determine what share of the business's profits and losses each member will receive. On the other hand, an S corporation dictates that the gains and losses be divvied up based on how much stock a member owns.

Another advantage is that LLCs enjoy the limited liability protection of a corporation. Owners and members can't be forced to use their personal assets to pay business debts, and any losses can be used as tax deductions against active income.

There are some restrictions on transferring ownership interests, though. In general, any member of a corporation can transfer his or her interest to another person without the permission or consent of the other members. An LLC restricts that privilege.

It is more expensive to form an LLC than a general partnership. It may run you as much as $2,500 to set up your organization. Some states charge an initial filing fee plus an annual fee. Consult your secretary of state's office for details and the necessary application forms.

Your club must file an article of organization with the state. Some states also require that you create an operating agreement—much like a partnership agreement—that spells out how you will conduct the affairs of the club.

OPERATING AS A LIMITED PARTNERSHIP

Limited partnerships often have been formed in real-estate deals in which property managers are the general partners and outside

investors, or investment club members, in this case, are limited partners. A limited partnership is a variation on the theme of a general partnership—there are some similarities as well as key differences.

This legal structure allows for two classes of partners: general partners, who handle all management duties of the business; and limited partners, who are strictly investors and have no control over the business's operations.

Limited partners have no personal liability except for the amount that they invest in the business. They cannot be sued for actions of the partnership. On the other hand, anyone who plays the role of general partner is personally responsible for liabilities—his or her house, car, bank account, and personal assets can be taken to satisfy any obligations of the partnership.

Like a general partnership, a limited partnership files tax information annually using Form 1065 and pays no taxes. All partners must report their share of income or loss on their individual tax returns and pay any taxes due. An exiting limited partner does not dissolve the business, but a general partner pulling out, unless the partnership agreement states otherwise, might mean the end of the business.

To form a limited partnership, you must obtain and file a certificate of limited partnership with the secretary of state's office. This document contains information about the partnership, including its name, address, purpose, and the names of the general partners. Requirements for filing a limited partnership certificate vary in each state.

CONCLUSION

Just keep in mind that your club may form a partnership starting out, especially given the amount of time and costs of administrative paperwork in setting up a corporation or any limited liability structure. As your club grows and seeks riskier ventures to invest in, you may opt for another legal structure that provides limited liability. This way, you can protect members from losing their personal assets and can better accommodate changes in your investment strategy.

5

RULES TO LIVE BY: DESIGNING OPERATING PROCEDURES

Ask for what you want and be prepared to pay for what you get.

—Maya Angelou

People don't plan to fail, they simply fail to plan.

—Unknown

Running an investment club isn't a sport, but you and fellow members must compete against yourselves in trying to pick the winners from the losers out of thousands of stocks that trade on the major exchanges. But before you get started, it's imperative that club members understand the rules and that they play by them. Much like a referee lays out the ground rules before a boxing match, the club needs to spell out some serious "do's and dont's."

For instance, members are allowed to miss only two meetings throughout the year, or members aren't allowed to withdraw their money in the first year. While members may verbally slug it out at meetings, it's important that there's a sportsmanlike atmosphere. Meaning that there shouldn't be any hard feelings when the group votes not to invest in a stock that an individual member recommends.

It's going to take camaraderie and a formal written agreement to run a profitable investment club. That said, the first bout is to iron out the thorny details on how the club is to operate and who is responsible for doing what at the club's start. "Let's get it on."

THE CLUB'S BYLAWS

With respect to the bylaws—a written agreement of your club's procedures and processes—there are several things you need to take into consideration.

Purpose of the Group

Are you going to invest strictly in bonds, and/or stocks, or in other securities, such as real estate? A good number of black clubs look beyond traditional securities—not only to invest gains they've made in the market, but as a means to give back to their communities. Take Detroit's Omega Diversified Investment Consortium. From the start, the frat brothers determined that they wanted to do more than invest in stocks to maximize their funds. Instead, they wanted to get involved in venture capital acquisitions. Initially, the club invested only in stocks and mutual funds, concentrating on building their portfolio by adopting a buy-and-hold strategy. The club was up and running for 10 years before ever purchasing its first broadcast property.

"We realized that most of us had investment portfolios at work and home," says the group's chairman of the board, Charles Hicks. "So, we didn't want to mirror image those portfolios. As a group we wanted to do something different and provide something extra. The way we approached our club was like a business: we wanted to develop some products that could help empower our communities."

Indeed, looking to build wealth within the African-American community, the Omega men created a nonprofit arm, the Omega Diversified Investment Foundation. Although it is still under development, the group's vision for the 501C.3 organization (a legal entity exempt from taxes), is to provide scholarships and internships to students majoring in communications at historically black colleges and universities.

How Often Will You Hold Meetings?

Biweekly, monthly, or bimonthly? Most clubs meet the first or third business day of each month. Make sure that everyone takes the meeting

place and time very seriously. Some clubs impose penalties for nonattendance.

For instance, members of the Windy City Investment Club, out of Chicago, start their meetings promptly at 4:00 P.M. In fact, the group uses a timer. Any member who is a minute late must pay a $2 fine. According to the bylaws of the Black Women Investment Corp. in Raleigh, North Carolina, members must attend 75 percent of the meetings throughout the year, although there are no penalties or punishments inflicted on no-shows.

How Will Decisions Be Made?

Each partner should participate in conducting the affairs of the club on an equal basis. Determine whether decisions require a majority vote or a two-thirds majority. Will you accept proxy votes cast by absent partners?

As with anything, there are exceptions. For example, you may run your club like a real corporation. "We are run by a board of directors much like any other corporation, such as Lucent Technology and AT&T," says Alliance Investment Group president Nathaniel "Nate" Watson. The AIG, comprised mostly of Lucent and AT&T employees, put all of its business affairs into the hands of its elected board of directors—which is made up of a president, first vice president, second vice president, secretary, treasurer, assistant treasurer, and three directors. Officers are elected every two years, and any AIG member can run for an elected office. While the board holds monthly meetings, the entire group meets annually and receives quarterly reports much like shareholders of the typical publicly traded company.

How Will Members Share in Club Profits and Losses?

In general, partners make a regular contribution at each meeting, usually a fixed amount. Still, you'll need to make allowances for members who wish to contribute more than their fair share. To prevent any member(s) from becoming a majority owner, you may limit the percentage of shares they may own. A capital account should be maintained in the name of each partner. Any increase or decrease in the value of the

club's portfolio must be credited or debited respectively to the value of each partner's account.

The AIG's bylaws offer three choices of investment levels to join. The first and lowest level of investment allows an individual to pay an initial $100 followed by $10 in monthly dues. The second level requires an initial payment of $250 and monthly contributions of $25. The third level allows those wanting to invest at a higher level to pay $500 followed by monthly payments of $50. The group ranges in age from toddlers (since many parents have opened up accounts for their children) to seniors. AIG recently formed the Alliance Kids Investment Club. Youth have the option of paying an initial $50 fee and $5 in monthly dues or $100 to join and $10 in dues.

There are some stipulations as to how much any one person can contribute: Members can't invest more than one year's worth of monthly contributions ahead of time. So, instead of paying $50 a month, you can pay a lump sum of $600 ($50 × 12 months).

How Will You Deal with Delinquent Contributions?

What fine will you impose on delinquent monthly contributions? What happens should a partner be delinquent in his or her monthly contributions for a period of 60 days; will that member be automatically terminated as a partner? If so, will that individual receive 100 percent of his or her total capital account or an amount equal to 95 percent (minus 5 percent for transaction fees) of his or her total stake in the club.

Every second Friday of the month the members of the Future-Vest Investment Club in New York meet. Anyone who fails to pay his or her $25 dues within the first 15 days of the month is charged a $25 late fee. So, that person has to pay twice as much that month. Moreover, if you miss three consecutive meetings you are ousted from the club. There is a 3 percent buyout fee to cover transaction costs.

How Will You Handle Members Who Leave or Join the Club?

Since change is inevitable, you need to address how and when partners can leave the group and new partners can be admitted. Not enough

clubs cover departing and joining members in their bylaws. How will you determine the value of new deposits? Will new members have to pay a lump sum to play catch up with existing members? What if someone experiences financial hardships and wants his or her share of the money right away? The club has to have enough cash reserve to cover the loss. Most clubs rely on a formula that is based on the overall value of the club's portfolio, years of membership, and number of shares owned.

In 1990, a group of 20 investors formed the M.O.D.E.L Club (Managing Our Dollars, Earnings and Learning) in Sacramento, California. Six years later, only eight members remained, none of whom were the founders. "Some of them left to join other clubs, others moved away," says Gary D. King, NAIC council and M.O.D.E.L club president. "Under the club's original agreement, we opted to pay out the fleeing club members in securities rather than cash. But whereas the club started out with ten stocks the group ended up with owning shares in only five companies."[1]

Many clubs require new members to pay a larger initial amount and attend at least two consecutive meetings prior to joining. This sort of probationary period helps to determine if prospective members have the time to fully participate in club activities and whether they are serious about investing.

How and When Will the Club Allow for Partial or Full Withdrawal of Funds?

A *partial withdrawal* means you take out part of your money. *Full withdrawal* means you divest all your capital from the club. The Alliance Investment Group made it mandatory for its members to stay in the club for a minimum of three years. Translation: A member could get out of the club at any time, but his or her money had to stay behind until the three-year period was up; at which time, a member could withdraw 100 percent of his or her funds minus a $25 transaction fee. "We wanted to make sure members got involved for the right reason," explains Watson. "We wanted people to understand this was a long-term investment and that they just couldn't up and leave after six months." Later, the Alliance amended its bylaws to institute a hardship withdrawal application, so that in an emergency a member could take out money before the three years expired.

How Will You Register the Stock?

Years ago, investors received stock certificates when they purchased securities. Nowadays, stocks are registered by a broker who makes book entries showing a computerized record of each stock transaction. If you like, you can register stocks in the club's name and have them sent to the treasurer's home. Another option is to purchase stocks in a *street name,* in which company reports and dividends are sent to the broker who forwards the info to the club and credits the money to the club's account. Accounts are insured by the federal government up to $500,000 to prevent brokerage fraud.

The Alliance opened an account with City National Bank of New Jersey, one of the nation's leading black-owned banks, and a brokerage account with A.G. Edwards. Each month, the treasurer deposits members' dues. Once the checks clear, the treasurer contacts the brokerage house and uses the money to buy securities. Many clubs have money automatically withdrawn from their bank accounts and deposited into their brokerage accounts, and sometimes a set portion is placed in a mutual fund account.

How Will the Club Handle Money?

Before investing, the club needs to open a checking account in the club's name (using its federal partnership ID number) and assign two or three members to sign checks, preferably the president and treasurer. Most clubs set up an account with enough cash on hand to take care of administrative expenses and pay any member who bails out.

What happens if a member does not pay dues because he or she is experiencing personal difficulty? Should you cash that member out or allow him or her to make up the difference once these personal matters are resolved? How might this impact the club's ability to purchase securities? In essence, the operating agreement must build in a contingency plan to address such issues.

"We had to pay $13,000 to one member who left the club (he moved out of state)," says Future-Vest's Monica Noel. "We had to raise cash to buy him out. Even though our bylaws provided for paying withdrawing members in stock or cash, most members usually opt for cash. Since we try to keep funds fully invested, we don't hold a lot of cash on hand. This forces us to have to sell shares in some of the stocks we own." Like most

clubs, Future-Vest tries to get rid of stocks that are the dogs of the industry or the club's portfolio at the time.

How Will You Terminate the Partnership?

Under what circumstance will the club cease to exist? Things happen, so you will want to prepare and have in writing how the group handles the club's demise—whether it's five days or fifty years after its formation. How will the club's portfolio be divvied up among members—what percentage of the total value and will they get their share of the pot in securities or cash?

In 1962, 13 men from the sales force of the Hamilton Management Corporation, a firm that sold mutual funds, formed the Progressive 20 Investment Club. Each member invested $10 a month—eventually $20—or $120 a year.

When the club was dissolved 27 years later, its money had increased to $75,000. The club's founder and presiding partner, Grafton J. Daniels received 7 percent of that amount, or about $5,250. He also garnered an average rate of return of $10,520 from his investment in the Progressive 20 club.

Undaunted, Daniels launched the St. George's Investment Club in Washington, DC, in 1983. The club has 30 members, most of whom belong to the congregation of St. George's Episcopal Church, including Daniels's daughter. Not including its octogenarian founder, the club's members range in age from 20 to 60 and its portfolio is valued at $300,000. If S.G.I.C. were to dissolve today, Daniels would get an equal share of the club's account—$9,000 or 3 percent per member.

Not all clubs divvy up their accounts 50/50. Several mandate that each member receives an amount proportionate to his or her contribution since inception. Thus, the club's newest members would get back less money than those who started out with the club.

WHO'S RUNNING THINGS?

As with any business entity, you need people to help run the organization. The activity level of your group will determine how many and what kind of officers are needed to accomplish your goals. All of your members should be encouraged to serve as officers, and your club's

officers should be elected annually. You may want to limit the secretary's term of office to less than a year, given the workload associated with the position.

You should count on electing at least five officers:

1. *President.* This presiding partner is responsible for setting the time and place for the meetings, appointing committees, ruling on procedural matters, presiding over meetings, and overseeing the activities of the club.

2. *Vice president.* This partner not only takes the place of the president when the president is unable to serve, but usually leads the investment education program. His or her responsibilities are to assign members to evaluate specific stocks and to report their findings to the club; lead the discussion of individual and group reports; and maintain and review the club's stock holdings and their present market position.

3. *Secretary.* This partner records minutes of the proceedings; reports on any unfinished business from the previous meeting; revises the minutes to include corrections and omissions; notifies members of the date, time, and place of each meeting; and sends copies of minutes to members. He or she also handles routine correspondence and maintains a membership roster.

4. *Treasurer.* This partner collects and disburses funds, oversees the club's banking and brokerage accounts, signs checks in the club's name, maintains a set of books showing the club's financial operations, coordinates preparation of the club's tax documents, deposits the club's monies as directed, and places buy-and-sell orders with a broker.

5. *Assistant treasurer.* This partner maintains the financial records of the club, keeps track of deposits and interest, and records all purchases. He or she prepares monthly statements showing cash on hand and the value of the club's portfolio. Recordkeeping includes an accounting of club receipts and disbursements, and calculation of each member's share of interest in the club.

The treasurer and assistant treasurer normally are responsible for developing a financial statement of the club's securities holdings—comparing what the club paid for each security with its current price. Some clubs appoint a separate recordkeeper whose job is to maintain a

list of all stocks, bonds, and so on, accompanied by the reason for the purchase.

It is not uncommon for clubs to have two secretaries: recording and corresponding. In these clubs, a recording secretary takes the minutes, provides copies to each member, and reports on unfinished business from the previous meeting. The corresponding secretary handles all correspondence, distributes club minutes, and maintains the membership roster.

Future-Vest and St. George's are not unlike many clubs that operate via a three- to five-tier committee structure. These groups can range from two or more members who are often responsible for specific areas. Should your club adopt this form, make sure each member of your club is required to serve on one of the club's standing committees. This ensures that everyone is involved in some phase of the club's activities.

Members should be encouraged to rotate committee assignments periodically, usually every two years, to enhance their knowledge of all phases of your club's investment activities. Committees generally meet once a month outside of the regular club meeting:

- *Executive committee.* This group is made up of the key officers (president, vice president, secretary, treasurer, and assistant treasurer. The executive committee is responsible for carrying out the club's overall goals and objectives. This group is charged with making sure all members adhere to the bylaws and—when necessary—updating those bylaws.

- *Education committee.* This group is responsible for gathering reading and research materials to keep members abreast of learning tools and resources that are available to them, such as NAIC's stock-study programs and council meetings. This arm of the club also arranges for members to attend special workshops, and sign up for classes on personal finance and investing, and encourages members to attend investors' fairs and conferences.

- *Investment or securities committee.* This group is responsible for taking the lead in setting the objectives for investing in the stock market, developing an investment strategy, selecting a broker, and buying or selling stocks and other securities. In general, individual members can make stock recommendations at any time, but the committee must compile and review the data to determine whether a particular security is a good buy.

Many investment clubs form committees to handle the group's more speculative, high return investments:

- *Real-estate committee.* Once club members determine whether they want to invest in residential, commercial, or resort properties, the real-estate committee is responsible for identifying potential real-estate properties. They must also decide whether the club wants to acquire local property, out-of-state property, or property outside of the country. In the case of the Alliance Investment Club, a single member of the board of directors will be in charge of overseeing real-estate investment as opposed to a group.

- *Entrepreneurial ventures committee.* This group is responsible for evaluating proposals for the club to invest in special projects or small businesses. This could involve any number of options, from putting up the funds for a local bazaar to buying a franchise to capitalizing a new software development firm. It's important that this group has someone on board who understands how to review business plans.

Over time your club will accumulate minutes, agendas, news and magazine articles, photographs, announcements, and so on. You may decided to appoint an official historian to collect and store these important documents, as well as to maintain and preserve the chronology of your investment club.

MEMBERS' RESPONSIBILITIES

Every member plays a critical and vital role in making your club successful.[2] It is important that members understand that each and every person is responsible for learning information on his or her own, as well as educating other members. Your club needs to spell out in the operating agreement the major tasks that members are required to perform:

- *Attending meetings.* Meeting are forums for discussing investment opportunities. Requiring attendance will ensure that every member has a voice in determining the club's short- and long-range goals. Require that your members attend a minimum number of meetings per year. This stipulation helps to

ensure participation. As harsh as it may sound, you may have to give members the boot if they are regular absentees.

- *Participating in meetings.* Members should come ready, willing, and able to fully discuss investment opportunities. The purpose of monthly meetings is to guarantee that every member obtains information that is necessary to make sound investment decisions. Members ought to feel free to voice reservations about specific investments or proposals, offer new ideas, and suggest alternative ways of accomplishing the club's investment objectives. Frank, lively discussions will help your club evaluate the strengths and weaknesses of each stock or security recommendation under consideration and to reach a consensus more quickly.

- *Selecting officers.* The club's officers may be elected by secret ballot or chosen by consensus. Officers must assume leadership roles and be committed to carrying out their duties for the duration of their term. While officers take charge of the club's operation, they must take into account all member input. In essence, they are the ones who should provide guidance and direction that is necessary for the club to accomplish its goals.

- *Researching investments.* The club should never purchase a stock (or securities) without formal analysis. Members are not expected to become professional analysts, however, each and every partner should become proficient in applying a few essential tests to enhance the club's prospects for success. This holds true regardless if your club has an investment committee that is calling the final shot on which stocks to buy, hold, and sell. Remember, a key component of investment clubs is learning to invest as a group, so that in turn, individual members can invest on their own.

- *Voting on investments.* Each member has the opportunity during a meeting to speak, argue, and vote on an investment opportunity being considered by the club. Prior to any vote, background information must be provided, questions answered, and discussions held. How can you expect members to cast well-informed votes when adequate information is not made available to them?

As a group, review and discuss issues covered in the bylaws. Consider adding a section on forbidden activities to prevent any one partner

from purchasing securities without club knowledge or authorization, binding or obligating the partnership in any transaction outside of the club, selling a part or all of his or her interest in the partnership to someone else, or using the club name to secure property or credit other than for the purposes of the partnership itself.

Make sure that the operating rules are acceptable to all members and that they comply with regulatory and tax requirements—consult an attorney. The club's operating agreement or bylaws may be between 15 and 25 pages long, whatever is necessary to cover the main points. Allow for amendments to the bylaws; situations change and unforeseen issues arise over time.

Alliance recently changed its bylaws so that one member of the board of directors would bear responsibility for real-estate development and another for business development. "Our group has grown in numbers and we have reached more than $200,000 in value. We expect to hit the $500,000 level in value by year 2001," adds Watson. For now, Alliance only owns stocks and mutual funds, although members have expressed to the board a desire to invest in some type of business venture. "One of the things our bylaws state is that we want to grow to a point where we can own businesses and provide jobs to people in our communities."

CONCLUSION

Keep in mind that the club's bylaws are not a one-shot deal. Update this document regularly. Some clubs revise their bylaws annually. Each year, members may learn something new about the nature of the club or encounter new issues they may have to deal with from a policy standpoint.

6

MEETING OF THE MINDS: RUNNING MEETINGS SMOOTHLY AND EFFECTIVELY

Persistence and positive attitude are necessary ingredients for any successful venture.

—L. Douglas Wilder

Organization is sacrifice. It is sacrifice of time, of work and money.

—W.E.B. Du Bois

Can you recall a circumstance in which you felt your time and money were totally wasted? Maybe it was a business deal gone sour, a lousy date, or a poor travel experience. Whatever the situation, you were left completely dissatisfied.

It's important that, each month, club members walk away from a meeting feeling their time was well spent. A successful club requires skillful organization and planning. Members will take their roles in the club seriously if matters are handled professionally. NAIC's Chairman of the Board of Trustees, Thomas E. O'Hara, says that it is no coincidence that clubs that hold well-run, organized meetings generally enjoy superior investment results.

GENERAL MEETING GUIDELINES

The following sections offer some helpful hints in running meetings smoothly and effectively.

Start on Time and Be Prompt

Send out a meeting notice (see Figure 6.1) to ensure that all members know the date, time, and location of the meeting. The president or vice president should call the meeting to order at the appointed hour. Reward members who show up on time, not stragglers. One club charges late members a dollar per minute. So, if you show up 10 minutes after the scheduled time, then that's an additional $10 out of your pocket—even though it goes into the club portfolio. The meeting should last as long as is necessary to cover all essential business. Ideally, it shouldn't take more than two-and-a-half hours.

Set an Agenda

Every meeting should have a game plan that is presented by the president (see Figure 6.2). It is a written tool that should help keep members focused. Of course, you want to follow a structured, yet flexible, agenda. But, in general, old and new business issues should be part of

Figure 6.1   Sample Meeting Notice

GENESIS INVESTMENT CLUB

Date:	Tuesday, June 15, 1999
Time:	7:00 PM
Host/Hostess:	Partner Jane Doe
Location:	130 Fifth Ave. New York, NY 10011 212-242-2000
Reminder:	If you cannot attend, please notify host/hostess.

Figure 6.2   Sample Meeting Agenda

GENESIS INVESTMENT CLUB
Agenda

June 15, 1999

Opening Remarks	President
Minutes	Secretary
Financial Report	Treasurer
Guest Speaker	John Doe, President of Delta Financial Services
Members' Reports	Vice President/Individual Members
Old Business	President
New Business	President
Announcements	Secretary
Adjournment	President

---

the agenda. The secretary should read minutes from the previous meeting (see Figure 6.3). The treasurer should review the club's portfolio, commenting on securities the club has already purchased, and give highlights of any discussions had earlier in the week with a broker. If the broker made a stock recommendation, then a member should be assigned to research and follow up on that particular stock.

Encourage Member Participation

Require involvement of all club members and reward member participation. Members should be allowed to express themselves without being pressured. It never fails that a handful of members end up doing 80 percent of the work, which can lead to resentment and fleeing club members. Make sure that members understand market declines, since those are the times when doubt sets in and members become impatient or complacent and participation tends to drag.

Figure 6.3   Sample Minutes

GENESIS INVESTMENT CLUB
Minutes

Meeting

The monthly meeting of the Genesis Investment Club was held on Wednesday, June 15, 1999 at 7:00 PM at the home of partner Jane Doe.

Attendance

The meeting was called to order at 7:15 by the president. All members were present. Guest speaker John Doe from Delta Financial Services was recognized.

Minutes

President approved minutes from last month's meeting.

Recommendations

We heard and discussed recommendations on three new stock candidates: Mobil, Intel, and Wendy's. The guest speaker John Doe of Delta Financial Services suggested that the club further diversify its portfolio by allocating 15% of its stock purchases to foreign stock. The following were cited as reasons:

- Allows investors to hedge against risk by profiting when U.S. currency is down.
- Allows investors to participate in regional trends (e.g., Asia).
- Allows investors to smooth out cyclical peaks and valleys in current portfolio.

Mr. Doe indicated that the best way to become involved in international investing is to purchase international stock mutual funds.

Treasurer's Report

Treasurer collected monthly dues from everyone present. He or she handed out copies of the club's current valuation statement and holdings report. The Liquidating Value Statement shows the value of the club's assets if they were to be liquidated (cashed in) that day. This valuation statement lists all of the club's assets valued at a date prior to the meeting. It also shows how many shares members' dues will buy at that point. The treasurer discussed other monetary news information, noting that the Federal Reserve announced it did not plan to raise interest rates. Also, he or she was informed by the broker that ABC Company plans to add a new product to its line that will increase sales by 30% over the next three years.

Figure 6.3   *(Continued)*

Vice President/Member Reports

The vice president asked members to present their stock study reports. Each member discussed the status of the stock he or she is responsible for covering, including historical earnings per share growth, estimated earnings per share growth, historical sales growth, and estimated sales growth. Members presented their monthly updates on their respective stocks, examining whether its current price was in line with the club's buy zone. Could the group buy more shares at a favorable price?

Most of the club's holdings showed revenues were up, earnings per share were up, sales were up, and growth rates were in line with past trends. A motion was made to buy more shares of all but one of the club's current holdings. Members voted to hold onto existing shares of that company stock pending further review at next month's meeting.

Old Business

Treasurer contacted broker about new stock purchases in Mobil, Intel, and Wendy's. The members were reminded that recommendations are needed for electing new club officers. Elections will be held at the August meeting.

New Business

Special consideration is being given to making stock purchases in the home improvement and medical supply industries. At the July 1999 meeting, the vice president will submit a formal recommendation regarding which stocks in those industries the club should review. Also, it was suggested that the committee assess whether foreclosure sales were a feasible way for the club to acquire real estate.

Announcements

None.

Adjournment

The meeting was adjourned at 9:30 PM

Respectfully submitted,

Secretary (name)
July 7, 1999

Present Securities Reports and Recommendations

Maintain a disciplined approach to studying and selecting stocks and portfolio-management procedures. Each member is responsible for researching a security. Pertinent information should be disseminated among members. Each member should report his or her findings: for instance, significant news about the company or industry, most recent quarterly sales and earnings figures, and a recommendation as to whether the stock is a candidate for purchase, hold, or sale. A formal presentation, including a table or chart, should be given to each member to review. Members must commit to doing research on their own time. Resources include *Standard & Poor's Stock Reports, Hoover's* business reports, *Barron's,* and *Better Investing* magazine, published by NAIC (all which are discussed in more detail in Chapter 12).

Vote on Securities

After updates on the portfolio and reports are made, a motion is made by the president or vice president, and members must vote on whether to buy what was presented or to buy more of what the club already holds. There should be an open floor discussion and thoughtful consideration of all issues and investment picks. There may be more than one course of action with regard to the club's current holdings—members may vote to buy additional shares of one stock and to sell shares of another stock that has underperformed.

You don't have to decide on any given security right away. If the club needs more information or time to decide, members can review that security again and vote on it at the next meeting. Some clubs starting out spend the first couple of meetings just researching securities before even purchasing their first share—though you don't want to waste months trying to decide on every candidate and let a good stock buy pass you by.

Call for Next Meeting

After the investment decision, the club should discuss any new business and recap any special items from the previous meeting. The president or

vice president should ask for suggestions for new companies or industries to be considered at the next meeting and make assignments for the following month's investment reports/presentations.

Invite Guest Speakers

Down the road, you may find your meetings are too predictable. To liven things up, invite outside speakers to attend the meetings to discuss trends and investment opportunities. Members can call on financial planners or NAIC regional council reps. A local economist, bank executive, or college professor can make for a great guest who can lead engaging discussions on regional, national, or even international economic outlooks. In addition to trying to relieve the monotony, use guest speakers to educate members in areas in which they may be lacking.

Maintain a Waiting List

A club should always have replacements on hand for when a member leaves the group—and eventually someone will depart. Occasionally invite potential members to sit in on the monthly meetings.

Keep Interest High

Many clubs break up because of lack of confidence if the club is not making money. The club *will* make money over time as long as members continue to choose good-quality companies and stick with them. Find ways to promote the spirit of enthusism, excitement, and enjoyment. Use aides such as computers, videotapes, and overhead projectors to facilitate member participation and understanding of market cycles.

EDUCATE AND MOTIVATE: THE BLACK WOMEN INVESTMENT CORPORATION

Perhaps the greatest challenge that every club faces is membership participation.[1] That's because it is always easiest at the beginning of a club. Whenever a new club meets, everyone is bustling with enthusiasm.

There's rarely a problem getting members to research and recommend stocks. There's a feeling, a spirit, that anything is possible.

Two years later—sometimes even after six months—members start singing a different tune. The excitement starts to fade and members start to slack off. They stop coming to the meetings. They do less work researching companies and recommending stock picks. In short, their idea of belonging to a club has narrowed to sending in a dues check each month.

It takes more than a monthly monetary contribution to accumulate wealth. You need members who are willing to devote their time to club activities. You need the group to pull together in order to hang in there long enough to reap financial rewards.

How can your club survive the down cycles of group investing? One strategy Black Women Investment Corp. (BWIC) uses to keep members motivated is training programs. Launched in 1988, every partner is required to complete a short session each month and attend an annual program that could last from one day to six weeks. The sessions cover a wide range of issues, such as using library resources to investigate companies, finding information on-line, and using NAIC tools to analyze and select stocks.

"Two years ago, we had six three-hour sessions because we had new people who wanted to join the club," says Saundra Wall Williams, past president of the investment club and NAIC council president for the eastern North Carolina region. "Before a new partner can join, we require her to take the training. This way, she is clear about what she is getting into. We started out with nine women who wanted to join the group; after the sessions, only six decided to sign on."

Williams points out that some measures clubs take to get members to participate are somewhat harsh, such as a club that stipulates that if a member misses three meetings out of the year, he or she is out of the club. Or, if you don't present a stock recommendation at least twice a year, you are out.

The idea is to bring together—from the start—people who are willing to work together and are committed to the club's success, she explains. Even if you don't exact any penalties, it is important to make sure the club's partnership agreement and bylaws clearly state that members must recommend stocks and attend meetings a certain number of times a year.

Today, BWIC comprises 15 women representing various professions, from educators to engineers, and ranging in age from 25 to 55. The

club's $75,000 portfolio, with an average rate of return of 28 percent, holds shares in 15 companies, including Nike, Home Depot, Microsoft, PepsiCo, and Cisco Systems. A company has to have a good track record for at least five years before the club will consider it. They watch a stock for three months before deciding if they want to buy it.

BWIC is strict on members who take partial or full withdrawals. A member can take out a part of her money—the minimum is $500—but she must have been in the club for at least two years. According to the club's bylaws, it will take 60 days for the club to get a departing member her money, since it must sell some of its securities if cash is not available. The member pays transaction fees associated with selling the securities—usually 3 percent to 5 percent. The club reduces the member's personal holdings by the amount withdrawn. However, members can put that portion of their money back into the club at any time.

"What makes our club successful is that we are consistent," says Williams. "We have always invested regardless of what was going on in the market or around us. When you invest that way, you see your club getting a constant return and you see your portion of the club's portfolio continue to grow. That's an incentive for partners to stay in the club to keep learning and to continue investing."

HAVE A LITTLE FUN

There is nothing wrong with having a little fun or socializing at meetings, but it should be done after the formal meeting is over. At that point, you can turn your attention to refreshments and casual conversation. Relaxing before going home helps end each meeting on a high note. Conversely, eating when you first arrive may leave everyone sapped before the important work begins.

Your club can host outside activities not related to investing. Most clubs sponsor two social events during the year, usually a Christmas party and summer picnic, to which spouses, children, and other family members are invited.

Some clubs hold a three-day or weekend annual retreat at a resort or elegant hotel. Your club could also give a party with one or more clubs in your region. Your club could consider a field trip to a financial institution, such as a stock exchange, which could prove educational. Take advantage of the visitor's gallery to learn firsthand how the market works.

Arrange a club visit to a company in which your club owns shares, so that members can see and possibly meet the people who supply the company's products or services. It's wise to have a member attend a company's annual shareholders' meeting and report on the management's message, business discussed and voted on, problems that were brought up and reported on, and any questions raised by other stockholders.

Think creatively: "How can we best meet the needs of our club?" Your club could put out a one- to two-page newsletter that discusses the club's portfolio performance, gives investment tips for members with personal portfolios, or announces special events in members' lives.

Chris Wilson, founder of the New Freedom Investment Club in Durham, North Carolina, produces a monthly investment newsletter, *Ebony Investor.com* (www.ebonyinvestor.com; 919-419-1318). Along with friends Robert Lancaster and Saundra Wall Williams of BWIC, he started the four-year-old African-American publication (formerly known as *Wall-Streetwise*), which offers stock analyses and model portfolios. Subscription to the newsletter is free, but it does require you to sign up via the Web site. The e-newsletter is e-mailed to subscribers each month and posted to the site a few days afterward.

During the week, the three independently gather information from the Web or the library and meet once a month to hash out which companies they will include in the newsletter's model portfolio. As editor, Wilson says the group's Saturday morning meetings are very pleasant, members take turns hosting the gathering while they sip tea and grapple with the numbers. The calm atmosphere doesn't necessarily make for lightweight picks. Since the trio have been long-time investment club members, they know the lay of the land.

Williams no longer contributes to the newsletter but Wilson and Lancaster are steadfast online stock pickers. *Ebony Investor.com*'s portfolio holds between 17 and 20 stocks, depending on how optimistic Wilson and his colleagues are about the economy. From there, the North Carolinians follow set criteria, such as hunting for companies with an average 10 percent or more annual increase in sales.

There's also research done on how efficiently the company is run, a conclusion Wilson says is easy enough to reach after working through annual reports and documents corporations must file with the Securities Exchange Commission (SEC). *Ebony Investor.com*'s portfolio has more than held its own, with a 23 percent average annual return, a figure that shames most mutual funds.[2]

CONCLUSION

For new clubs, a lot of time will be spent studying stocks and other securities the club is considering for purchase. As the club gets older, members will spend more time hearing updated reports on stocks and other securities the club already owns. Your goal as a member is both to get a good return on your investment and to learn how to judge a stock's growth potential.

Well-organized meetings will keep members acquainted with the stocks they own and will assure your club's success. Run your club following these guidelines and each and every member will learn a great deal about stock values, make some money, and have fun doing it.

7

SEVEN KEYS TO A PROFITABLE CLUB: FOLLOWING THE RIGHT PATH TO INVESTING

Tell me, and I forget. Teach me, and I may remember. Involve me, and I learn.

—Benjamin Franklin

Today's most prosperous investment clubs—those with assets of several thousand to more than a million dollars—started out years ago with only a few dollars and little or no prior experience. Yet these novice investors managed to achieve results that would make many professional money managers green with envy.

Your club can apply the same tested and proven standards that have made these clubs profitable. Like the tortoise in Aesop's fable, all you need is to be patient—slow and steady wins the race—and to avoid a few hare traps. Rabbitlike investors end up with sleepy portfolios when they develop a basic plan, yet fail to stick with it through thick and thin.

Most clubs are not profitable in the first two to three years. Starting out, club members may not have large sums of money to invest, but this is fine, since most members are spending a good deal of their time educating themselves during the early years.

"My belief is to make mistakes while the club is still young," advises Saundra Wall Williams, who is one of 20 members of NAIC's national board of directors, the governing body responsible for making the rules for member councils. "If you are going to lose money, let it be in the early stages while you are still learning as opposed to waiting until you have a lot of money to lose."

The knowledge gained by investing the whole time is key to a club's success in building wealth. Don't operate in a vacuum. There's an old saying: "Learn from the mistakes of others, because you won't live long enough to make them all yourself." Simply put: Follow the lead of other successful clubs if you want yours to be profitable.

SEVEN KEY PRINCIPLES

A good place to start is to adhere to seven key principles set forth by *Black Enterprise* magazine and the National Association of Investors Corporation, which all winning investment clubs follow rigorously.[1]

Key #1. Practice Dollar-Cost Averaging

It doesn't matter whether the market is in a boom or bust, club members must commit to investing a set amount of money in the market each month—a practice known as *dollar-cost averaging*. This way, you buy more shares when prices drop and fewer shares when prices go up (Figure 7.1). The reason being that, when prices are lower, your money buys more shares for the same fixed amount; when those shares are overpriced, your set monthly amount of money buys fewer shares. The average cost per share of the investment is less than the average market price per share over the period you are investing, enabling you to capitalize on price fluctuations.

With this approach, you're virtually certain to purchase stocks at a bargain, and profit significantly when prices move upward. This doesn't mean that you won't ever lose money. However, it does mean that your losses will be less if your club starts investing at a bad time *(bear market)* and your club will have gains if it starts investing at a good time *(bull market)*.

You may ask: Why not just wait around to buy shares when they are really cheap and sell them when they are too expensive? The

Figure 7.1   Dollar-Cost Averaging

Date of Meeting	Amount Invested ($)	Share Price ($)	Shares Purchased	Shares Owned
January 15	250.00	15.00	16.67	16.27
February 15	250.00	14.00	17.86	34.53
March 15	250.00	12.00	20.83	55.36
April 15	250.00	10.00	25.00	80.36
May 15	250.00	12.00	20.83	101.19
June 15	250.00	14.00	17.86	119.05
July 15	250.00	16.00	15.63	134.68
August 15	250.00	17.00	14.71	149.39
September 15	250.00	18.00	13.89	163.28
October 15	250.00	21.00	11.90	175.16
November 15	250.00	22.00	11.36	186.54
December 15	250.00	24.00	10.42	196.96
Totals:	3,000.00	195.00	196.96	

Average cost per share: Total amount invested divided by shares owned
$3,000 ÷ 196.96 = $15.23

Average price per share: Total share price divided by number of purchases
$195 ÷ 12 = $16.65

Value of portfolio: Number of shares owned multiplied by the current price
196.96 × $24.00 = $4,727.04

Net profit: Total value minus total amount invested
$4,727.04 − $3,000 = $1,727.04

answer is that you don't have the foresight to know when those situations will arise. Not even professional money managers know how to time the market.

The Washington Metropolitan Investment Club uses dollar-cost averaging to make the most of a turbulent market. Launched in 1992, the club's portfolio dropped 28 percent when the market hit a downturn in 1998—as did many other investors.

"We decided to stick with our goal of investing a set amount per person each month," says the club's past president Gerald Coles. "We aren't bothered by market fluctuations. Because we dollar-cost average, we were able to use the same monthly contributions to purchase more shares in our current holdings since stock prices were low."

In fact, Washington Metro doubled the number of shares owned in several companies, including Colgate-Palmolive, Lucent Technologies, and Waste Management. When the market turned around, the club's portfolio profited handsomely.

By constantly buying shares using dollar-cost averaging, your club will end up buying more shares at lower costs over the long haul. Market tides may cause speculators or inexperienced investors to bail out, but astute club members welcome dips as buying opportunities.

Key #2. Invest in Growth Companies

Investment clubs can almost assure solid returns by investing in companies whose sales and earnings are increasing at a rate faster than their industries in general. These companies reinvest most of their earnings in the business to expand operations and to generate new and improved products through research and development.

Growth in a business comes in many ways. One is a growing industry in which those companies that offer products, materials, or services grow as they fill that market. Companies introducing new products or services that satisfy an unmet market need stimulate growth. Sometimes, companies find a new use for an old product which then spurs growth. Most investors concede though that the most reliable and long-lasting growth is driven by good, solid management.

With about $80,000 under management, the Madison Area Investment Club owns shares in 15 companies. Some of its biggest winners and long-term holdings are McDonald's, Merck, Cisco Systems, and PepsiCo. Like most member clubs, Madison uses NAIC's *Stock Selection Guide,* a customized methodology designed to help investors pick growth stocks.

The club's president, Robert Wynn, explains, "The guide helps determine (1) Is this a good company, meaning, has it been growing at 15 percent a year and will it continue to grow at that rate over the next five years and (2) is it currently selling at a good or reasonable price? If we buy a company that is too high in price, it could substantially set back our opportunity to have appreciable gains in the near term."

Madison uses industry reports (available at your local library) published by big investment advisory firms such as Standard & Poor's and Value Line to examine a company's growth rate in terms of sales and earnings over the past five to ten years.

Key #3. Diversify Investments

A club should invest in different-sized companies in different industries. "Aim for holdings in eight core industries: Consumer staples,
technology, consumer cyclical, capital goods, communications, health
care, financial services, and energy," recommends Simone A. Thompson, investment representative with New York-based Edward Jones, a
financial services company.

You can check size by the market capitalization or the number of
shares outstanding times the stock price. Consider a balanced portfolio in which 50 percent of the club's holdings are in medium-sized
companies (those with annual sales between $400 million and $2 billion), 25 percent in large companies (those earning $2 billion or more in
annual sales), and the remaining 25 percent in small companies (those
with sales under $400 million and rapid rates of growth).

This ratio may differ depending on a given club's risk-tolerance
level. Madison tries to get a good mix by investing half its money in small
and mid-sized companies and the other half in large firms or blue chips—
major, well-established companies in top industries that have long records
of earnings growth and dividend payments in good and bad times.

The club's portfolio extends across different industries from technology to consumer household goods to pharmaceuticals. "We took a
bottom-up approach, meaning we looked at individual companies first
as opposed to a top-down approach where you would choose a certain
industry first and then go after companies within that area to invest,"
Wynn says. The club tries not to have more than two to three stocks
within the same industry.

Key #4. Create Study Teams

"Each one teach one" is the motto of the typical investment club. That's
because experienced or knowledgeable members often teach what they
know to others. One way to assist club members in understanding how
to pick a company stock is to develop stock-study groups. This is where
you have teams of two or more members research stocks together, prepare reports, and present their findings to the group.

"When we started out, most of us were really naïve and somewhat
afraid to invest in the stock market," admits Washington Metro's Coles.
"So, we paired off to research stocks. We try to have strictly educational

meetings about three times a year. We also use a portion of our club's funds to send members to workshops." One of the hardest things, as far as any club is concerned, is getting members on the same page. So, the club is working on a Web site (www.icinvest.com) to keep members up to date on the stocks in their portfolio, meeting dates, and how-to guidelines for selecting stocks.

Initially, each member brings a different understanding or level of knowledge about the stock market to the group. It is important that the club provides ongoing education.

Many clubs have a stipulation in their bylaws that partners must continuously develop their skills when it comes to picking stocks. Members must be willing to learn the rigors of evaluating a company's stocks, says Baunita Greer, president of Cromwell, Miller and Greer, a New York-based brokerage firm and active member of the Coalition of Black Investors. "Club members need to understand what fundamentals to consider, such as sales, prices, earnings, betas, dividends, and industry trends. But they also need to know how to interpret this information, so that they will better understand when to buy, hold, or sell a security," adds Greer, who also belongs to the CMG Investment Club, a small group of Wall Street professionals.

Greer and other NAIC representatives can't stress enough that member participation is the lifeblood of your club. It's important that the group solicits ideas from every member about companies to look into for possible purchases.

Key #5. Reinvest All Earnings and Dividends

A club's money grows faster when earnings are reinvested. The club maximizes its profits through compounding. Moreover, those clubs that flourish do so because they tend to stay fully invested at all times. Meaning, they rarely turn over their portfolios, instead reinvesting all returns, including dividends and interest.

Professional money managers may sell and buy their holdings more than once—possibly even three times—during the course of a year, in hopes of garnering higher profits. This short-term trader mentality doesn't quite mesh with the long-term growth objective of investment clubs. Members minimize risks and maximize gains when they purchase shares they intend to hold onto as long as the business is operating smoothly and making money.

CMG is not unlike most clubs that concentrate on increasing their ownership of the best performers, substituting the better stocks for those that fail to live up to expectations. "Clubs continue to hold onto quality companies that they own as long they exhibit high growth potential," says Greer. "When a club sells a stock, it's generally because of trailing earnings, where the company has lagged behind its peers for an extended period of time and no longer has a high growth potential."

Once they crunch the numbers, members don't see anything that would change that company's growth rate. Another time clubs sell shares is when the stock becomes grossly overpriced (or overvalued), generally taking one-quarter to one-third of their profits.

Key #6. Evaluate the Club's Portfolio

You're not expected to become a professional analyst. However, you should become proficient in applying a few essential tests to enhance your club's prospects for success. At every monthly meeting, your club should review the securities it owns to determine if it wants to buy, hold, or sell investments based on both fundamental and technical research.

* * *

In *fundamental research,* members study the company, industry, and market, trying to understand what makes a company run and what its future will be. You are looking for companies to grow and increase in value over a long period of time. In *technical research,* members pay more attention to the stock market and stock price, with the hope of making money from price moves caused by conditions in the stock market itself rather than any one company's progress.

Each month, Washington Metro evaluates its holdings using both technical and fundamental analysis. This requires members to draw a graph that plots each company's sales, earnings, and stock-price fluctuations, so that the group can get a visual analysis to determine if a company is meeting its projected growth rate of 15 percent or above. In their fundamental analysis, the group looks at the company's price-to-earnings (P/E) ratio and where it stands in its respective industry.

While Washington Metro tries to stay fully invested at all times, the club did sell its shares in Upjohn, opting to buy Pfizer. Explains Coles, "These are two companies in the same sector, but we felt Pfizer had a better growth and earnings projection."

In general, your best strategy is to purchase companies with good fundamentals at a reasonable price, keeping in mind that stock prices fluctuate and that, though downward trends can last for a while, the overall movement in the market has been upward.

Look at management's capabilities as evidenced by growing sales and earnings, pretax profit margin (sales − costs ÷ sales), and superior return on stockholders' equity (net earnings divided by the sum of the value of preferred stock, common stock, and retained earnings).

Key #7. Be Patient and Invest for the Long Term

Ideally, you should plan to maintain member status in a club until your retirement years. It is crucial for clubs to stay together for a significant period of time, otherwise, their ability to achieve long-term gains will vanish. According to the NAIC, club members who begin their program in their twenties and maintain it until their departure from the labor force 40 years later could amass $1.9 million at a rate of return of 10 percent (barring withdrawals over the four decades).

Washington Metro's bylaws call for a minimum 20-year goal for the club to stay together. This is in spite of the fact that the 29-member club's broad group of investors range in age from midthirties to retirees. The group represents several different sectors of the population, including corporate professionals, government workers, senior officers in the U.S. military, and small-business owners. Coles says members formed the club to do smart investing so that they could in turn build a nest egg for themselves, their children, and their families. Members must learn to be patient—remember, "slow and steady wins the race."

EIGHT IS ENOUGH: HOW MANY STOCKS SHOULD YOUR CLUB OWN?

By now, you know that spreading around the holdings in your portfolio increases your gains and reduces your risk. But, how many stocks does it take to have an optimal diversified portfolio? Moreover, how much do you really need to reach that mark?[2]

Your first instinct may well be to opt for a mutual fund or two. Many clubs starting out park their cash in mutual funds until making

that first stock purchase. If your club wants substantial exposure to overseas market opportunities, then you may want to invest in an international or global mutual fund. Or, if your club wants to invest in a very high-growth industry sector like biotechnology or the Internet, you may want to gain exposure in those sectors via a mutual fund.

Don't settle just for mutual funds. Your club should jump headlong into the stock market, say experts like NAIC Chairman Thomas E. O'Hara. In his eyes, investment clubs aren't the place to put the bulk of your savings and shouldn't be treated as such. Instead, clubs are a great place for individuals to learn the ups and downs of investing in stocks, but only if they thoroughly research companies before purchasing shares.

The average investment club is nine years old, with a portfolio amounting to $89,000, a sum that can easily be spread about a number of companies in a variety of industries. Members of newer clubs may think that this is out of their reach, given that year-old clubs likely have a portfolio amounting to $2,000 to $5,000. O'Hara stresses that's still no reason to lump all of your investment dollars in one place.

When New Jersey-based Ebony Prospectors Investment Club was formed, diversification was one of the first issues the group's 13 members grappled with. By October 1995, just two months after the club was established, members made their first investments with just $780. Member Ann Joyner says Ebony Prospectors divided the money among McDonald's, AFLAC, and Motorola.

At first glance, dividing $780 among three companies may seem like a stretch but, according to NAIC, the average one-year-old club holds eight companies in its portfolio. Later, they concentrate on increasing the ownership of those investments offering the better returns. Generally, clubs not yet ten years of age will own no more than 20 to 25 stocks and other securities.

Adding a number of stocks means you're open to less risk of one company sinking and taking you under with it. To achieve true diversification, you need to concentrate more on making investments in various industries that move at different parts of the economic cycle. Ebony Prospectors did that by investing in the fast-food, insurance, and semiconductor industries at first, then adding oil, financial, and technology to the mix when they purchased shares in Mobil, Synovus Financial, and Intel in January 1996. To date, the club's total return has been 14 percent.

It doesn't take a lot of companies to successfully diversify a portfolio. There are limits. "During the first year for the average club, I

wouldn't advise going beyond 12 stocks," advises O'Hara. "The more stocks you have, the harder it is for individual members to keep track of them."

On the flip side, Randall Ely, president of the Edgar Lomax Co., a 12-year-old money management firm based in Springfield, Virginia, says your portfolio should contain no less than eight stocks. According to Ely, the ideal number is 10, because it gives you a large enough portfolio that, if one stocks goes down, it will affect only 10 percent of your portfolio.

Even if you buy a couple of stocks at a time, aim toward owning *lots* (100 shares) in a company, advises Cheryl Broussard, a registered investment advisor and principal of Broussard & Douglas Inc., an Oakland-based money-management firm. Your club should not be as concerned with how many stocks it does or does not own, but that each holding has the potential to reach its projected growth rate.

"Select a downside and upside percentage. In other words, if a stock drops 15 percent to 20 percent, the club agrees to sell the stock and take the loss, or if it is up 50 percent, the club agrees to take the profit," adds the author of the *Black Woman's Guide to Financial Independence*. "Once you have made your decision don't look back. There are plenty of stock opportunities out there."

As you begin to operate as a club and purchase your first few shares of stock, there are a few points that you should consider:

- *Be aware of the state of the market when you first start to invest.* If you start buying during a period of high prices, keep investing during the period of low prices which is almost sure to follow. This will help your club average some of the high prices members paid for stocks. When stock prices turn around, your club will see the advantage it gained during the down cycle.

- *Don't get too confident too soon.* Some clubs that start investing during a market down period start crediting themselves too much when prices head upward. This can make a new club careless and lead to future losses.

- *Put each stock/security you buy to a test.* Remember, the club's overall goal is to achieve 100 percent appreciation at each market peak. Thus, every stock you buy should have the potential to double in price and sales and earnings per share every five years. Many members may fret at how stock prices fluctuate, but they must always remember that, historically, stocks have

always recovered from declines and moved on to new highs. Your club will experience both. To accomplish this, members must consistently conduct formal analysis of each stock purchase.

NINE UP, TEN DOWN: EDUCATING MEMBERS

Chances are that if your club has nineteen members, ten people are going to keep up on the latest company news, trends, and information, while the other nine are totally clueless—they still think P/E stands for physical education.

Logically enough, the most knowledgeable members tend to be the most committed to the club. In short, they're the ones who do all the work. With that in mind, it's in your club's best interest to continuously increase members' knowledge about investing.

Encourage members to participate in NAIC regional council meetings, and to attend stock-study classes that the NAIC sponsors, a series of twelve lessons on selecting and evaluating stocks. "Many council presidents will actually go out and tutor a new investment club," adds Baunita Greer, a member of NAIC's New York regional council. Council directors also serve as a sounding board for local clubs, many of which sponsor open forums in which club members get to ask questions and address their needs. Just about all host an annual investors' fair, where four to five companies of different sizes make presentations.

Another key in boning up on the market is reading. Members should routinely read at least one business or investment publication, advises Greer. Some members, if not all, should subscribe to financial newsletters for ideas on investing.

The local library is the best place to start to develop club resources. Develop a relationship with the reference librarian and have him or her give your club a tour of the reference section and expose you to the services and resources available. The most widely used tools among investment clubs are *Value Line Investment Survey, Standard & Poor's Stock Reports, Morningstar Mutual Fund* newsletter, and *Better Investing* magazine, published by NAIC. There also are a number of Web sites that provide investment news and pointers (see Chapter 11).

Once you become a stockholder, you automatically receive company reports. But, before you even make your first stock purchase, call the investors' relations department of the prospective company

and ask for the annual report and most recent company quarterly report free of charge, which is also available via the Securities Exchange Commission (SEC).

CONCLUSION

Early on, the biggest advantage to joining an investment club is that everyone is learning about investing together. To ensure that members are indeed learning, it is crucial to set some time aside during meetings for the sole purpose of introducing something new about the market, securities, and investing in general. Equally important, members must be willing to carve out time from their busy schedules to learn outside regular club meetings.

Whatever standards your clubs sets, you have to be consistent and make sure that everyone buys in. How well your club's investments perform will hinge on each member's level of competence and cooperation. Your club will prosper as long as everyone is in it to win for the long haul.

8

SWEAT THE SMALL STUFF: RECORDKEEPING AND OTHER TAXING ISSUES

If you want to know the ending, look at the beginning.

—African Proverb

There are three kinds of people in the world: those who make things happen, those who watch things happen, those who wonder what happened.

—Unknown

The daily mantra for the millions of fans—especially talk-show queen Oprah Winfrey—of author Richard Carlson is "don't sweat the small stuff." But, for investment club members, survival depends on how well they pay attention to every little detail when it comes to keeping accurate records.

The last time you probably kept a diary was your teen years. It told the story of every one of the crucial events in your life: first date, first kiss, first love. Throughout the life of your investment club, you will most definitely have to keep a diary. No, you won't have to write in detail about the first time everyone met. You *will* have to maintain a

financial journal that tracks every single cash transaction in chronological order.

Moreover, you will have to keep ledgers that calculate each member's share, which will constantly change, since new people will come aboard as others jump ship. Your club also will have to keep an individual record of each stock purchased and dividends received. And since there are no guarantees in life but death and taxes, your club will have to file both partnership and individual tax forms.

Granted, this is a not-so-sexy chapter of the book, dealing with the issues of bookkeeping and taxes; it is one of the most important. Forget whatever inhibitions you may have about anything that smacks of mathematics. The longer you put off understanding the basics of accounting procedures, the costlier it will be for your club down the road.

KEEPING THE CLUB'S BOOKS

The financial partner or treasurer is ultimately responsible for handling the books, but all club members should be familiar with the process of recordkeeping to protect themselves and the club, advises Thomas E. O'Hara, chairman of the NAIC board of trustees. "Every member should also be prepared to audit the work of the financial partner or treasurer if asked to do so," he says.

When starting out, the club's organizers should seek someone who has some experience in bookkeeping and accounting, advises Jerrilyn O. Collier, financial partner for New York's TIF Investment Club, currently a budget manager for NYC's Human Resources Administration. Collier, along with an assistant, is responsible for recording all payments and collecting fees at the monthly meetings, executing stock trades, reconciling the books and brokerage statements, preparing a valuation statement on the club's holdings as well as an individual's share of the pot, and handling tax forms.

The cornerstone of club accounting is the journal. Collier points out that it helps that much of her work life has been as a fiscal officer for nonprofits and city agencies. "But, even with my own personal bank statements I have to prove everything I spend right down to the penny. So, you need someone in place as a financial officer who has that kind of mindset, where he or she has to check out everything." Even in cases in which no one in the club was prepared to handle the books, most members found they had access to a CPA, either through a

spouse, family member, or friend, who was willing to work pro bono with the financial partner or treasurer.

Help is readily available. In addition to a number of books on the subject, NAIC offers training classes and an accounting manual, featuring forms for recording financial data by hand. NAIC also provides a club accounting-software program, although the treasurer can use any of a number of spreadsheet programs, such as Excel or Lotus 123, to handle the club's bookkeeping needs.

Another option is hiring an outside accountant or bookkeeper to maintain the club's books, but keep in mind that an accountant isn't cheap. Some of the large, national accounting firms charge $50 to $125 an hour for their services. An independent bookkeeper may charge up to $25 an hour, depending on your region.

As with most clubs, TIF uses NAIC's accounting-software program, which makes it a lot easier, yet still time consuming, says Collier. "One week after each meeting, my assistant and I update everything. Once a month we evaluate our portfolio. We have a separate committee that performs an annual check-up of the accuracy of the club's books and then prepares and signs off on a verification report that is kept on record. Also, at the end of the year, I get the necessary forms from the state or IRS and give them to each person to fill out."

Usually several days before each meeting, the financial partner/ treasurer prepares a valuation statement that shows the number of shares of each security owned by the club, the average cost per share, the total cost of the purchase or purchases, the current market price of the share, and the current value of each security. Most clubs base valuation on the closing price of listed securities and the bid price of over-the-counter stocks. The valuation statement also reports the total value of the club's portfolio to date and the amount of cash on hand.

You may wonder: Why the need for complex calculations, since the monthly ante required of each member is the same? Bottom line: Your club won't be able to maintain identical share values among all members. First, there's bound to come a time when some club members will wish to contribute more than the set amount. Second, you need to adjust the account and record when members withdraw any of their shares or a new member joins the group.

Each member's account consists of two parts: (1) the accumulation of cash deposits and (2) the valuation of his or her deposits, which includes the sum of profits and losses. All the club's assets are valued monthly—each time members deposit additional funds.

Figure 8.1 The Club Valuation

The Story of Investment Club #600

There are 12 members in Investment Club #600. Each month members contribute $30 in dues, or $360 in total. In return, each member will get three valuation units (a unit has an arbitrary value of 10). In this case, a total of 36 units (12 × 3) was issued by the club.

At the July meeting, Investment Club #600 decides to purchase 20 shares of Moore Steel for a total investment of $344.80, or $17.24 per share, including fees and taxes. This leaves the group with a cash balance of $15.20 (total amount on deposit minus the total investment; $360 − $344.80).

Since Moore Steel is trading at $16.125, the current value of the club's portfolio is $322.50 ($16.125 × 20). Add the $15.20 cash on hand and the total value is $337.70.

The actual dollar price of a valuation unit is $9.38 ($337.70 divided by 36). So, the number of units for every $10 paid into the club would purchase is 1.0661 valuation units ($10.00 divided by $9.38).

Investment Club #600 also decided to purchase 22 shares of XG Company at $16.10 per share. The following is the August Valuation Statement in an expanded version.

Company	Div'd/Exch.	Est. 5 Year Hi	Est. 5 Year Low	P/E	No. of Shares	Cost per Share	Total Cost	Price per Share This Date	Total Value
Moore Steel Co.	1.20-NYSE	$36.00	$15.00	16	20	$17.24	$344.80	$16.125	$322.50
XG Co.	1.10-NYSE	33.00	12.00	14	22	16.10	354.20	15.00	330.00
Cash on Hand									21.00
Total Value of Club to Date									673.50

Total Number of Valuation Units to Date 74.3796

Value of One Unit $ 9.05

Number of Units $10.00 Purchases 1.1050

Members' Total Investment $720.00

Purchases Last Month:

XG Co. @ $16.10

Members Name	Invested Last Month	Total Invested	Value Units Purchased Last Month	Total Value Units
Bob Smith	$ 30.00	$ 60.00	3.1983	6.1983
Frank Vestor	30.00	60.00	3.1983	6.1983
Arthur Black	30.00	60.00	3.1983	6.1983
William Brown	30.00	60.00	3.1983	6.1983
Keith Shatley	30.00	60.00	3.1983	6.1983
Joe Kriss	30.00	60.00	3.1983	6.1983
Tom Januszek	30.00	60.00	3.1983	6.1983
Andy Park	30.00	60.00	3.1983	6.1983
Jerry Schulte	30.00	60.00	3.1983	6.1983
Matthew O'Brien	30.00	60.00	3.1983	6.1983
Bryan Reccord	30.00	60.00	3.1983	6.1983
Chris Burger	30.00	60.00	3.1983	6.1983
	$360.00	$720.00	38.3796	74.3796

Source: Accounting Manual: *The Handbook for Investment Club Accounting,* National Association of Investors Corporation. Reprinted by permission, all rights reserved.

The valuation of an investment club member's interest differs from the valuation of other businesses since the worth of the club's assets constantly fluctuates due to stock-market changes. Moreover, most clubs are partnerships, so each person owns part of the total assets rather than shares of stock, as in a corporation.

There are two methods for keeping track of members' equity in the club. With the first, each member's account is credited or debited in proportion to the value change of the club's assets as of the last statement. This way, each member can see what he or she would receive if the club were to liquidate his or her assets on that date. The second method follows NAIC's system for determining club member ownership based on *valuation units,* which NAIC substitutes for members' shares. Typically, each unit represents an arbitrary value set at $10 (see Figure 8.1 on page 107).

FILING PARTNERSHIP AND INDIVIDUAL TAX RETURNS

Benjamin Franklin once said their are no guarantees in life except death and taxes. April 15 seems like doomsday for most of us, as we scramble about trying to file our tax returns—looking for every tax-deductible item possible—and rush out to the mailbox before midnight.[1]

Tax reporting is a chore for individuals and businesses alike, because it requires keeping complete, meticulous records, comprehending endless forms and regulations, and meeting deadlines, says NAIC's O'Hara. "Investment clubs, just like any other entity, must file taxes."

Given that the legal structure of most clubs is a partnership, your club will have to calculate and report all profits earned during the year. The club does not have to pay federal income taxes, but must report the overall portfolio results to the IRS, as well as each member's portion of the total account.

This applies to income from dividends from securities owned by the club, and interest and capital gains from the sales of securities. Club members are personally liable for payment of their share of the club's income. If your club forms a limited partnership, members are personally liable for payment of their share of the club's income tax.

Tax Form 1065 (see Figure 8.2) is what every partnership must file if it engages in business or derives gross income, deductions, gains, or losses from the operation of a partnership. This form is used

Figure 8.2 Tax Form 1065

Form **1065**				U.S. Partnership Return of Income		OMB No. 1545-0099
Department of the Treasury Internal Revenue Service			For calendar year 1999, or tax year beginning ...., 1999, and ending ...., ... ▶ See separate instructions.			**19 99**

A Principal business activity	Use the IRS label. Other- wise, please print or type.	Name of partnership	**D** Employer identification number
B Principal product or service		Number, street, and room or suite no. If a P.O. box, see page 12 of the instructions.	**E** Date business started
C Business code number		City or town, state, and ZIP code	**F** Total assets (see page 12 of the instructions) $

G Check applicable boxes: **(1)** ☐ Initial return **(2)** ☐ Final return **(3)** ☐ Change in address **(4)** ☐ Amended return
H Check accounting method: **(1)** ☐ Cash **(2)** ☐ Accrual **(3)** ☐ Other (specify) ▶ ....
I Number of Schedules K-1. Attach one for each person who was a partner at any time during the tax year ▶ ....

Caution: Include **only** trade or business income and expenses on lines 1a through 22 below. See the instructions for more information.

Income	**1a** Gross receipts or sales	**1a**		
	b Less returns and allowances.	**1b**		**1c**
	2 Cost of goods sold (Schedule A, line 8)			**2**
	3 Gross profit. Subtract line 2 from line 1c.			**3**
	4 Ordinary income (loss) from other partnerships, estates, and trusts (attach schedule). . .			**4**
	5 Net farm profit (loss) (attach Schedule F (Form 1040))			**5**
	6 Net gain (loss) from Form 4797, Part II, line 18.			**6**
	7 Other income (loss) (attach schedule)			**7**
	8 **Total income (loss).** Combine lines 3 through 7			**8**
Deductions (see page 14 of the instructions for limitations)	**9** Salaries and wages (other than to partners) (less employment credits)			**9**
	10 Guaranteed payments to partners			**10**
	11 Repairs and maintenance			**11**
	12 Bad debts			**12**
	13 Rent			**13**
	14 Taxes and licenses			**14**
	15 Interest			**15**
	16a Depreciation (if required, attach Form 4562)	**16a**		**16c**
	b Less depreciation reported on Schedule A and elsewhere on return	**16b**		
	17 Depletion **(Do not deduct oil and gas depletion.)**			**17**
	18 Retirement plans, etc.			**18**
	19 Employee benefit programs			**19**
	20 Other deductions (attach schedule)			**20**
	21 **Total deductions.** Add the amounts shown in the far right column for lines 9 through 20 .			**21**
	22 **Ordinary income (loss)** from trade or business activities. Subtract line 21 from line 8 . .			**22**

Please Sign Here	Under penalties of perjury, I declare that I have examined this return, including accompanying schedules and statements, and to the best of my knowledge and belief, it is true, correct, and complete. Declaration of preparer (other than general partner or limited liability company member) is based on all information of which preparer has any knowledge.	
	▶ Signature of general partner or limited liability company member	▶ Date

Paid Preparer's Use Only	Preparer's signature ▶	Date	Check if self-employed ▶ ☐	Preparer's SSN or PTIN
	Firm's name (or yours if self-employed) and address ▶		EIN ▶	
			ZIP code ▶	

For Paperwork Reduction Act Notice, see separate instructions.   Cat. No. 11390Z   Form **1065** (1999)

(continued)

Figure 8.2 *(Continued)*

Form 1065 (1999)   Page **2**

Schedule A   Cost of Goods Sold (see page 17 of the instructions)

1	Inventory at beginning of year	**1**	
2	Purchases less cost of items withdrawn for personal use	**2**	
3	Cost of labor	**3**	
4	Additional section 263A costs *(attach schedule)*	**4**	
5	Other costs *(attach schedule)*	**5**	
6	**Total.** Add lines 1 through 5	**6**	
7	Inventory at end of year	**7**	
8	**Cost of goods sold.** Subtract line 7 from line 6. Enter here and on page 1, line 2	**8**	

9a Check all methods used for valuing closing inventory:
    (i)   ☐ Cost as described in Regulations section 1.471-3
    (ii) ☐ Lower of cost or market as described in Regulations section 1.471-4
    (iii) ☐ Other (specify method used and attach explanation) ▶ ....
   b Check this box if there was a writedown of "subnormal" goods as described in Regulations section 1.471-2(c) . . . . ▶ ☐
   c Check this box if the LIFO inventory method was adopted this tax year for any goods *(if checked, attach Form 970)* . . ▶ ☐
   d Do the rules of section 263A (for property produced or acquired for resale) apply to the partnership? . . . ☐ **Yes** ☐ **No**
   e Was there any change in determining quantities, cost, or valuations between opening and closing inventory? ☐ **Yes** ☐ **No**
      If "Yes," attach explanation.

Schedule B   Other Information

		Yes	No
1	What type of entity is filing this return? Check the applicable box:		
	a ☐ General partnership **b** ☐ Limited partnership **c** ☐ Limited liability company		
	d ☐ Limited liability partnership **e** ☐ Other ▶		
2	Are any partners in this partnership also partnerships?		
3	Is this partnership a partner in another partnership?		
4	Is this partnership subject to the consolidated audit procedures of sections 6221 through 6233? If "Yes," see **Designation of Tax Matters Partner** below		
5	Does this partnership meet **ALL THREE** of the following requirements?		
	a The partnership's total receipts for the tax year were less than $250,000;		
	b The partnership's total assets at the end of the tax year were less than $600,000; **AND**		
	c Schedules K-1 are filed with the return and furnished to the partners on or before the due date (including extensions) for the partnership return.		
	If "Yes," the partnership is not required to complete Schedules L, M-1, and M-2; Item F on page 1 of Form 1065; or Item J on Schedule K-1		
6	Does this partnership have any foreign partners?		
7	Is this partnership a publicly traded partnership as defined in section 469(k)(2)?		
8	Has this partnership filed, or is it required to file, **Form 8264,** Application for Registration of a Tax Shelter? . .		
9	At any time during calendar year 1999, did the partnership have an interest in or a signature or other authority over a financial account in a foreign country (such as a bank account, securities account, or other financial account)? See page 18 of the instructions for exceptions and filing requirements for Form TD F 90-22.1. If "Yes," enter the name of the foreign country. ▶		
10	During the tax year, did the partnership receive a distribution from, or was it the grantor of, or transferor to, a foreign trust? If "Yes," the partnership may have to file Form 3520. See page 18 of the instructions		
11	Was there a distribution of property or a transfer (e.g., by sale or death) of a partnership interest during the tax year? If "Yes," you may elect to adjust the basis of the partnership's assets under section 754 by attaching the statement described under **Elections Made By the Partnership** on page 7 of the instructions		

Designation of Tax Matters Partner (see page 18 of the instructions)
Enter below the general partner designated as the tax matters partner (TMP) for the tax year of this return:

Name of designated TMP ▶		Identifying number of TMP ▶	
Address of designated TMP ▶			

Form **1065** (1999)

for reporting purposes only. A partnership passes through any profits or losses, whether or not distributed, to its partners, who then add these items to their personal tax returns.

Each club member must file a K-1 Form on his or her individual tax returns. While Schedule K (see Figure 8.3) of Form 1065 includes the total of all profit and loss items of the partnership, Schedule K-1 (see Figure 8.4) represents each partner's pro rata share of those profits or losses.

When the Form 1065 and each partner's K-1s are finished, one copy of the Form 1065 and one copy each of the K-1s should be sent to the IRS by the due date. All partners should also receive a copy of their respective Schedule K-1s for use in filing their personal tax returns. This copy is kept with their tax records; it is not filed with their tax returns. The club should also keep a copy of all the forms with the club records for future reference.

Each member, in addition to a K-1 form, is given a Earnings Distribution Statement that contains all of the information he or she needs to file a personal tax return. Paper gains and losses for securities still held by the club are not taxable. In general, dividends paid in the form of additional shares rather than cash are not taxable. Costs incurred in connection with investing, such as subscriptions to financial publications, are deductible as itemized deductions on Individual Tax Form 1040, Schedule A.

Capital gain income and loss are reported on Schedule D, Form 1065 (see Figure 8.5). Short-term capital gains are entered under Part I of Schedule D on the line for partnership items. Long-term capital gains are entered in Part II. The individual's share of club expenses is shown in column 6 of the Earnings and Distribution Statement, listed as a separate item in the Miscellaneous Deduction section of Schedule A as a "share of investment club expenses."

If your club received interest during the year, it is shown as a separate item on the Income and Expense Statement and in a special column of the Earnings Distribution Statement. You report interest on Schedule B, Part I of Form 1040 if over $400 and line 8a of Form 1040 if under.

Some clubs are under the misconception that if they have a net loss for the year, they do not have to file. This is not true. The character of the taxable items cannot be netted against the expenses or deductions. The items flow through to the partners and are commingled with the same items earned at a personal level.

Figure 8.3 Schedule K

Schedule K	Partners' Shares of Income, Credits, Deductions, etc.		
	(a) Distributive share items		(b) Total amount

Income (Loss)	**1** Ordinary income (loss) from trade or business activities (page 1, line 22)	**1**	
	2 Net income (loss) from rental real estate activities *(attach Form 8825)*	**2**	
	3a Gross income from other rental activities	**3a**	
	b Expenses from other rental activities *(attach schedule)*	**3b**	
	c Net income (loss) from other rental activities. Subtract line 3b from line 3a	**3c**	
	4 Portfolio income (loss):		
	a Interest income	**4a**	
	b Ordinary dividends	**4b**	
	c Royalty income	**4c**	
	d Net short-term capital gain (loss) *(attach Schedule D (Form 1065))*	**4d**	
	e Net long-term capital gain (loss) *(attach Schedule D (Form 1065)):*		
	(1) 28% rate gain (loss) ▶ .... **(2)** Total for year ▶	**4e(2)**	
	f Other portfolio income (loss) *(attach schedule)*	**4f**	
	5 Guaranteed payments to partners	**5**	
	6 Net section 1231 gain (loss) (other than due to casualty or theft) *(attach Form 4797)*	**6**	
	7 Other income (loss) *(attach schedule)*	**7**	
Deduc-tions	**8** Charitable contributions *(attach schedule)*	**8**	
	9 Section 179 expense deduction *(attach Form 4562)*	**9**	
	10 Deductions related to portfolio income (itemize)	**10**	
	11 Other deductions *(attach schedule)*	**11**	
Credits	**12a** Low-income housing credit:		
	(1) From partnerships to which section 42(j)(5) applies for property placed in service before 1990	**12a(1)**	
	(2) Other than on line 12a(1) for property placed in service before 1990	**12a(2)**	
	(3) From partnerships to which section 42(j)(5) applies for property placed in service after 1989	**12a(3)**	
	(4) Other than on line 12a(3) for property placed in service after 1989	**12a(4)**	
	b Qualified rehabilitation expenditures related to rental real estate activities *(attach Form 3468)*	**12b**	
	c Credits (other than credits shown on lines 12a and 12b) related to rental real estate activities	**12c**	
	d Credits related to other rental activities	**12d**	
	13 Other credits	**13**	
Invest-ment Interest	**14a** Interest expense on investment debts	**14a**	
	b (1) Investment income included on lines 4a, 4b, 4c, and 4f above	**14b(1)**	
	(2) Investment expenses included on line 10 above	**14b(2)**	
Self-Employ-ment	**15a** Net earnings (loss) from self-employment	**15a**	
	b Gross farming or fishing income	**15b**	
	c Gross nonfarm income	**15c**	
Adjustments and Tax Preference Items	**16a** Depreciation adjustment on property placed in service after 1986	**16a**	
	b Adjusted gain or loss	**16b**	
	c Depletion (other than oil and gas)	**16c**	
	d (1) Gross income from oil, gas, and geothermal properties	**16d(1)**	
	(2) Deductions allocable to oil, gas, and geothermal properties	**16d(2)**	
	e Other adjustments and tax preference items *(attach schedule)*	**16e**	
Foreign Taxes	**17a** Type of income ▶		
	b Name of foreign country or U.S. possession ▶		
	c Total gross income from sources outside the United States *(attach schedule)*	**17c**	
	d Total applicable deductions and losses *(attach schedule)*	**17d**	
	e Total foreign taxes (check one): ▶ ☐ Paid ☐ Accrued	**17e**	
	f Reduction in taxes available for credit *(attach schedule)*	**17f**	
	g Other foreign tax information *(attach schedule)*	**17g**	
Other	**18** Section 59(e)(2) expenditures: **a** Type ▶ .... **b** Amount ▶	**18b**	
	19 Tax-exempt interest income	**19**	
	20 Other tax-exempt income	**20**	
	21 Nondeductible expenses	**21**	
	22 Distributions of money (cash and marketable securities)	**22**	
	23 Distributions of property other than money	**23**	
	24 Other items and amounts required to be reported separately to partners *(attach schedule)*		

Figure 8.3 *(Continued)*

Analysis of Net Income (Loss)

1 Net income (loss). Combine Schedule K, lines 1 through 7 in column (b). From the result, subtract the sum of Schedule K, lines 8 through 11, 14a, 17e, and 18b **1**

2 Analysis by partner type:	**(i)** Corporate	**(ii)** Individual (active)	**(iii)** Individual (passive)	**(iv)** Partnership	**(v)** Exempt organization	**(vi)** Nominee/Other
a General partners						
b Limited partners						

Schedule L — Balance Sheets per Books (Not required if Question 5 on Schedule B is answered "Yes.")

Assets	Beginning of tax year (a)	(b)	End of tax year (c)	(d)
1 Cash				
2a Trade notes and accounts receivable				
b Less allowance for bad debts				
3 Inventories				
4 U.S. government obligations				
5 Tax-exempt securities				
6 Other current assets *(attach schedule)*				
7 Mortgage and real estate loans				
8 Other investments *(attach schedule)*				
9a Buildings and other depreciable assets . . .				
b Less accumulated depreciation				
10a Depletable assets				
b Less accumulated depletion				
11 Land (net of any amortization)				
12a Intangible assets (amortizable only).				
b Less accumulated amortization				
13 Other assets *(attach schedule)*				
14 **Total** assets				
Liabilities and Capital				
15 Accounts payable				
16 Mortgages, notes, bonds payable in less than 1 year .				
17 Other current liabilities *(attach schedule)* . . .				
18 All nonrecourse loans				
19 Mortgages, notes, bonds payable in 1 year or more .				
20 Other liabilities *(attach schedule)*				
21 Partners' capital accounts				
22 **Total** liabilities and capital				

Schedule M-1 — Reconciliation of Income (Loss) per Books With Income (Loss) per Return
(Not required if Question 5 on Schedule B is answered "Yes." See page 29 of the instructions.)

1 Net income (loss) per books . . . . .

2 Income included on Schedule K, lines 1 through 4, 6, and 7, not recorded on books this year (itemize): ....

3 Guaranteed payments (other than health insurance) . . . .

4 Expenses recorded on books this year not included on Schedule K, lines 1 through 11, 14a, 17e, and 18b (itemize):

a Depreciation $ ....

b Travel and entertainment $ ....
....

5 Add lines 1 through 4 . . . .

6 Income recorded on books this year not included on Schedule K, lines 1 through 7 (itemize):

a Tax-exempt interest $ ....
....

7 Deductions included on Schedule K, lines 1 through 11, 14a, 17e, and 18b, not charged against book income this year (itemize):

a Depreciation $ ....
....

8 Add lines 6 and 7 . . . .

9 Income (loss) (Analysis of Net Income (Loss), line 1). Subtract line 8 from line 5 . . . .

Schedule M-2 — Analysis of Partners' Capital Accounts (Not required if Question 5 on Schedule B is answered "Yes.")

1 Balance at beginning of year . . . .

2 Capital contributed during year . . . . .

3 Net income (loss) per books . . . . .

4 Other increases (itemize): ....

5 Add lines 1 through 4 . . . .

6 Distributions: **a** Cash . . . .
b Property . . . .

7 Other decreases (itemize): ....
....

8 Add lines 6 and 7 . . . .

9 Balance at end of year. Subtract line 8 from line 5

Figure 8.4 Schedule K-1

SCHEDULE K-1 (Form 1065)	**Partner's Share of Income, Credits, Deductions, etc.**	OMB No. 1545-0099
Department of the Treasury Internal Revenue Service	► See separate instructions.	**1999**
	For calendar year 1999 or tax year beginning , 1999, and ending ,	

Partner's identifying number ►	Partnership's identifying number ►
Partner's name, address, and ZIP code	Partnership's name, address, and ZIP code

A This partner is a ☐ general partner ☐ limited partner
  ☐ limited liability company member
B What type of entity is this partner? ► ....
C Is this partner a ☐ domestic or a ☐ foreign partner?
D Enter partner's percentage of: **(i)** Before change or termination   **(ii)** End of year
  Profit sharing . . . . % .... %
  Loss sharing . . . . % .... %
  Ownership of capital . . . . % .... %
E IRS Center where partnership filed return:

F Partner's share of liabilities (see instructions):
  Nonrecourse . . . . $ ....
  Qualified nonrecourse financing . . $ ....
  Other . . . . $ ....
G Tax shelter registration number . . ► ....
H Check here if this partnership is a publicly traded partnership as defined in section 469(k)(2) . . . . . ☐
I Check applicable boxes: **(1)** ☐ Final K-1 **(2)** ☐ Amended K-1

J Analysis of partner's capital account:

(a) Capital account at beginning of year	(b) Capital contributed during year	(c) Partner's share of lines 3, 4, and 7, Form 1065, Schedule M-2	(d) Withdrawals and distributions	(e) Capital account at end of year (combine columns (a) through (d))
		( )	( )	

	(a) Distributive share item		(b) Amount	(c) 1040 filers enter the amount in column (b) on:
Income (Loss)	**1**	Ordinary income (loss) from trade or business activities . . .	**1**	See page 6 of Partner's Instructions for Schedule K-1 (Form 1065).
	2	Net income (loss) from rental real estate activities	**2**	
	3	Net income (loss) from other rental activities	**3**	
	4	Portfolio income (loss):		
	a	Interest	**4a**	Sch. B, Part I, line 1
	b	Ordinary dividends	**4b**	Sch. B, Part II, line 5
	c	Royalties	**4c**	Sch. E, Part I, line 4
	d	Net short-term capital gain (loss)	**4d**	Sch. D, line 5, col. (f)
	e	Net long-term capital gain (loss):		
		(1) 28% rate gain (loss)	**e(1)**	Sch. D, line 12, col. (g)
		(2) Total for year.	**e(2)**	Sch. D, line 12, col. (f)
	f	Other portfolio income (loss) *(attach schedule)*	**4f**	Enter on applicable line of your return.
	5	Guaranteed payments to partner	**5**	See page 6 of Partner's Instructions for Schedule K-1 (Form 1065).
	6	Net section 1231 gain (loss) (other than due to casualty or theft) .	**6**	
	7	Other income (loss) *(attach schedule)*	**7**	Enter on applicable line of your return.
Deductions	**8**	Charitable contributions (see instructions) *(attach schedule)* . .	**8**	Sch. A, line 15 or 16
	9	Section 179 expense deduction	**9**	See pages 7 and 8 of Partner's Instructions for Schedule K-1 (Form 1065).
	10	Deductions related to portfolio income *(attach schedule)* . . .	**10**	
	11	Other deductions *(attach schedule)*	**11**	
Credits	**12a**	Low-income housing credit:		
		(1) From section 42(j)(5) partnerships for property placed in service before 1990	**a(1)**	
		(2) Other than on line 12a(1) for property placed in service before 1990	**a(2)**	Form 8586, line 5
		(3) From section 42(j)(5) partnerships for property placed in service after 1989	**a(3)**	
		(4) Other than on line 12a(3) for property placed in service after 1989	**a(4)**	
	b	Qualified rehabilitation expenditures related to rental real estate activities	**12b**	
	c	Credits (other than credits shown on lines 12a and 12b) related to rental real estate activities.	**12c**	See page 8 of Partner's Instructions for Schedule K-1 (Form 1065).
	d	Credits related to other rental activities	**12d**	
	13	Other credits	**13**	

For Paperwork Reduction Act Notice, see Instructions for Form 1065.   Cat. No. 11394R   Schedule K-1 (Form 1065) 1999

Figure 8.4 (Continued)

(a) Distributive share item		(b) Amount	(c) 1040 filers enter the amount in column (b) on:
Investment Interest	**14a** Interest expense on investment debts . . . . `14a`		Form 4952, line 1
	b (1) Investment income included on lines 4a, 4b, 4c, and 4f . . `b(1)`		See page 9 of Partner's Instructions for Schedule K-1 (Form 1065).
	(2) Investment expenses included on line 10 . . . . `b(2)`		
Self-em-ployment	**15a** Net earnings (loss) from self-employment . . . . `15a`		Sch. SE, Section A or B
	b Gross farming or fishing income . . . . `15b`		See page 9 of Partner's Instructions for Schedule K-1 (Form 1065).
	c Gross nonfarm income . . . . `15c`		
Adjustments and Tax Preference Items	**16a** Depreciation adjustment on property placed in service after 1986 `16a`		
	b Adjusted gain or loss . . . . `16b`		See page 9 of Partner's Instructions for Schedule K-1 (Form 1065) and Instructions for Form 6251.
	c Depletion (other than oil and gas) . . . . `16c`		
	d (1) Gross income from oil, gas, and geothermal properties . . `d(1)`		
	(2) Deductions allocable to oil, gas, and geothermal properties `d(2)`		
	e Other adjustments and tax preference items *(attach schedule)* `16e`		
Foreign Taxes	**17a** Type of income ▶		Form 1116, check boxes
	b Name of foreign country or possession ▶		
	c Total gross income from sources outside the United States *(attach schedule)* . . . . `17c`		Form 1116, Part I
	d Total applicable deductions and losses *(attach schedule)* . . . `17d`		
	e Total foreign taxes (check one): ▶ ☐ Paid ☐ Accrued . . . `17e`		Form 1116, Part II
	f Reduction in taxes available for credit *(attach schedule)* . . . `17f`		Form 1116, Part III
	g Other foreign tax information *(attach schedule)* . . . . . . `17g`		See Instructions for Form 1116.
Other	**18** Section 59(e)(2) expenditures: **a** Type ▶		See page 9 of Partner's Instructions for Schedule K-1 (Form 1065).
	b Amount . . . . `18b`		
	19 Tax-exempt interest income . . . . `19`		Form 1040, line 8b
	20 Other tax-exempt income . . . . `20`		See pages 9 and 10 of Partner's Instructions for Schedule K-1 (Form 1065).
	21 Nondeductible expenses . . . . `21`		
	22 Distributions of money (cash and marketable securities) . . . `22`		
	23 Distributions of property other than money . . . . `23`		
	24 Recapture of low-income housing credit:		
	a From section 42(j)(5) partnerships . . . . `24a`		Form 8611, line 8
	b Other than on line 24a . . . . `24b`		

Supplemental Information	**25** Supplemental information required to be reported separately to each partner *(attach additional schedules if more space is needed):*
	....
	....
	....
	....
	....
	....
	....
	....
	....
	....
	....
	....
	....

Figure 8.5 Schedule D Form 1065

SCHEDULE D (Form 1065) Department of the Treasury Internal Revenue Service	**Capital Gains and Losses** ▶ Attach to Form 1065.	OMB No. 1545-0099 **1999**

Name of partnership	Employer identification number

Part I Short-Term Capital Gains and Losses—Assets Held 1 Year or Less

(a) Description of property (e.g., 100 shares of "Z" Co.)	**(b)** Date acquired (month, day, year)	**(c)** Date sold (month, day, year)	**(d)** Sales price (see instructions)	**(e)** Cost or other basis (see instructions)	**(f)** Gain or (loss) ((d) minus (e))	
1						

2	Short-term capital gain from installment sales from Form 6252, line 26 or 37	**2**	
3	Short-term capital gain (loss) from like-kind exchanges from Form 8824	**3**	
4	Partnership's share of net short-term capital gain (loss), including specially allocated short-term capital gains (losses), from other partnerships, estates, and trusts	**4**	
5	**Net short-term capital gain or (loss).** Combine lines 1 through 4 in column (f). Enter here and on Form 1065, Schedule K, line 4d or 7	**5**	

Part II Long-Term Capital Gains and Losses—Assets Held More Than 1 Year

(a) Description of property (e.g., 100 shares of "Z" Co.)	**(b)** Date acquired (month, day, year)	**(c)** Date sold (month, day, year)	**(d)** Sales price (see instructions)	**(e)** Cost or other basis (see instructions)	**(f)** Gain or (loss) ((d) minus (e))	**(g)** 28% rate gain or (loss) *(see instr. below)
6						

7	Long-term capital gain from installment sales from Form 6252, line 26 or 37	**7**	
8	Long-term capital gain (loss) from like-kind exchanges from Form 8824	**8**	
9	Partnership's share of net long-term capital gain (loss), including specially allocated long-term capital gains (losses), from other partnerships, estates, and trusts	**9**	
10	Capital gain distributions	**10**	
11	Combine lines 6 through 10 in column (g). Enter here and on Form 1065, Schedule K, line 4e(1) or 7	**11**	
12	**Net long-term capital gain or (loss).** Combine lines 6 through 10 in column (f). Enter here and on Form 1065, Schedule K, line 4e(2) or 7	**12**	

*28% rate gain or (loss) includes all "collectibles gains and losses" as defined in the instructions.

For Paperwork Reduction Act Notice, see the Instructions for Form 1065. Cat. No. 11393G Schedule D (Form 1065) 1999

Say, for example, a club earned $100 in dividend income and $150 in expenses resulting in a net loss of $50 for the year. Partner A is given a K-1 showing dividend income of $10 and expenses of $15. He also earned $60 worth of dividends income from his personal portfolio. The two amounts are added together and Partner A must report $70 worth of dividend income on his personal tax return. The same holds true for expenses or any other item assigned to the partner and appearing on his or her K-1.

Many clubs, though, forget to file their partnership returns, Form 1065, or to give K-1 forms to members to file on their individual tax returns. They tend to file when they sell stock but not when they are just getting dividends or interest, but anything over $10 in interest income must be reported, say financial experts.

Make sure you file Form 1065 promptly and completely. In fact, the IRS can fine each partner for late or incorrect tax returns, especially if an extension was not requested—around $50 each for every month the return is filed late.

Form 1065 and Schedule K-1 are available by contacting your local IRS office, post office, or library or by calling 800-TAX-FORM. You also can access the IRS's Web site at www.irs.ustreas.gov. The NAIC offers a seminar on preparing the K-1 and 1065 forms.

Most clubs elect to use an accountant for tax purposes only, says Walter Clark, president of Clark Capital Investments L.L.C. Clark acts as a financial advisor for several investment clubs in Maryland and Virginia. He notes that these clubs, like any other entity, have to be aware of tax rules that apply to them and their members.

If you haven't done so already, get a tax identification number (Form SS-4) from your nearest U.S. Treasury office. You will be asked for the officers' names, addresses, and Social Security numbers.

This tax ID number should be used on all tax filings, and should be given to your broker for the securities your club buys. When individual members report their share of income or loss on their individual tax return, the tax ID number is included so that the reported amounts can be cross-referenced to the club's partnership returns.

Keep in mind that members might be required by state and local law to file state and city income taxes and intangible property tax returns. Some areas allow partnerships to pay taxes as an organization, exempting individual members. It usually costs less to pay such taxes at the club level rather than individually.

PAYING MEMBERS IN CASH OR STOCK

A member withdrawing either all or part of his or her account value may be paid in cash or stock. There are different rules for taxation and treatment of investment-club withdrawals, depending on whether the withdrawal is partial or full.

The transfer of stock is advantageous to both club and member if the member is making a full withdrawal. The club transfers the stock to the partner and the stock picks ups the member's tax basis in the club, less any cash received. Since this is not a taxable transaction until the member sells the stock, this method is becoming increasingly popular.

When a club sells securities it owns to pay a withdrawing member, tax liability rises for the remaining members. The club fares best by selling stocks with a loss, and transferring stocks held at a profit. Withdrawing members are liable in all instances for any profit in their accounts.

Generally, clubs apply a 3 percent charge to a withdrawing member. The costs to a club of funding a withdrawal can range from 3 percent to 10 percent; if there is no levy on the withdrawn funds, those costs must be borne by the remaining partners.

The Windy City Investment Club incorporated into its partnership agreement a graduated scale, so, if a member elects to leave the club within five years of joining, he or she must pay a penalty. "We encourage members to stay in the club for the long term and let them know up front that we have a minimum five-year commitment. So, if they leave before then, the club will keep 45 percent of their portion of the portfolio invested up to that point," notes club treasurer Ron Haskins. "After five years, members get 95 percent of their funds when they leave, paying a 5 percent penalty."

The 14-member group has yet to address the issue of partial withdrawals. Having lost members in the past, the club now requires potential candidates to attend three meetings, after which they are put on probation for three months before becoming full members.

GIVING UNCLE SAM HIS DUE[2]

If you're in investment club, there's more to November 26 than Thanksgiving and a turkey dinner. For many investors, the date marks the opening of tax-selling season. Between November 27 and December 27,

in fact, many clubs sell stock or mutual funds that have posted losses to offset some of the capital gains other holdings have made.

Patricia Boyd, a partner with the New York CPA firm Kahn, Boyd and Levychin and a member of Wall Street's CMG investment club, says companies that pay dividends are obligated to determine which shareholders are eligible by a certain record date—often toward the end of the year. That affords an investment club enough time to hold a stock until a November record date in order to qualify for the capital gains declared by the company. Afterwards, stockholders are free to sell and lock in any profit they've made.

There is a down side. If your club sells a stock too early, it may not be able to qualify for the dividends, warns Boyd. Also, by waiting until November to sell, you run the risk of seeing the stock depreciate in value. "There's always the chance that if you paid $25 four years ago for a stock, it might be up as high as $58 in April and then swoon to $43 a share in November."

Don't jump headlong into selling every position in your investment-club portfolio, cautions Clark. "Tax selling is a strategy for more sophisticated clubs that have done exceptionally well; they have several realized gains in their portfolio." It's time to give a stock the once over only if it has gains of 30 percent from your initial investment.

Say you still like a stock, but want to net the fruits of a sizable increase. If your club is still enthusiastic about a stock's long-term prospects, you can always consider selling it and then buying it back after 31 days. For instance, says Clark, "If you sell a stock on November 20 and you buy it back on December 22, you may be able to repurchase the stock at or below the price you paid for it because others are liquidating."

Historically, the stock market starts to recover at the beginning of a new year, which Wall Street calls the *January effect*. Investors start bottom fishing, buying back stocks at a lower price, adds Clark. "They look for undervalued stocks that were oversold for tax selling." The down side to this strategy, though, is obvious: You'll pay a total of four brokerage commissions to buy, sell, buy, and later sell, instead of the usual two transactions.

Boyd says that clubs should keep on top of their investments to know a good time to sell. Most young clubs hold their stocks too long or sell too quickly. The capital gains rules say that investors have to hold appreciated property for at least 18 months to get the tax savings. Previously, it was a year.

As your club grows, you may decide to broaden your investment choices, to include real-estate properties, which will certainly have other tax implications. Beyond tax purposes, however, there's another important reason for keeping track of your club's account: to measure how well it is doing.

SURVEYING YOUR CLUB'S RESULTS

Will Rogers used to say: "Even if you are on the right track, you'll get run over if you just sit there." This is good advice for any investment club that has been around for more than a year. Simply put, even if you buy and hold a portfolio of well-researched stocks, you can't merely leave it there and wait for it to grow.

Running an investment club is no dog-and-pony show. There's no trick shooting, roping, or riding to growing your funds. You must constantly reevaluate things to make sure your investments are meeting the club's goals.

Does reassessing things sound like a tall order? Start with your portfolio. NAIC's O'Hara suggests that members look at their portfolio at least once a year:

- First, for diversity's sake, you want to check to make sure the stocks you hold are in a wide range of industries.
- Second, you'll want to see that you have companies of varying sizes—small, large, and medium capitalization.
- Third, it's good to go over your portfolio to check on each stock's growth potential. Remember, things change over the course of a year.

"When a new investment club is formed, there is very little thought given to diversification both by industry and by size," says NAIC's president and CEO of the board of trustees Kenneth S. Janke Sr. "You buy one or two stocks and that's your portfolio. You aren't really looking at whether you are diversified properly or not. That's why we suggest that at the end of the year you evaluate your portfolio."

MEASURING PERFORMANCE BY INDUSTRY

"Often club members will see great returns in a particular sector, and they will stay in that industry because they feel comfortable with it,"

observes Simone A. Thompson, investment representative with Brooklyn, New York-based brokerage firm, Edward Jones. Even though your club may be heavily weighted in a particular sector, Thompson says clubs should shoot for owning shares in companies that span several core industries.

Many experts point to those industries where earnings per share (EPS) growth rates are higher. EPS is used to value stock given that a company's profitability directly affects its stock price. A chart published by David L. Babson & Co. shows the correlation between earnings growth and price appreciation by industry. Those industries with low EPS growth rates had poor price appreciation. Conversely, industries with high EPS growth rates tended to have stronger price appreciation.

Using Standard & Poor's Industry Groups based on annual rates of growth from 1960 to 1995, the chart (see Figure 8.6) looks at growth rates and price appreciation in over 20 sectors, including:

- Soft drinks, with an earnings growth of 12.9 percent and stock price appreciation of 13.4 percent.
- Tobacco, earnings growth 11.8 percent and stock price appreciation 11.7 percent.
- Pharmaceuticals, earnings growth 11 percent and stock price appreciation 10.8 percent.
- Household products, earnings growth 9.6 percent and stock appreciation 9.2 percent.
- Food, earnings growth 9.4 percent and stock appreciation 9.2 percent.
- Department stores, earnings growth 9.4 percent and stock price appreciation 9.4 percent.

Your club should decide to invest in a company first, after doing its homework. After which, members must determine if they want to be represented in that particular industry. People may say they want to invest in Internet stocks, because they are very popular. But, as a group, they have been very volatile. You have to invest company by company.

Investing in companies in different industries shields you from market swings. "Look at those mutual funds that concentrate on a particular sector," says Janke. "For instance, those funds that specialize in banking have not done well because bank stocks have performed poorly. But if your club's portfolio is only weighted 5 percent in bank stocks,

Figure 8.6   Standard & Poor's Industry
Group's Annual Rate of Growth (1960–1995)

Industry Group	Earnings Growth	Stock Price Appreciation
Soft Drinks	12.9%	13.4%
Tobacco	11.8	11.7
Pharmaceuticals	11.0	10.8
Household Products	9.6	9.2
Food	9.4	9.2
Department Stores	9.4	9.4
Aerospace and Defense	9.1	8.6
Electrical Equipment	8.5	9.2
Computer Systems	8.1	4.8
Chemicals (Basic)	7.2	5.7
Railroads	7.2	8.4
Grocery Stores	7.2	7.5
S&P 500	6.9	7.0
Machinery	6.6	6.6
Oil-International	6.6	8.0
Banks (Money Center)	6.1	6.4
Oil-Domestic	5.8	6.3
Forest Products and Paper	5.8	5.6
Gas Pipelines	5.9	5.9
Airlines	5.8	6.0
Autos	5.6	4.5
Telephone	5.1	5.0
Textiles & Apparel	5.1	5.5
Electric Utilities	3.3	2.3
Steel	0.0	0.0
AVERAGES	6.9	7.3

Source: David L. Babson & Co., Inc., *Better Investing* magazine, March 1999.

then you still have 95 percent invested in stocks that are going up or at least are not going down." Bear in mind that the industries your club invests in will change from time to time.

MEASURING PERFORMANCE BY COMPANY SIZE

You can check size by the market capitalization or the number of shares outstanding times the stock price. Consider a balanced portfolio where 50 percent of the club's holdings are in medium-sized companies

(those with annual sales between $400 million and $2 billion), 25 percent in large companies (those earning $2 billion or more in annual sales), and the remaining 25 percent in small companies (those with sales under $400 million and rapid rates of growth).

This ratio differs depending on individual member's risk tolerance. Those who are younger, in their twenties and thirties, are inclined to assume more risk and invest in small, aggressive companies, while clubs with older members will tend to stay with large capitalization companies.

As the stock market continued its meteoric rise in 1999, small capitalization stocks were like poodle skirts and the pet rock: out of fashion. Gargantuan companies—particularly those with "dot com" trailing their names—ascended to nosebleed heights, while small caps languished.

These stocks are sure to make a comeback. There have been times when small- and mid-sized companies were in vogue and their larger counterparts were safe buys but not in style. Some investors view picking small caps similarly to finding out about a sale before the rest of the world takes notice.

"Again, you are diversifying because you never know when a particular segment is going to be popular and rise in price," asserts Janke. "Most stocks jump in spurts. A stock may average 10 percent or 15 percent growth rate a year; it will go along its merry way and then suddenly shoot up 80 percent in a period of months. You want to make sure you are in those stocks when that happens."

The Washington Metropolitan Investment Club tries to achieve a sort of bell curve by investing half of its money in small- and mid-sized companies and the other half in large firms or blue chips.

"We know that with the blue chips, they may not make as much money in returns, but we know those companies have been out there for a while and they are the ones we can count on," says Gerald Coles, past president of the Dumfries, Virginia-based club. "With the smaller stocks, we know we can make more money with them but we might also lose money on them because they are high risk."

Washington Metro has stuck with this strategy since 1992 and is proof that it does work; it was top gun among all clubs in its home state of Virginia in 1996 and an elite member of the top 30 clubs overall in the United States, as ranked by NAIC and Value Line Publishing Inc.'s annual outstanding club performance contest. Washington Metro's portfolio soared in 1995 and 1996, posting an average annual rate of return of 32 percent and 52.7 percent, respectively.

Today, the club's portfolio is worth $500,000 with 24 holdings. The top ten are:

- Colgate-Palmolive.
- Cisco.
- AT&T.
- Lucent Technologies.
- Waste Management.
- McDonald's.
- Pepsico.
- Quaker Oats.
- Wal-Mart.
- Pfizer.

The club recently raised its monthly contribution from $25 to $50, of which 40 percent (or $20) is invested in a mutual fund for future investments. Explains Coles, "We are considering buying a franchise or buying some real estate."

MEASURING PERFORMANCE BY A STOCK'S GROWTH POTENTIAL

When it comes to growth, review each stock and see if it has the potential to double in value over the next five years (or whatever goal you set for your club). "You want to look at fundamentals of the company to see if sales and earnings have and will continue to grow," says Janke. "Is management doing the job they are supposed to, is the price reasonable, and has the company continued to grow as you anticipated it would when it was first purchased?"

Don't make the mistake of concentrating only on a stock's price. You want to focus on the structure of a company, its earnings, and its management. Search for companies that have continuous growth of earnings and sales.

A good growth rate for a small company is 25 percent to 40 percent or even higher in sales; a medium-sized company should be expected to grow 17 percent to 25 percent; and a large, established company should grow 10 percent to 15 percent. For the past five years, earnings growth for the S&P 500 has skipped along at a 10 percent rate.

Some companies can increase earnings in the short time by cutting costs. In the past decade, corporations have sold factories, sent workers packing, created spinoff divisions, or acquired the competition. In the end, they saw fabulous results in the stock market. You want see a company creating something substantive for the future. For instance, you want a company to have solid sales growth over the long term because it has good products that are seizing market share or dominant products in a given sector.

NAIC teaches that if a company's management is able to increase sales and earnings on a consistent basis, your club has a much better chance of making money on the stock. Many clubs look for companies that have a 10-year history. This way, the company will have gone through two cycles of the economy (in general, a cycle runs every five years). If a company continues to increase sales and earnings through down cycles, it shows that management is able to make it through the hard times.

EVALUATE YOUR CLUB'S EARNINGS

For your club's portfolio review, create a table for each stock holding, displaying the current price, five-year low and high price, and columns showing each stock's size and industry classification.

You especially need to review your club's portfolio as old club members leave and new members join. The same holds true for members. You want to give them an annual checkup. It's necessary to review members' attitudes and desires about investing from time to time.

At the formation of your club, members should have filled out a survey as a way to determine their risk tolerance (see Figure 3.2 in Chapter 3). Remember the purpose of these surveys was to help in the diversification and allocation of assets in your club's investment portfolio.

Review the pyramid model in Chapter 3 to guide any readjustments of the club's portfolio. Gauge to see if members still feel the same about certain types of securities. Members' attitudes may change as they become more familiar and comfortable with investing.

Not to sound like a recording, but your club should shoot for doubling its money every five years. This five-year interval spans the average time between market ups and down. As mentioned earlier, in order for your club to double its money every five years, it must achieve a

compound annual return around 15 percent. It may take as little as three years or as a long as eight years for your club to realize its goal.

You can maximize profits by applying value tests not only to the stocks you are thinking about buying but the stocks you already own. One measure that tells how well your club is doing is the rate of return—a numerical factor that summarizes the growth of investments over time.

Each year, hundreds of clubs participate in NAIC's Investment Club Earnings Survey of investment performance. This survey, which dates back to 1960, is an opportunity for clubs to learn or verify the rate of return earned on their portfolios. It is also an opportunity to see how that performance compares to both the S&P 500 Index and the record of other investment clubs in the same age category and state, both over the 12-month period and for the lifetime of the club.

Results are shown on an earnings certificate, which is sent to every club that participates in the survey. Special prizes and recognition are awarded to top-performing investment clubs by Value Line. The most outstanding clubs across the nation, in terms of lifetime investment performance, receive cash payments of up to $1,200.

You want to perform better than the market in general, but that is not always an easy task. "What would your portfolio look like had you invested in the S&P 500 index of stocks? That is what you are measuring your club's performance against," Janke explains.

"But this can also be an unfair comparison. If you are in an investment club that has been in existence five years and the market has been up for five consecutive years, then your rate of return will be high as opposed to a club that started around 1987 when the market was in a down cycle. Consequently," says Janke, "that club's portfolio would have tanked some. Even if you invest in the best companies of the world, if the market is down, they are down. IBM is a consistent performer but it too will suffer in a declining market."

CONCLUSION

The important thing is that you set a goal, give yourself a measurement and focus. As long as your club produces a higher rate of return than you could have achieved through other forms of investing, then you are doing a great job. If you can double your money between market peaks, your club is well on its way down the road to success.

9

DO YOU NEED A BROKER? BUYING AND SELLING SECURITIES

Many receive advice. Only the wise profit by it.

—Publilius Syrus

Just as you would scrutinize a surgeon's credentials before scheduling an operation, you should be choosy when finding professionals to tend to your club's financial health. Financial advisors range in reputation from highly trained professionals to fly-by-night con artists. So, how can you separate the helpers from the hucksters?

First, your club must decide whether it even needs someone to advise members on how to invest its money. You definitely want to invite financial planners and stockbrokers to speak before the group at regular club meetings and to provide a few pointers, but don't feel pressured into turning your portfolio over to a stockbroker.

Traditionally, many clubs have relied on good advice from brokers who agreed with members' basic investment philosophy. However, some clubs don't believe they need advice beyond the research efforts of members and, instead, use discount or deep-discount brokers to place orders. Still other clubs invest directly through the companies in which they want to invest via dividend reinvestment plans and direct stock purchase programs.

Initially, when AT&T employees formed the Alliance Investment Group, club president Nate Watson was one of two people who had previous experience investing in the stock market. In order to make the other members feel more comfortable about picking stocks, the group chose to work with a full-service broker who could provide a little hand holding. A year later, the group was left feeling emptyhanded. Dissatisfied with the lack of services they received, they opened an account with another full-service broker. The group has been with A.G. Edwards ever since.

"A.G. Edwards was better in terms of providing the services and resources we needed—like analysts' reports," says Watson. "But the main service our broker Isreal Maldonado provides is that he will give us a complete analysis of our portfolio and make suggestions on what we should buy, hold, or sell based on asset allocation. He will provide a very extensive report for us annually, and more frequently if we request it. He is always there to help us when we need it."

Watson admits that once trading on the Internet became a big craze, the group considered cutting loose their broker and trading strictly online. Reluctant to sever the relationship that the club had formed, the group decided to leave well enough alone. Besides, "we realized that we weren't going to cut down on costs significantly by buying and trading online," he adds. "It was worth it to pay a couple percentage points more for the kind of service that we were getting."

Watson says that it's important that club members weigh all options before deciding which course is best for the group. Members may feel confident in their ability to make investment decisions without the advice of a full-service broker and choose to save money in commissions by investing with a discount broker the first couple of years. After which, say the third year of operation, the club may wish to switch to a full-service broker who can provide broader investment choices as well as another perspective on the market and the long-term growth of its portfolio.

On the other hand, if all the members of your club are inexperienced investors, the group might consider using a full-service brokerage firm for the first couple of years, then move to discount brokers when they have gained more experience.

There's no getting around the fact that in order to buy and sell stock, your club must establish an account with a broker. However, you do have your pick: full-service, discount, and deep discount. Keep in mind that while there are independent brokers—those who don't work for a firm—most are affiliated with a major house.

FULL-SERVICE BROKERS

Plain and simple: A stockbroker buys and sells securities (e.g., stocks and bonds) and provides financial advice. They are commission-only advisors, meaning they will make investment recommendations but they won't charge you for the advice. Should you go ahead and purchase a security a broker recommends, he or she will receive a commission. Typically, a broker pockets around 30 percent to 40 percent of the commission made on a trade. The rest of it goes into the firm's coffers. The more trades you make, the more money the full-service broker makes. If you don't act, that broker won't be compensated regardless of the time spent and the advice given.

Full-service brokers such as Merrill Lynch, Morgan Stanley Dean Witter, and Prudential Securities supply their clients with everything, including in-house research reports, new stock and bond offerings, client meetings, and professional advice on which stocks to buy and sell.

A good broker will alert you to industry trends or news that might favorably impact a particular company and he or she will give opinions about specific investments that are in line with the club's investment objectives. Many of the large national and international brokerage firms offer a full range of products including a selection of in-house mutual funds.

DISCOUNT BROKERS

If your club needs professional advice and doesn't mind paying for it, look into a full-service brokerage firm. Otherwise, go with a discount brokerage firm. You can save up to 60 percent on commissions with discount brokers, since they don't employ commissioned reps.

Discount brokers such as New York's Charles Schwab & Co. essentially offer do-it-yourself investing: They don't tell you how to invest your club's money. However, they do provide some personal advice, news, investment materials, and a few perks at a lower cost, including money-market accounts and mutual funds.

Discount brokers offer just about everything a full-service broker provides in terms of resources. In fact, you can request the same type of research reports that you would receive from a full-service brokerage firm, with all the same analyst's recommendations and opinions.

Most of this information is easily accessible online, since every firm now has its own Web site.

The biggest differences are higher commissions and investment advice—a discount broker won't review your club's portfolio and advise you as to when to buy or sell a security. In the past, full-service brokers had a reputation for calling clients, including investment clubs, and trying to promote a particular security—especially an investment product that the brokerage firm offered.

The more popular discount brokers are Fidelity Investments (www.fidelity.com or 800-544-8888), Quick & Reilly (www.quick-reilly .com or 800-672-7220), and Charles Schwab & Co. (www.schwab.com or 800-435-4000). Usually, you can contact a discount broker 24 hours a day, seven days a week, to place trades. As with a full-service broker, you call a discount broker to place an order and receive a trade confirmation in the mail. Plus, many discount brokers now let you monitor and execute investment decisions online via their Web site.

While you don't get hand holding from a discount broker, they are cheaper than a full-service firm. Full-service brokers charge commissions ranging from 1.5 percent to 3 percent per trade—that's $51 to $30 off top of a $1,000 investment (the larger the investment, the smaller the commission). Discount brokers, though, will apply the same fixed fee every time you purchase stock, charging anywhere from $20 to $40 per trade.

DEEP-DISCOUNT BROKERS

Minimum commissions are often the same for discount and full-service brokers when you are investing in small amounts—a couple hundred or a thousand dollars. An alternative is deep-discount brokers. These firms are the cheapest of the investment spectrum. You can save up to 80 percent, sometimes more.

Deep discounters such as Brown & Co. and Ameritrade Securities execute trades at a rock-bottom price. At the same time, these firms offer bare-bones services—no research, no advice. So, you won't get an actual person to work with, but you will get the lowest overall dollar amount for trades.

Contrary to their competition, deep-discount brokers don't have scores of offices across the country, and they mostly conduct business over the phone or through the mail. Such firms include TD Waterhouse

(800-233-3411), Brown & Company (800-225-6707), and Dreyfus (800-421-8395). Each broker offers a different combination of services and features.

Both discount brokers and deep-discount brokers take and promptly execute buy and sell orders, and they are large enough to handle transactions on days when everyone is trading, from financial tycoons to typists. However, you could end up paying twice as much for a trade using a discount broker, since the firm doles out more services, including 24-hour telephone access to a variety of information services as well as online trading. With deep-discount brokers, there are no bells and whistles, no added value to the investor.

Much like discount brokers, deep-discount firms charge minimum transaction fees between $10 and $40. The difference between the two lies in whether the brokerage firm charges on a per share basis or on a value basis. Some deep-discount brokers charge a flat $.05 to $.08 per share, no matter if you buy 10,000 shares of ABC Company stock or only 100 shares of the same company. Others may charge you based on how much you trade.

Once you begin investing in blocks (100 shares), the discount on commissions becomes more significant, explains Thomas E. O'Hara, chairman of the NAIC. The less often you trade and lower your volume of trading, the higher your commission per share.

For example, if you buy just a few shares of a low-priced stock, at $10 per share, you may pay a commission of up to 40 cents per share. However, if you were to buy several hundred shares of high-priced stock at $75 per share, you may pay as little as ten cents per share commission.

Check out the following scenario in order to understand what some of the largest full-service, discount, and deep-discount brokerage firms charge in commissions on transactions. Say you buy 100 shares of ABC Company stock at $30 per share. How much will the commissions be? A full-service broker's commission would be $83 to $100; a discount

Figure 9.1 Company ABC Commission Comparisons

Broker	100 Shares	500 Shares	1,000 Shares
Full Service @ $30–$40 share	$100.00	$354.00	$559.00
Discount	27.92	28.79	30.35
Deep Discount	16.43	16.43	17.93

Source: Edward Jones, New York, 1969; Mercer Partners (www.askmercer.com), New York, 1999.

broker, $27.92; and, a deep-discount broker, $16.43 (Figure 9.1). If you were to buy 300 shares of ABC Company at $40 per share, commissions for a full-service broker would be roughly $354; for a discount broker, $28.79; and a deep discounter, $16.43.

SHOPPING FOR A BROKER

You should understand what to look for in a broker before you hire someone to advise your club. First and foremost, realize that brokers are salespeople. A full-service broker may want to help your club achieve its goals but, because they are usually paid entirely in commissions and make money only on stock transactions, they will often encourage you to buy and sell stocks when you really ought to hold onto the ones you have.

In selecting a broker, the club president and other officers should seek recommendations from established clubs or experienced individual investors. Don't hire the first broker who comes along.

Develop a list of five to ten names. Club officers should call and visit these brokers, or invite them to attend the club's initial meetings. Talking to the broker face to face is crucial. You want to find someone with whom you are comfortable and that you can afford.

Also, check credentials. Ask what professional degrees or certifications your broker has earned. Look at his or her work history. Make sure he or she is established and does not move from firm to firm. Brokers go through training and testing to qualify for various kinds of securities licenses. One organization that administers proficiency exams is the National Association of Securities Dealers (NASD). To find out if your broker is a registered representative or has committed fraud or any other serious violations, contact the NASD (800-289-9999).

Should you choose to use a full-service broker, be sure to find one who is compatible with your overall investment philosophy and is willing to conduct business within your guidelines. He or she should be familiar with your risk tolerance before making recommendations. Working with a full-service broker essentially boils down to establishing a personal as well as professional relationship.

When meeting with prospective brokers, ask what attributes they will bring to the table. Take interview notes (Figure 9.2). Find out whether they will provide your club with extra services at no extra charge. You want someone who is truly going to add value to your club's portfolio.

Figure 9.2 Interview Your Broker

ADVISOR INTERVIEW NOTES: These sheets are designed to help you record information from your interviews with financial advisors. Additionally, you may want to bring relevant information about your club's investment goals to help the advisor better understand your financial situation.

Advisor's Name: _____ Advisor's Phone: _____

Advisor's Firm: _____ Date of Interview: _____ Time: _____

1. What is your educational and professional background?
   _____
   _____

2. What size is your firm and how many clients do you have?
   _____
   _____

3. What types of services do you offer?
   _____
   _____

4. What is your management style and philosophy?
   _____
   _____

5. Do you have a preference for specific types of investments?
   _____
   _____

6. What has your past performance been for clients with investment needs and risk tolerances similar to mine?
   _____
   _____

7. How are you companionated?
   _____
   _____

8. Who will we be working with?
   _____
   _____

9. Who will maintain control of our assets and where will they be held?
   _____
   _____

Additional questions and notes:
   _____
   _____
   _____

Source: © 1998 Charles Schwab & Co., Inc. Used with permission.

In your quest for a full-service broker, find someone who has worked with investment clubs before and understands their general inner workings. You want someone who will take the time to listen to fellow club members, attend meetings, and educate club members on the ins and outs of investing.

"Brokers should have a high level of patience in working with investment clubs," advises Walter L. Clark. "They should understand that their job is to help your club achieve its overall goals." He notes that there are two types of personalities: Some brokers try to take over, others are very passive. "You don't want either of these," says Clark, who is an advisor to the Washington Women's Investment Club, as well as individual investors. "You want someone who knows how to make recommendations but allows members to pick their own stocks."

Club members should decided which stocks to buy or sell. The broker should be at your disposal. If you aren't sure as to when to buy or sell a particular investment, your broker can help you. However, make sure your broker is working in your best interests.

A full-service brokerage firm usually has a staff of investment analysts assigned to follow various industries and companies in order to compile investment information. A full-service broker will advise your club based on these reports and will tell you whether the analysts' research indicates that a company's stock seems to be overvalued (overpriced), undervalued, or fairly valued.

If you have the time and discipline to research and follow stocks, then your club could get by using a discount broker, whose primary job is to execute orders, says Michael Hall, an investment specialist with Charles Schwab in New York, who works with four investment clubs in the surrounding area.

"I also act as an advisor in that I help club members with research, including how to use NAIC's stock selection tools," says Hall, "which consists of a short and a long version to determine if a stock makes sense for purchase. But many members don't get it. I will show them what the analysts' reports say about a particular stock, industry overviews and so forth. I do everything but actually push or recommend a stock, because it is important that members do the legwork. A big part of belonging to an investment club is the learning component."

Hall points out that a deep-discount broker may be appropriate for your club if you don't need that face-to-face interaction or to have live discussion with a financial advisor, you want to reduce your

overall transaction costs and expenses, and you are comfortable finding research material online.

The downside to this investment approach is that many clubs do a great job at choosing which stocks to buy, but will overreact to rumors or stock fluctuations and sell a stock sometimes at bargain basement prices when they should hold onto it. A full-service broker can help guide a club.

Once you choose a broker, make sure that authorization is given to designated club members who will be placing buy and sell orders, usually the treasurer and assistant treasurer. All members must sign a broker–club agreement when the account is opened. The treasurer should be responsible for sending checks to the broker.

Pay on time. If the money doesn't reach the firm three days after the buy order, your club may be fined or penalized and put on a restricted list. In other words, you'll have to pay *before* the broker can accept any of your club's orders.

STOCKING UP

Once your club opens a brokerage account, you can place orders over the telephone or by computer. There are two basic types of accounts you can open with brokerage firms: (1) cash and (2) margin accounts.

As newcomers, your club should have a cash account, which means that you will be required to pay for your security purchases within three business days of your order. Margin accounts are for sophisticated investors who are actually borrowing money from the brokerage to purchase securities. Discount brokers usually offer cheaper margin rates than full-service brokers.

There are three different kinds of orders:

1. *Market order.* Here you try buy or sell certain stocks at the best current available price and assume your order will be executed as soon as possible.

2. *Limit order.* In this case, you instruct your broker to buy or sell when the stock reaches a certain set price. The broker won't place the order if the specified price is not reached. For example, you may place a limit order to buy ABC Company at $30. Even if the stock is selling at $30¼, the broker will not execute the trade. Similarly, if you put in a limit order to sell ABC

Company at $33, the trade will not be executed until the stock
reaches that price.

3. *Stop order.* Here you instruct your broker to execute your order
to buy or sell a certain stock at the current market price, but
only after the stock has reached a specified price or better.

In addition to these three basic orders, there is the day order,
which is good only on the day it is placed. When the market closes at
the end of the day, the order expires. A combination of the stop order
and limit order is the stop-limit order, where you buy or sell a stock
only after a given stop price has been reached or passed.

Stocks are often ordered in even hundreds of shares (e.g., 200,
500, 1,000). When you order this way, it is called a *round lot.* An order
that is not in even hundreds (e.g., 60, 128, 235) is called an *odd lot.* It
usually costs more in commissions to buy and sell odd lots.

In general, your order goes in a matter of minutes from your broker to the appropriate stock-market exchange (which is much like an
auction market—you know "going once, going twice, sold to the gentle-
man down front in the green suit"). If the security you are interested in
is listed on the New York Stock Exchange or the American Stock Exchange, your order will be handled by a specialist there.

On a stock exchange, a specialist acts as an agent, matching buy orders and sell orders. When you are buying, you pay the asking price.
When you are selling, you receive the bid price. Sometimes, the specialist will buy or sell from his own account to maintain an orderly market.

If you are interested in buying stock in a company not listed on
AMEX or the NYSE, your order will go to a dealer in the over-the-
counter market. In the NASDAQ and over-the-counter markets, a
dealer handles the buying and selling. He or she acts not as an agent
but as a principal using his or her own funds.

Approximately 75 percent to 80 percent of all stock-market trading is done by institutional investors. Usually, they are large companies
with professional staffs dedicated to investment decisions like banks,
trust departments, mutual-fund companies, pension funds, and insurance companies. Because of the size of their purchases, these institutions have a lot of influence on stock prices.

Once the account is open, your club's stockbroker transmits your
bid (or price you are willing to pay), to the brokerage firm's trader who
is located on the trading floor of the stock exchange. The trader will

then try to match your bid to the best offer (the lowest price for which someone is willing to sell the same stock).

When a price between a buyer and seller is agreed on, the transaction is concluded. A confirmation statement is mailed to you. This written document summarizes the transaction—the number of shares of a certain security you bought or sold, the price, date, commission, transaction fees, the amount you owe or will receive if the security is sold, and the settlement date.

Remember, the stock certificates you buy may be registered in the club's name or in a street name—the name of your brokerage firm. If they are registered in the club's name, your club will receive a stock certificate several weeks after the transaction date. If the stock remains with the broker in an account, the firm acts as a custodian. Each month, when the club purchases securities, they are registered in the broker's name. The broker sends members a monthly account statement itemizing transactions and listing securities in the club's account.

When securities are registered in a street name, you cannot physically hold your own stock certificates. This offers some convenience, because club members don't have to worry about safeguarding or paying to store the stock certificates. However, most companies now provide electronic records, making storage less of an issue.

Your broker receives all stockholder notices, such as annual and quarterly reports and proxy statements, which he or she then forwards to the club's president or treasurer. The club can request to have these documents mailed directly by putting it in writing and sending it to the investors' relations department, explaining that they own that company's stock in a street name.

Dividend payments are sent directly to the broker and credited to your club's account. A downfall is that when you hold securities in a street name, you are not allowed to participate in the company's dividend reinvestment plan (DRIP), by which you buy stock directly from that company.

DRIPS AND OTHER COST CUTTERS

For new clubs, cost is a big concern, given limited financial resources starting out. Many end up working with a discount broker rather than a full-service firm because they don't want the advice nor do they want

to feel pressured to make decisions or pushed to buy the brokerage firm's stock of the day.

There are avenues your club can pursue to keep the costs of investing as low as possible. You can take advantage of special investment programs such as DRIPs, direct stock purchase programs, and the NAIC's low-cost investment plan.

DIVIDEND REINVESTMENT PLANS (DRIPs)

One of the easiest and most affordable ways to build an investment portfolio is through a program called the dividend reinvestment plan (DRIP). This low-cost way of buying stocks allows you to purchase just one share of a company's stock from a broker (you can purchase the single share from a deep-discount broker to keep costs to a bare minimum). After your initial purchase, any additional shares can be bought directly through that company.

Rather than pay out dividends, DRIPs automatically reinvest your stock dividends to purchase more company shares. Even better, many companies offer discounted shares through DRIPs, taking 3 percent to 10 percent off a stock's trading price. This enables you to accumulate a growing number of shares of a company's stock without paying high commissions. If the company does charge a fee, it's typically quite nominal.

The concept of a DRIP dates back to the 1950s, from a program called the *monthly investment plan* sponsored by brokerage firms of the New York Stock Exchange. Customers in these member firms were allowed to invest a minimum of $40 in the plan.

This plan was the precursor to the first DRIP that was offered by AT&T in the 1960s. In the past, the strongest emphasis on DRIPs was placed on purchasing a few shares of stock at a time instead of receiving a cash dividend (a company could offer a dividend to its shareholders in the form of cash or stock). So, instead of receiving a dividend check in the mail for a measly $1.50, you invested that amount back into the company.

Today, more than 1,000 companies and closed-end mutual funds allow investors to buy single company shares through DRIPs. Many of these companies offer perks and other little goodies to shareholders. For example, if you invest in the Wrigley Company's DRIP program, you'll get a container with 20 packs of chewing gum.

You can call or write to a company to request an enrollment form and prospectus for their DRIP plan (contact the investors' relations or shareholder services department). Read the prospectus to determine whether there are any fees or charges, the minimum and maximum optional cash payments, and when they place the buy orders.

Make sure you take physical possession of the stock, registering it in the club's name, not in the brokerage firm or street name. Have the brokerage firm send the stock certificate directly to the club's treasurer via certified mail. Make sure the spelling of the club's name is correct and that a current address appears on the front of the stock certificate. In order to sell you need to contact the DRIP plan administrator, mail in the certificates, and have them sold on the specific sell day set by the plan.

Most DRIPs permit investors to send in an optional cash payment (OCP), which could be as low as $10. This enables you to purchase additional shares. For example, if a company's stock was trading around $50 and you sent in only $25, you'd receive a fraction of a share—in this case, half a share. These fractional shares continue to build over time.

Keep in mind that when you send in additional payments, your account isn't usually credited immediately. Many companies invest DRIP payments once a month or every quarter. That's why it's important to time your purchases.

For example, if you place an order the first of the month and that company's investment date is the 25th of each month, your cash sits there for 24 days. The company is just holding onto it until the investment date. More important, the group's money will buy whatever number of shares it can afford at the current price, not the price at the time of the stock order.

Moreover, you will be getting separate paperwork for all these different transfers. So, each and every month you will have to maintain different records on each and every DRIP stock holding (as opposed to the consolidated statement a broker provides). This can become very cumbersome.

There are several newsletters and even software programs for people interested in DRIPs. The best source to keep up with the latest DRIP information is the monthly publication *DRIP Investor* (219-931-6480), which is your guide to buying stocks without a broker. This newsle' updates each month which DRIPs are worth looking into.

DRIP Investor publisher Chuck Carlson also provi' subscribers the *Directory of Dividend Reinvestment Pl.*

the industry. This more-than-140-page directory sums up everything you need to know about all DRIPs, including tidbits such as minimum and maximum OCPs, fees and charges if any, and a special performance rating.

Direct Stock Purchase (DSP)[1]

Over 1,500 companies have these plans, sometimes called *optional cash purchases,* which are often offered as a feature of their DRIP program. Most companies have employee stock-purchase programs. Since they had they necessary procedures to sell in house, many decided they might as well offer direct stock purchased as a benefit to individual shareholders.

Unlike DRIPs, these companies don't require you to buy one share through a broker in order to participate in their stock-purchase plans. However, some companies require that you reside in the state in which the company is headquartered.

Moreover, most DSPs require a minimum investment of least $250. Others, like Lucent Technologies, ask you to plunk down $1,000. Some companies, like IBM, will waive their minimum initial investment if you join their automatic debit plan. IBM's requires $50 a month for ten months in lieu of a $500 minimum investment.

The desire to cut out the middleman has fueled the proliferation of Web sites devoted to both DSPs and DRIPs. Many of these sites charge fees to provide this service. They range from being transaction related, such as Netstock Direct (www.netstockdirect.com), to purely informational, like DRIP Central (www.dripcntral.com).

Bellevue, Washington-based Netstock Direct boasts that its site is the only one that does not charge investors a fee. The firm currently has 1,600 companies offering their DSPs on the sites, but charges a minimum fee to only 250 of those companies, which post their enrollment on site (see Figure 9.3). They include such well-known companies as General Electric and Home Depot.

Low-Cost Investment Plan[2]

Another alternative to sidestepping brokers is to invest through NAIC's low-cost investment plan (see Figure 9.3). Established in 1979, this plan

Figure 9.3 Buying Stock Directly from a Company

Bypass Your Broker

Want to buy shares of your favorite company directly without paying a broker's fee? So do some other individual investors. The following stocks were the top 10 most sought after no-load stocks by visitors to www.netstockdirect.com as of June 1, 1999.

Company/Ticker	Minimum Initial Investment	Minimum Reinvestment	Stock Price*	Web Site
Fannie Mae (NYSE:FNM)	$ 250	$ 25	$ 67.31	www.fanniemae.com
General Electric Co. (NYSE:GE)	250	10	102.56	www.ge.com
Home Depot Inc. (NYSE:HD)	250	25	55.81	www.homedepot.com
IBM Corp. (NYSE:IBM)	500	50	112.00	www.ibm.com
Lucent Technologies Inc. (NYSE:LU)	1,000	100	56.00	www.lucent.com
Merck & Co. Inc. (NYSE:MRK)	350	50	68.13	www.merck.com
Wal-Mart Stores Inc. NYSE:WMT)	250	50	43.45	www.wal-mart.com
Walgreen Co. (NYSE:WAG)	50	50	23.75	www.walgreens.com
Walt Disney Co. (NYSE:DIS)	1,000	100	28.81	www.disney.com
Warner-Lambert Co. (NYSE:WLA)	250	50	61.81	www.warner-lambert.com

*Closing price as of 6/1/99.
Source: Netstock Direct.

For First-Share Buyers

If you don't have a single share of a company's stock and want to avoid high initial investment fees, first-share purchase plans can help. The following are the stocks bought the most by members of the National Association of Investors Corp., a trade group for investment clubs, through its Low-Cost Investment Plans.

Company/Ticker	Number of Purchases*	Minimum Reinvestment	Stock Price**	Web Site
Intel (Nasdaq:INTC)	11,000	N/A	$50.69	www.intel.com
Wendy's International Inc. (NYSE:WEN)	7,900	$ 20	27.81	www.wendys.com
Diebold Inc. (NYSE:DBD)	7,000	10	28.25	www.diebold.com
RPM Inc. (NYSE:RPM)	4,600	25	13.69	www.rpminc.com
AFLAC Inc. (NYSE:AFL)	4,300	50	49.19	www.aflac.com
AT&T Corp. (NYSE:T)	2,600	100	55.06	www.att.com/ir
Emerson Electric Co. (NYSE:EMR)	1,900	N/A	65.25	www.emersonelectric.com
GTE Corp. (NYSE:GTE)	1,800	25	63.56	www.gte.com
Newell Corp. (NYSE:NWL)	1,600	10	43.00	www.newellco.com

*As of September 30, 1998, end of NAIC fiscal year; excludes stocks with minimum initial investment and other conditions.
**As of 6/1/99.
Source: NAIC (www.better-investing.org).

141

allows club members to enroll in a company's dividend-reinvestment plan and eliminate many broker and transaction fees. NAIC's plan permits clubs to save as much as 10 percent in commissions the first year, an amount that can mean the difference between profit and loss in many cases. NAIC charges a one-time set-up fee of $7 per company.

Essentially, the club forwards its money to an escrow agent in care of NAIC for investment in a particular company or companies. Members receive a prospectus and authorization form for each company (which must be signed and mailed back to NAIC).

Note that your order is not processed right away. NAIC accumulates additional stock orders from other clubs and investors until the date the corporation has set for the acceptance of funds to its DRIP program before sending in any money.

Once the club makes its first purchase of a stock through the NAIC and the transfer of the stock is complete, the group can deal directly with individual companies and send future cash contributions to their transfer agents. The initial transaction takes 8 to 12 weeks from the time your check is mailed until you can transact directly with the company's transfer agent.

NAIC has joined the dividend reinvestment program of 150 corporations, including blue chips like AT&T, Exxon, Kellogg, Quaker Oats, Motorola, and Upjohn. The downside is that you are limited to investing only in those companies listed by NAIC.

Bear in mind that NAIC does not act as a broker. Its role is to transfer investors' money into the company DRIP account. Also, each company has a limited amount of money it will accept at one time for investment; therefore, NAIC can invest only up to that limit for all of its members wishing to own that stock.

Once NAIC receives the statement from the transfer agent confirming the purchase, it executes the transfer of stock and forwards the signed authorization form for each agent. From there, you must transfer the shares out of NAIC's account into the club's own account, established with that company's transfer agent, after which your club will receive a monthly statement from each company's transfer agent. You can sell your stock directly through the agent, or you can request a stock certificate and sell through a broker.

Also available through the NAIC is a stock-service program that allows investors to purchase stocks in 200 companies, including Ford Motor, Campbell Soup, Coca-Cola, Disney, Hershey Foods, Microsoft,

Sprint, and Wal-Mart. For an additional $25 fee, you can purchase stocks not on the list.

Established in 1998, NAIC's stock service offers three different plan options: Platinum, Gold, and Silver Plans (Figure 9.4). These plans differ in the annual fee and purchase fee applied to each transaction. All three plans have a small cents-per-share fee ranging from 3 cents for 1,501 shares or more, to 8 cents for one to 500 shares. So, if you purchased $200 of a $50 stock, you would have 4 shares and the total cents-per-share fee would be no more than 32 cents.

Under the Platinum Plan, the annual fee is $200 and there are no purchase fees. With the Gold Plan, which has a $60 annual fee, the more stocks you purchase each month, the less you pay in purchase fees per stock. Thus, you pay $3.50 each for 26 purchases or more compared to $4.50 for 6 purchases or less. The Silver Plan has a lower annual fee of $36, but charges an $8 purchase fee for every transaction.

All transactions are completed through MMS Securities Inc., a specialized discount broker for the program, which minimizes many transaction fees. Investors can make initial stock purchases, additional cash contributions, reinvest dividends, and sell stock through this service.

To participate in the program, you simply select the stocks you wish to purchase, fill out a purchase form indicating the dollar amount you want to go into each stock, and mail it in with a check for your order. The minimum investment required for each stock purchase is $10.

As with DRIP programs, your club's order is added to those of other participating members purchasing the same stock. On the 22nd of each month (the set purchase date), a block of stock is purchased for each of the NAIC companies for which orders were received.

From then on, your club receives one monthly statement for all investments, consolidating all investment activity and tax information, and detailing the number of whole and fractional shares purchased on your club's behalf. You have the option of reinvesting stock dividends or having a money-market account to hold funds that aren't being invested. You can sell stocks in the NAIC stock service at any time by completing and sending in an instruction form. Your order is executed only upon receipt of your written instructions.

A word to the wise when it comes to fees: Monitor your broker transaction fees as often as you do your investments. Why? Because not only are there commissions that you pay when you trade investment securities in your accounts, there are also maintenance fees.

Figure 9.4 Stock Service List

These are some of the companies featured in the NAIC Stock Service:

Amoco Corporation

Anheuser-Busch
Companies, Inc.

The Boeing Company

Bristol-Meyers Squibb
Company

Campbell Soup
Company

Chrysler Corporation

Coca-Cola Company,
Inc.

Cooper Tire & Rubber
Company

The Disney (Walt)
Company

Ford Motor Company

General Electric
Company

General Motors
Corporation

The Gillette Company

Hershey Foods
Corporation

Johnson & Johnson

Merck & Co., Inc.

Microsoft Corporation

NIKE, Inc.

Pfizer, Inc.

Philip Morris
Companies, Inc.

Rubbermaid, Inc.

Sprint Corporation

Starbucks Corporation

Tyson Foods, Inc.

Wal-Mart Stores, Inc.

Whirlpool Corporation

Worldcom, Inc.

This is not a complete list. For a complete list of companies in the
NAIC Stock Service—call 888-780-8400.

	Platinum	Gold	Silver
Annual Fee	$200	$60	$36
Purchasing Costs			
• Purchase fee	0	1–6 purchases = $4.50 each	$8 each
		7–25 = $400 each	
		26 or more = $3.50 each	
		(per Purchase Date)	
• Cents per share fee	3 to 8 cents	3 to 8 cents	3 to 8 cents
Automated Dividend Reinvestment Costs			
• Purchase fee	0	0	0
• Cents per share fee	3 to 8 cents	3 to 8 cents	3 to 8 cents

The cents per share fee is based upon the total number of shares per security purchased by all investors for that month. The more shares purchased, the lower the fee:

Shares	Per Share Fee
1 to 500	8 cents
501 to 1000	6 cents
1001 to 1500	4 cents
1501 & up	3 cents

These maintenance fees—which can run as high as $50 per year—are simply added to your account just for having it at any type of brokerage firm.

Other fees to watch for are postage and handling fees. When you buy or sell investments, you'll receive a trade confirmation in the mail. This is just a notice confirming the transaction. Many times a postage and handling fee is added to your transaction. Some of these fees can be as high as $4 per transaction. Also, many full-service brokerage firms will charge you an inactivity fee if you do not generate at least $100 worth of commissions to the firm.

ONLINE TRADING

With the advent of online services, you may find electronic discount brokers with fees even lower than your local discount broker. Online trading allows you to access your brokerage account at any time of the day, rectify statements, and execute transactions.

By utilizing this technology, you can stay on top of Wall Street—all from the ease of your armchair. Anyone can do their own research and move their own money with the click of a mouse and for a fraction of the cost of going to a brokerage firm. More and more investors are abandoning professional advice and are guiding themselves. An estimated five million people now take advantage of the convenience of online brokers, compared to 250,000 four years ago.

The more widely used online brokerages are Charles Schwab (800-435-4000), E*TRADE (800-786-2575), TD Waterhouse (800-238-3411), Datek (800-823-2835), Ameritrade (800-669-3900), and Suretrade (401-642-6900).

The issues in selecting a Web broker are trading speed, low commission costs, and good customer service. Massive volume can cause costly delays by slowing online traders to a halt. To attract and keep customers, many retail online brokerages are adding research tools to their sites. Datek was one of the first online sites to offer after-hours trading—from 8 A.M. to 8 P.M. Eastern Standard Time.

You can trade right online—buy and sell shares, move money between accounts—all for a fee, of course, usually under $10. Often the costs involved with online trading are posted right on the home page, along with basic information about the company, its products, quote services, and security transaction information.

The Black Business Investment Group participates in DRIPs to bypass heavy commissions. To cut costs and expedite orders, the club uses such online services as Datek and E*TRADE—at about $9.99 per trade. "We started out with a full-service broker for advice and research. But once we became accustomed to investing on the Internet, we decided to trade strictly online," says club president Rod Carter.

"We meet on Saturdays. We decide what stocks to buy or sell. We deposit the checks for our monthly dues into our brokerage account. We are able to trade right away," he says, adding that the club has a margin account which allows them to purchase stocks even if members come up short in their dues that month. Carter maintains that even though the club is capable of doing day trading, the group still practices an investment strategy of buy and hold. Choosing to ride out the market has paid off; the club's portfolio has an average a rate of return of 33 percent.

Savings and discounts, convenience, and easy access to research materials: Those are the biggest pros when it comes to online trading. The main concern is reliability of the service—whether it's your Internet service provider (ISP) or the broker firm you are dealing with—how often are their systems down? Is this the only way I can make a trade if the system is down, or, can I call up and make a trade on the telephone? Security is another concern. Does the company scramble your data so that no one can access your information?

Find out if your broker has touch-tone service or online trading, automated features you can use around the clock if you'd like. Besides, these little perks often can shave 10 percent or more off of your commissions, since your orders are directly entered into the trading system.

INVESTING FOR THE MILLENNIUM

Investing on the cheap has been the goal of the Women of the Millennium Investment Club in New York, but the group is experiencing growing pains as do most clubs when it comes to trying to get the most for their money.

The 11-member group consists of professional women ranging in age between their mid-twenties and mid-fifties, with backgrounds varying from homemakers to computer analysts to real-estate agents. The group was formed in June 1997, with members contributing an initial minimum investment of $200 each (monthly dues are now set at $50). As of January 2000, the club's portfolio was valued at $18,000, with ten

company holdings: Avery Dennison (office paper supplies), CVS, Compaq, Emerson Electrics, Lucent, MCI Worldcomm, McDonald's, Wal-Mart, Cisco, and Sun Microsystems.

Starting out, the group decided to invest through NAIC's Stock Service program. "We chose that service because it was the easiest way out," says Arletha Allen Vickers, the club's assistant treasurer for two years. "We thought that it would be cheaper using NAIC. We bought the Platinum plan, which consisted of a yearly fee ($200) and no purchase fees" (unless they purchased a stock not listed on NAIC's recommended sheet).

The group purchased its first five stocks all at once. With an investment amount of $5,412, they were able to buy 20 shares of Avery at $54.59 a share, 14 shares of CVS at $74.50 per share, 17 shares of Emerson at $65.38, 26 shares of Diebold at $42.69 (the club later sold the stock), and 18 shares of McDonald's at $61.81 per share.

"We gave NAIC the check and told them we wanted to buy shares in these five companies and that we wanted the money divided among them," Allen explains. "They came back and told us how many shares of each company we could get."

Prior to participating in NAIC's stock service, members had the opportunity to hear from various brokers who attended preliminary meetings and spoke before the group. "Once we learned how much money it was going to cost in commissions and transfer fees, we decided it might not be worth it to us to go with a full-service broker," says Allen. "Also, some members feared the brokers would give us advice that was not in line with our investment goals. However, if we did it ourselves—chose all the stocks—we wouldn't have to worry about someone misleading us."

The Women of the Millennium stayed in NAIC's program for a little over a year before moving to a discount broker, Charles Schwab, in March 1999. The main reason for the big switch—transactions weren't made in a timely manner. "MMS Securities did their transaction once a month, so, if something was happening in the market before that time and you wanted to trade right away you blew it," explains Allen.

For example, the group got wind that one of its stocks was going to split. "We thought we had put our money in time to buy shares when Compaq split, but by the time the securities company made the transaction we had missed it. They had us down for a date after the fact."

That was enough to convince Allen and the other members to look at an alternative route to trading. They settled on using a discount

broker. "Our reasoning was that we could see a stock going up in price every day but we couldn't get in on it when we wanted to, because the transaction wasn't going to happen until a month later," says Allen, who adds that club members didn't always wait for their own monthly meetings to make trades. "If a member came up with a stock she thought the group should be buying based on the numbers and some timely event or news, we would contact one another over the phone and do a telephone poll to determine if the group wanted to buy that stock."

That was how the women investors ended up with two of their holdings: Lucent and CVS. "Following NAIC's principles, we would not have bought shares in those companies because they wouldn't have had the numbers—they didn't fit within the realm of NAIC's formula for picking stocks. CVS was another company that we learned was going to split," Allen says. "And Lucent is a company that was spun off from Bell Labs, so there wasn't a lot of history on them, at least not five years' worth in terms of Value Line Surveys, which is what NAIC recommends."

The group decided to go with a discount broker over a full-service broker to save on costs. They were referred by another investment club to a broker at Charles Schwab who was offering a personal touch, by attending club meetings and helping members with their research material.

In particular, the broker has been very helpful in showing Allen and her investment comrades how to make better use of NAIC's stock selection tools. The Women of the Millennium joined NAIC membership around August 1997, attending the organization's three-part seminar series and purchasing their stock-selection video. Still, the group found the forms too complicated—too number intensive.

"Now we see our broker as someone we can call up who can make the transaction that same day, not 30 days from now," adds Allen. "With Charles Schwab, we also have the option of trading online and we have access to a lot of research materials. There is a down side: You can either allow all the club members to have access to the system and hope that no one will make a transaction on her own without authorization or you can designate a select number of people to have access to the account. There is no read-only service. Only the president and treasurer know the password to our account."

The group transferred their funds from an account with a major commercial bank to a money-market fund at Charles Schwab. The advantages: checking privileges, lower fees, and interest-bearing account.

The group is now looking to further diversify its portfolio by adding mutual funds—a service that more and more discount brokers like Charles Schwab are offering.

CONCLUSION

Whether you use a full-service or discount broker or trade online, it is important that members do the research on those companies the club currently invests in or is considering for purchase. Even if a broker recommends a stock, have members follow up on the tip. Never give broker carte blanche over your club's account.

Part II

HOW TO BUILD A PROSPEROUS INVESTMENT PORTFOLIO

10

GRAB THE BULL BY THE HORNS: INVESTING IN THE STOCK MARKET

Prosperity is when the prices of things that you sell are rising; inflation is when the prices of things you buy are rising. Recession is when other people are unemployed; depression is when you are unemployed.

—James D. Gwartney and Richard L. Stroup
Economics: Private and Public Choice

Every day you wake up, rub your eyes, brush your teeth, percolate the coffee, and turn on the tube. Often, the first words to greet you are: "The Dow is up 50 points" or "the market is down." We just can't seem to start our day without knowing two key bits of information: What's the weather and what's happening on Wall Street?

What's the big deal about Wall Street? Why is it such a part of American lingo? Why are books written on it and movies made about it? Who are these so-called market movers and shakers? What is the Dow and who cares if it's up or down?

The answer your high school economics teacher would have given you is that the stock market and Wall Street are considered the backbone of the American free-enterprise system, whereby companies are launched to meet consumer supply and demand. Management raises and risks capital for the purpose of making a profit. Tomorrow's profits can result in higher wages, more employees, greater opportunities, and

prosperity at home and work. Investing in the market gives you the opportunity to own a slice of an American business corporation and to share in the success of American industry. Hurrah for capitalism.

Going beyond this primary lesson, the stock market remains one of the greatest places where you and fellow club members can make money. It comprises over 45 million investors, from the little old lady in Pasadena to big institutions like banks and insurance companies.

The stock market is the general term used to refer to the organized trading of securities through the various exchanges and the over-the-counter market. The Dow, which is the nickname for the Dow Jones Industrial Average of thirty stocks (see Figure 10.1), is the most widely

Figure 10.1 Dow Jones Industrial Average

Company Name	Exchange/Symbol
1. Alcoa Inc.	NYSE:AA
2. American Express Co.	NYSE:AXP
3. AT&T Corp.	NYSE:T
4. Boeing Co.	NYSE:BA
5. Caterpillar Inc.	NYSE:CAT
6. Citigroup Inc.	NYSE:C
7. Coca-Cola Co.	NYSE:KO
8. DuPont Co.	NYSE:DD
9. Eastman Kodak Co.	NYSE:EK
10. Exxon Mobil Corp.	NYSE:XOM
11. General Electric Co.	NYSE:GE
12. General Motors Corp.	NYSE:GM
13. Home Depot	NYSE:HD
14. Honeywell International Inc.	NYSE:HON
15. Hewlett-Packard	NYSE:HWP
16. International Business Machines Corp.	NYSE:IBM
17. Intel Corp.	NASDAQ:INTC
18. International Paper Co.	NYSE:IP
19. J.P. Morgan & Co.	NYSE:JPM
20. Johnson & Johnson	NYSE:JNJ
21. McDonald's Corp.	NYSE:MCD
22. Merck & Co.	NYSE:MRK
23. Microsoft Corp.	NASDAQ:MSFT
24. Minnesota Mining & Manufacturing Co.	NYSE:MMM
25. Philip Morris Co.	NYSE:MO
26. Procter & Gamble Co.	NYSE:PG
27. SBC Communications Inc.	NYSE:SBC
28. United Technologies Corp.	NYSE:UTX
29. Wal-Mart Stores Inc.	NYSE:WMT
30. Walt Disney Co.	NYSE:DIS

quoted economic measurement. It is a symbol of the rise and fall of stock prices, and an indication of how the economy is doing in general.

For some of us, the stock market can be intimidating or overwhelming, but just think of it along the lines of a modern supermarket, which contains an amazing abundance of products and brands. There's an aisle for various categories. You know what you'll find in the produce section.

The stock market is an open market where, instead of goods, there are companies that are sold. Your club's portfolio is a shopping cart of a variety of companies. Sometimes you pay the full or regular price for them, other times you can take advantage of sales or discounts. Wall Street is where all the big supermarket chains and smaller grocers are located.

Okay, that might be stretching it a bit. Wall Street is really the financial district in lower Manhattan, where the stock exchanges and numerous brokerage firms are headquartered. The goal of everyone working on Wall Street is to make money hand over fist by buying and selling everything from gold to pork bellies.

HOW YOUR CLUB CAN MAKE MONEY ON WALL STREET

Back in 1986, long-time friends Lillian Heard and Joan Ford were looking for a way to line their pockets with a little extra cash. Their initial thoughts were to invest in real estate by buying and renovating boarded up, abandoned buildings in Brooklyn, New York, then renting out the properties. "But it would have been too costly for us to do and neither one of us is good with a hammer and nails, so we started an investment club instead," jokes Heard.[1]

Heard and Ford held three exploratory meetings in which they invited 15 to 20 family members and friends. Ten people actually signed on to form the Unity Investment Partnership, contributing $35 a month to buy stocks. All but one of the original members is still with the club. Many of them, like Heard, who formerly worked with the Department of Social Services, are retired civil workers who are investing to create a nice nest egg.

As with most fledgling investment clubs, Unity Investment Partnership was totally green when it came to the stock market and investing. As fate would have it, the club got its most valuable lesson on value buying when the market crashed in October 1987, on what is

now colorfully referred to as Black Monday. "For us, it was probably a blessing in disguise. We were able to buy some of our better stocks at a good price. One was Pfizer, which has grown 100-fold," says Heard.

Indeed, the group bought 100 shares at $2.75 per share. Today their holdings in the pharmaceutical company—made popular recently by the wonder drug, Viagra—is worth more than $10,000. Their second stock pick was Pespi, which they bought 400 shares of at $15 a share; it is valued today over $14,000.

Getting a group of like-minded folks to form an investment club is the easy part. Deciding what to invest in is difficult, in spite of numerous guides, including ones the NAIC puts out. Heard and fellow Unity Investment members know the decision about which companies to give the once over is a big step.

"It took us almost a year to develop the partnership and purchase our first stock," adds Heard. "We would do our research each month, following NAIC's stock selection guide. But we just kept putting the money away."

To date, Unity Investment Partnership, which trades through discount broker Charles Schwab, has 21 holdings, including Pfizer, Pepsi, Disney, Colgate-Palmolive, Motorola, and Staples. The club's portfolio is worth $150,000.

Heard did get her chance to own real estate through a REIT (real-estate investment trust). The group owns 100 shares of New Plan Reality, which manages a portfolio of supermarkets, shopping malls, and apartments.

Though you are investing as a group, it's important that each member researches and recommends stock(s). There are no exceptions to the rule. Let's use our supermarket analogy again. Just as you wouldn't trot off to the market without knowing what items you need and a general idea of how much they cost, you shouldn't invest in the stock market totally clueless. Then again, there are those of us who are impulse buyers who never shop with a list.

Remember the "ab" machine you purchased at 4 A.M. after being enticed by some infomercial promising a better looking you. This handy item was all yours in five easy payments of $29.99 per month or a total retail value of $149.95, plus add on $10 for shipping and handling. Five months later, instead of a six-pack stomach, you have yet another unused piece of exercise equipment cluttering up the closet.

Investing in the stock market is no different. If you follow whims and hot tips, you could end up wasting or losing your money. There are various styles and strategies for picking stocks, including looking at

various industries, your own personal tastes as consumers, and members' professional experiences.

CONSIDER THE PRODUCTS YOU CONSUME

Kellogg's Corn Flakes, Heinz Ketchup, Hanes Underwear, Coca-Cola Classic, Campbell Soup, Sara Lee Cheesecake, and Clorox Bleach. Sounds like a shopping list? Well, in a way, it is. Anyone who is in the market for stocks ought to check out a list of leading brand-name products and the companies that own them.

If your club has new parents who just love Huggies diapers, you may want to look into Kimberly-Clark, which owns the number one diaper brand in the United States. Kimberly-Clark is also the world's top provider of personal care, paper, and consumer products, including Kleenex Cottonelle and Scott brands of facial tissue, bathroom tissue, and paper towels.

Equally, no Saturday afternoon would be complete for some families without a trip to the mall and later a fast-food pit stop. So, it's fitting that many club members are eager shoppers at and investors in McDonald's and The Gap. According to NAIC's Top 100 listing of the most popularly held stocks among investment clubs and their members nationwide in 1999, other club favorites include Intel, Pepsi, Motorola, Home Depot, Microsoft, Disney, MCI, Compaq, Gillette, and Pfizer (see Figure 10.2).

Often, those companies that are market leaders offer growing income and earnings per share for savvy investors. And why not? Year in and year out, consumers reach first for those household names that they know and love, even if those products come at a premium price.

Club members should start by looking around them—say, your bathroom, kitchen cupboards, refrigerator, and clothes closet. The products that fill your homes and the corporations that provide services that your families can't do without yield great investment ideas.

"The question on everyone's mind when we started out was 'How do you know when and what to buy?' I told people to research something that they have an interest in or a product that they use," explains Carolyn Williams-Robinson, president of Investors 2000 Plus, a group of men and women out of Richmond, Virginia.

Hershey is one of Investor 2000's picks, thanks to one member's fondness for chocolate candies. Another member was a big Wal-Mart shopper, a major group holding. Investor 2000 Plus' portfolio has ten

Figure 10.2 Most Popular Held Stocks among Clubs

Better Investing's TOP 100 for 1999

Company	Rank by # of Clubs Holding	Number of Clubs Holding Stock	Rank by Total Shares Held	Number of Shares Held by NAIC Members	Rank by Total Value of Shares Held	Total Value of Shares Held by NAIC Members on 12-31-98	Investor Contact
Intel Corporation	1	12,423	3	3,629,616	3	$430,336,347	Alex Lenke
PepsiCo, Inc.	2	11,446	2	4,461,204	9	182,351,714	Margaret Moore
Merck & Co., Inc.	3	8,581	13	2,460,845	4	362,974,638	Laura Jordan
** Lucent Technologies	4	7,959	11	2,894,502	5	318,214,314	Andrew Backman
** The Home Depot, Inc.	5	7,136	5	3,331,571	8	203,850,501	Kimberly Shreckengost
** Cisco Systems, Inc.	6	7,130	8	3,083,521	6	286,189,293	Lisa Magleby
AFLAC Incorporated	7	6,926	1	18,322,079	1	803,881,216	Kenneth S. Janke, Jr.
Diebold, Incorporated	8	6,913	15	2,166,965	20	77,333,563	Sandy Upperman
Motorola, Inc.	9	6,894	23	1,414,310	19	86,361,304	Tim Callard
Clayton Homes, Inc.	10	6,311	10	2,898,419	40	40,034,412	Carl Koella
Tricon Global Restaurants	11	6,200	55	506,530	54	25,389,816	James Alterman
The Coca-Cola Company	12	5,971	14	2,293,494	11	153,664,098	Nancy Ford
Microsoft Corporation	13	5,857	6	3,248,583	2	450,537,855	Carla Lewis
McDonald's Corporation	14	5,696	19	1,826,241	13	140,278,137	Barbara VenHorst
RPM, Inc.	15	5,268	4	3,614,691	26	57,835,056	James A. Karman
General Electric Company	16	4,819	12	2,461,668	7	251,090,136	Jo Anna Morris
Johnson & Johnson	17	4,538	21	1,525,094	14	127,917,259	Helen Short
Wendy's International Inc.	18	4,266	17	1,927,177	37	42,047,455	Marsha Gordon
Abbott Laboratories	19	4,036	9	3,030,870	12	148,512,630	Stacey Tischler
The Walt Disney Corporation	20	4,029	18	1,877,322	27	56,319,660	Jennifer LaGrow
Oracle Corporation	21	3,607	24	1,256,116	29	54,170,003	Tanya Barberena
** Pfizer Inc.	22	3,286	25	1,232,039	10	154,004,875	Ron Aldridge
** Compaq Computer Corporation	23	3,280	22	1,449,230	25	60,867,660	Alice McGuire
Hewlett-Packard Company	24	3,186	32	941,354	24	64,306,245	Angel Massey
AT&T Corp.	25	3,075	26	1,209,084	17	91,588,113	Thomas Rozycki
Wal-Mart Stores, Inc.	26	3,059	28	1,107,157	18	90,164,098	Stephen Hunter
The Boeing Company	27	3,032	7	3,145,289	16	102,615,054	Paul Gifford
* MCI WorldCom, Inc.	28	3,012	29	1,048,523	21	75,231,525	Michael Broden
Walgreen Company	29	2,979	20	1,756,421	15	102,860,405	John Palizza
Amgen Inc.	30	2,584	52	526,330	28	54,837,007	Denise Powell
Century Telephone Enterprises, Inc.	31	2,570	30	1,007,197	22	67,985,798	Jeff Glover
Invacare Corporation	32	2,436	39	687,757	71	16,506,168	Robert Gudbrausota
Synovus Financial Corporation	33	2,224	16	1,995,293	33	47,887,032	Patrick Reynolds
Newell Co.	34	2,149	41	677,295	50	27,938,419	Ross Porter
** The Gillette Company	35	2,055	33	836,433	41	39,991,953	Everett R. Howe
** Medtronic, Inc.	36	1,881	40	678,219	31	50,357,761	Dale Beumer
** Sara Lee Corporation	37	1,841	42	858,000	56	24,184,875	Janet Bergman
** Starbucks Corporation	38	1,826	71	364,361	62	20,449,761	Tracy Moran
* Schlumberger Ltd.	39	1,814	64	409,843	67	19,006,469	Mary Birch
Callaway Golf Company	40	1,747	74	344,421	98	3,530,315	Krista Mallory
The Procter & Gamble Company	41	1,734	50	561,672	30	51,287,675	James Martis
* Citigroup, Inc.	42	1,573	36	791,774	42	39,341,271	Heidi Miller
ConAgra, Inc.	43	1,560	27	1,135,231	43	35,759,777	Walter Casey
** Staples, Inc.	44	1,560	48	590,025	53	25,776,717	Catharine Woods
Biomet, Inc.	45	1,553	43	656,552	52	26,426,218	Gregory Sasso
Harley-Davidson, Inc.	46	1,526	53	525,948	55	24,916,787	Rod Copes
Colgate-Palmolive Company	47	1,519	58	470,928	35	43,737,438	Anne Crawford
* ADC Telecommunications Inc.	48	1,345	60	467,996	70	16,575,611	Mark Borman
SYSCO Corporation	49	1,332	34	827,618	57	22,707,769	Toni Spigelmyer
* Safeskin Corporation	50	1,272	61	457,133	76	11,028,334	Mark Francois

* New to the Top 100 listing.   ** Advanced five positions or more in rank since 1998.

Figure 10.2 *(Continued)*

Shown on these two pages are the 100 most popular
and widely held stocks among investment clubs and
their members nationwide in 1999.

Company	Rank by # of Clubs Holding	Number of Clubs Holding Stock	Rank by Total Shares Held	Number of Shares Held by NAIC Members	Rank by Total Value of Shares Held	Total Value of Shares Held by NAIC Members on 12-31-98	Investor Contact
Automatic Data Processing Inc.	51	1,265	47	601,384	32	$48,223,480	John Maxwell
Bank One Corporation	52	1,245	35	805,690	38	41,140,546	Jay Gould
Stryker Corporation	53	1,225	46	610,628	45	33,622,704	David Simpson
Cracker Barrel Old Country Stores	54	1,225	75	329,260	87	7,675,874	Michael Woodhouse
Dana Corporation	55	1,181	31	1,000,236	39	40,884,647	Gudrun Carr
* Dollar General Corporation	56	1,171	49	565,688	73	13,364,379	Kiley Fleming
Exxon Corporation	57	1,162	65	408,558	47	29,875,804	David Henry
** Schering-Plough Corporation	58	1,131	44	623,500	44	34,448,375	Geraldine V. Foster
* Applied Materials, Inc.	59	1,118	62	449,663	64	19,194,989	Lorri Gross
* Deere & Company	60	1,098	93	200,002	91	6,575,066	Marie Ziegler
** Global Marine, Inc.	61	1,091	69	384,642	99	3,461,778	David Herasimchuk
Philip Morris Companies, Inc.	62	1,078	37	787,356	36	42,123,546	Nicholas Rolli
* Office Max, Inc.	63	1,078	67	385,987	92	4,728,341	Michael Weisbarth
** United States Filter Corporation	64	1,058	73	350,545	85	8,018,717	Tim Traff
Mylan Laboratories Inc.	65	1,051	63	417,454	75	13,149,801	JoAnne Carrozza
** Avery Dennison Corporation	66	1,024	98	174,941	86	7,916,080	Charles Coleman
* The Federal National Mortgage Association	67	1,021	81	286,288	61	21,185,312	Greg McDouough
Hannaford Brothers, Inc.	68	1,020	45	611,333	46	32,400,649	Charles Crockett
SBC Communications, Inc.	69	1,011	66	407,654	60	21,860,446	Patrick Anderson
* MBNA Corporation	70	1,010	38	773,300	65	19,090,844	Brian Daiphon
* People Soft, Inc.	71	1,010	92	203,436	95	3,852,569	Ronald Codd
Applebee's International, Inc.	72	1,004	70	367,292	88	7,575,398	William Lackey
Network Associates, Inc.	73	1,004	80	286,930	66	19,009,113	Prabhat Goyal
** Sun Microsystems, Inc.	74	997	86	256,448	59	21,958,360	Denise Peck
Emerson Electric Co.	75	944	57	479,782	49	29,026,811	Nancy Wulf
Albertson's, Inc.	76	944	82	284,039	69	18,089,734	Renee Bergquist
* 3Com Corporation	77	930	100	72,544	100	3,250,878	Bill Slakey
Texaco, Inc.	78	904	68	384,841	63	20,396,573	Doug Czarnecki
Johnson Controls, Inc.	79	896	99	140,383	84	8,282,597	Denise Zutz
Mobil Corporation	80	890	87	254,601	58	22,182,112	Gordon Garney
Bristol-Myers Squibb Company	81	884	56	484,462	23	64,827,071	Timothy Cost
Thermo Electron Corporation	82	877	51	528,358	82	8,949,064	Beat Lehmann
Gateway 2000 Inc.	83	863	84	259,400	74	13,278,038	Megan Robertson
Nucor Corporation	84	803	96	195,102	83	8,438,162	Samuel Siegel
Modine Manufacturing Company	85	776	83	261,017	80	9,461,866	Gerald Sweda
International Business Machines Corp.	86	763	85	258,637	34	47,686,197	Douglas Maine
Federal Signal Corporation	87	756	78	294,882	89	6,892,867	Henry Dykema
Campbell Soup Company	88	743	95	195,889	77	10,773,895	Leonard Griehs
* Claire's Stores, Inc.	89	736	94	199,058	94	4,080,689	Glenn Canary
* Andrew Corporation	90	716	89	220,524	97	3,638,646	Tami Kamarauskas
Monsanto Company	91	710	91	203,636	79	9,672,710	Andrew Kuchan
* American Power Conversion Corporation	92	703	77	296,569	72	14,365,061	Debbie Grey
Kellogg Company	93	689	97	193,174	90	6,592,063	John H. Bolt
Atmos Energy Corporation	94	682	79	291,146	81	9,389,459	Lynn Hord
Linear Technology Corporation	95	669	90	208,104	68	18,638,315	Paul Coghlan
* Wolverine World Wide, Inc.	96	663	72	353,798	93	4,687,824	Tom Mundt
ServiceMaster Company	97	629	59	470,647	78	10,383,649	Bruce Duncan
* Thermo Instrument Systems, Inc.	98	629	88	249,259	96	3,754,464	John N. Hatsopoulos
* American Home Products Corporation	99	616	54	520,888	48	29,365,061	Thomas Cavanagh
* Eli Lilly & Company	100	616	76	298,738	51	26,550,340	Patricia Martin

Reprinted from the April 1999 *Better Investing* magazine with permission.

holdings, including JCPenney, Intel, Evergreen Utility, Disney, Hannaford, DuPont, AFLAC, and Wendy's. (The group owned significant shares in BET before it reverted to a private entity.)

The six-year-old group set a one-year time table before buying its first stock, America's Utility Fund (offered by their local utility company). "We noticed in our bills it was offering customers a plan to buy into this mutual fund," says Williams-Robinson. A team of members researched the fund and presented their findings. The group voted in favor of investing.

The 15-member club ranges in age from 30 to 50, with diverse backgrounds, from nurses to bankers. In addition to a combined compound annual return of 70 percent for 1996 and 1997, the group's youth and community advocacy was a factor in the Coalition of Black Investor's selection of Investors 2000 Plus as Investment Club of the Year in 1998.

Club organizers, including Williams-Robinson, say that searching for companies among the places, products, and services that everyday folks use will make it easier and more appealing to members to do the necessary research. Plus, members have a better chance at aiding in the club's portfolio value increasing over time.

PAY ATTENTION TO YOUR SURROUNDINGS

One of the best ways to learn how to choose investments comes from observation. Many times, a good stock choice will come from members paying attention to their surroundings—again, the places where they shop, eat, and entertain. If it seems that everyone is drinking Starbucks café lattes and mochas, and it looks like it's not just a fad but a habit that's here to stay, invest in the coffee franchise. See what type of information you can find about the company. Indeed, Starbucks Corporation happens to be one of the top stock holdings of investment clubs.

Many folks have made money by checking out their surroundings and following trends. Peter Lynch, former portfolio manager of the world's largest mutual fund, Fidelity Magellan, bragged that he came across one of his best stocks by noticing his wife's preference for L'Eggs hosiery and how she could conveniently pick up the egg-shaped cartons at the supermarket. Lynch scored big with his legendary investment in Sara Lee Corporation, the product's manufacturer.

Still today, there's nobody who doesn't like Sara Lee, ranked number 37 on the NAIC Top 100 list (see Figure 10.2). You can eat Sara

Lee products (baked goods and packaged meats, such as Ball Park and Hillshire Farm), drink them (Douwe Egberts coffee and Pickwick tea), clean with them (Endust), wear them (Hanes and Wonderbra), or carry them (Coach leather goods).

Another way to search for stocks worth buying is to find out what people are talking about, and to look at the goods your friends and family are hooked on. Every product and the companies that make them are fair game from razors to rollerblades to computers to cell phones to micro-brewed beer. Also, pay attention to companies that are expanding or introducing new product lines.

"If your teary-eyed five-year-old is begging for the latest pair of Nike Air Jordans, chances are that other parents will be shopping for that same product," says Pierre Dunagan, managing partner of Dunagan, Robinson & Isbell Financial Services, a Chicago-based advisory firm. "Take a trip to retail stores and check to see how many people are buying the product," he advises. "Stand in the aisles for a little while and just observe. Talk to the store manager and ask how well a particular product is selling." If a company is large and has a broad product line, a new product may not greatly impact the bottom line, he cautions. "But for a small company, a new, hot-selling product could boost earnings significantly."

Investment advisor and author Cheryl D. Broussard recalls a woman making a lot of money in the early 1980s when the *Star War* movies first came out. The woman noticed the long lines at the theaters, checked out the film's producer, Twentieth Century Fox Film Corp., and invested in that company.

"We keep our eyes attuned to what's happening around us," explains Dr. Reginald L. Parker, vice president of the Columbia, South Carolina Group, Minority Empowerment for Tomorrow. "When we looked at recent statistics, we saw that two-thirds of the gross domestic product was primarily consumer driven. And, as consumers, we like stores that have a lot of products at a good price. That's how we ended up with Wal-Mart as one of our holdings." The group also owns shares in 12 other holdings, including Home Depot, MCI Worldcom, Immunex, AT&T, AOL, and Cisco Systems.

Of course, popularity alone doesn't make a company a good investment. You have to do both technical and fundamental analysis to make sure that the company has a good balance sheet, solid management team, consistent sales, and strong earnings growth (which you will learn more about in Chapter 12).

CONSIDER THE INDUSTRIES YOU WORK IN

Chris Wilson was working 2,000 miles away from the Redmond, Washington-based Microsoft Corp. But, from the way he forecast the company's growth, you might have thought he was a key player on its strategic-planning team. Banking on an educated hunch that the then $1.5 billion software giant had hit pay dirt with its newly released revolutionary Windows operating system for personal computers, Wilson advised his New Freedom Investment Club to buy $742.75 worth of Microsoft stock.

That was in August 1990. In just two years, the investment had doubled in value, up 126 percent and worth $1,677. Today, the club's overall portfolio is worth more than $250,000, and $19-billion Microsoft is the number one software maker, with co-founder and CEO Bill Gates the richest man in the world.

Like most successful strategic investors, New Freedom strongly believes in using "insider's knowledge" to make investments. For New Freedom (named in honor of the long-awaited release of former South African president Nelson Mandela from prison in 1990), this philosophy means sticking to industries that its 21 current members are familiar with, such as technology and health care. That's because, like Wilson, most New Freedom's members work in Research Triangle Park, a high-technology business research center near Durham, North Carolina.

"Working in the high-tech field helped many members understand the significance of Windows' initial popularity," says Wilson, a manager in Information Management at Glaxo Wellcome.

As a result of this thinking, the nine-year-old club's portfolio is invested 100 percent in 20 stocks, including Microsoft, Oracle Systems, Lucent Technologies, MCI Worldcom, and Cisco Systems. To balance its portfolio, New Freedom has incorporated a few nontech stocks, such as CVS Corp., the drugstore chain; State Street, a financial services company; The Gap, and Merck.

The real big money is made by people who are in an industry and have the smarts to realize that something new is going to mean a company will be making more money down the road. This legal version of insider trading is only one of a host of strategies for beating Wall Street at its own game.

While hot industry trends can be a source of stock picks, you don't want to follow the herd, chasing after the latest craze sectors, like health care or biotechnology, unless a member of your club is familiar with the business.

Industry experts say that studying companies in your own and fellow club members' industries or about which you have some "insider's knowledge" increases the likelihood of investment success. If you're a computer technician, look at what new software is making your life easier, find out the manufacturer, and if that company is publicly traded. It doesn't matter whether you are a construction worker, doctor, or a store clerk, you can grasp your own industry as surely as any Wall Street pundit.

When considering industries there are a few areas with which you should familiarize yourself:

- *Defensive industries,* such as food and drug companies, tend to offer stability, because they can weather poor economic conditions better than other types of industries.

- *Cyclical industries,* which include automobile manufacturing, steel, housing, and paper companies, tend to grow with an expanding economy but fare poorly during an economic downturn. Thus, any company that is closely tied to the ups and downs of the economy is considered cyclical.

  When the economy is growing, production is up, and consumers are utilizing the products these companies produce to meet increasing demand. If the economy isn't doing well and consumer demand is down, company earnings can drop.

- *Growth industries,* include such sectors as computers, robotics, biotechnology, health-maintenance organizations, and retailing stocks. Just think Wal-Mart, Xerox, Eastman-Kodak, and Abbott Laboratories. These companies expand when there is a growing demand for goods or services they produce. Over the past few years, growth companies have exhibited faster-than-average gains in earnings and profits and average annual returns between 12 percent and 15 percent.

The obvious downside to any homespun research is that you could come in on the late end of the cycle, when the buying frenzy is ending. And, of course, you risk a glitch cropping up in the product, slowing down sales. For this reason, your club should stick with industries in which there is continuous consumer demand.

Among the most promising consumer-driven sectors are household and personal products, food, beverages, textiles, apparel, shoes, and accessories. "We are always shopping for ourselves and our families," says First of Michigan's Gail Perry-Mason. "No matter what the market is

doing: We always eat. We clean our homes. We bathe ourselves and our children. Whatever age or size we are, we still shop for clothes."

Perry-Mason offers some advice on how to pick some winning stocks: "In your club's quest for investments, look at those companies that are well diversified and produce those products that we will always use and need regardless of how the economy is doing."

STICK WITH TRIED AND TRUE STOCKS

Many investment clubs find themselves blue, not because they are physically sick, but meaning that they tend to invest heavily in blue-chip stocks. Named for the most expensive poker chips, these stocks have a reputation for solid management and a history of profitability. They have long records of earnings and growth and pay dividends in good and bad times.

In seeking long-term investments that provide quality, growth, and income, blue chips are a great bet. A bit of a conservative investment, blue-chip stocks are issued by the nation's top corporations, including such household names as American Express, General Electric, Quaker Oats, and Johnson & Johnson.

Moreover, many of the blue chips have DRIPs, which, you may recall, absorb brokerage fees by automatically reinvesting dividends to buy more shares of company stock. Greer says typically 25 percent to 33 percent of a club's portfolio should be blue. Among investment clubs' more popular picks are AT&T, IBM, Bristol-Myers Squibb, Exxon, Ford, and Procter & Gamble.

"Because many blue chips are companies club members are familiar with, it gives them a comfort level in choosing such stocks for their portfolios," says Baunita Greer of Cromwell, Miller & Greer. "It makes it easier for them to understand what those companies do and, therefore, to monitor them. With new and emerging companies, they don't usually have a track record yet for members to follow."

However, the stock prices for these premium brands tend to be higher than smaller issues and it may take longer for new clubs to purchase significant shares in these companies. While blue chips usually withstand economic downturns, Greer cautions, don't ever buy a stock, even a blue chip, and then never look at it again.

"We have always been heavy on blue chips," says Heard, whose club owns shares in such companies as Colgate-Palmolive and Walt

Disney. When choosing stocks, Unity Investment Partnership considers two things: the size of the company and the industry it is in.

The group invests in few small- and mid-sized companies. "We own stock in a broad range of industries, including supermarkets, pharmaceuticals, household products, chemicals, beverages, entertainment, manufacturing, office products, and telecommunications," adds Heard.

The group got rid of its one health-care stock, First Health Group. "It did very well in the beginning but once the company got involved with HMOs it took a nosedive," says Heard. Two areas that the club is now focusing on are financials (e.g., banks, mortgage, and insurance firms) and energy (e.g., oil and utility companies). "We look at how much each stock represents. If it's more than 15 percent of our portfolio, we won't buy more shares of that stock or another in that sector."

Make Your Money Talk: Shareholder Activism

A community organizer and Pan-Africanist, Kamau Odinga has been a political activist for the past 27 years. In 1995 he co-founded the PULA Project Investment Club in Luling, Louisiana. "I wanted to help teach brothers and sisters that ownership is the key to success. I wanted to show them how to locate the very best minds and to put them to work. For instance, our club just employed Bill Gates; he now works for us because we own shares in Microsoft," says Odinga.

Odinga stands strong in his conviction that shareholder activism is the new civil-rights movement. The members of PULA, who purchase most of their stocks through DRIPS, own shares in 15 companies, including Monsanto, Home Depot, Union Carbide, AT&T, Lucent Technologies, Citigroup, PepsiCo, Exxon, and Bell South. The club invests 100 percent of its portfolio in stocks.

It was during the height of apartheid that Odinga attended a shareholders' meeting at Monsanto, demanding that they divest from South Africa. Members also wrote letters to the board of directors and management of Home Depot and Winn Dixie with respect to their policies and practices as they relate to race and sex discrimination.

"Our position is that when you own shares of a company, you are part owner of the company itself. You can now go to the CEO and say, 'I don't like the way you are managing my company,'" says Odinga. "When I sit back at the end of the day, I want to know that the CEO of Coca-Cola is vigorously competing with the CEO of PepsiCo, and that

when my friends, enemies, or those who are undecided drink a Coke or a Pepsi, they are putting money in my pockets, because I own shares in both companies."

Publicly held companies are required by the Securities and Exchange Commission to hold annual meetings attended by shareholders, company executives, boards of directors, and other interested parties. During this open forum, the CEO delivers his message on the company's direction and shareholders receive an annual report, vote on issues, and voice their concerns.

You may also cast your vote by mailing in a *proxy,* a written authorization indicating how you would like to vote on various issues. In reality, a small number of large shareholders can possess enough voting power to decide the outcome of an issue presented for the shareholder vote. If an investor wants to challenge these stockholders, they'll have to convince many other shareholders to vote in their favor by waging a proxy fight.

Barbara Talley, who has always been a political activist, lost the mayoral election a year ago by 97 votes in her hometown of Southfield, Michigan. While she has invested in the stock market for years, Talley never gave a second thought to shareholder activism, at least, not until the winter of 1999 when she and 39 other African-American women boarded a Detroit bus to Sara Lee Corp.'s annual shareholders' meeting.[2]

As do many investors, Talley always voted by proxy. "I consider myself an astute investor. Still, this was my first time ever attending a shareholders' meeting" says Talley. Together the group of 39 women owned 25,000 shares of Sara Lee common stock, a company that delivers big brand names such as Coach bags, L'Eggs pantyhose, Playtex bras, and Hanes underwear.

"It is important to expose shareholders to the benefits of being a partial owner of a company," says Gail Perry-Mason, the trip's organizer and a financial advisor with First of Michigan. "Their votes needed to be counted, their faces seen, and their voices heard."

These sisters turned heads at the gathering of 5,000 investors. Talley was among those to speak before the entire group, suggesting that Sara Lee add a woman of color to its board. Prior to the meeting, she contacted the office of John Bryant, the board's chairman.

"I told them that I wanted to learn more about Sara Lee's commitment to diversity in terms of African Americans in management and their vendor-supply program," she explains. "I also wanted to know how much of their sales were derived from African Americans. It was

important to me to see the direct correlation between the number of dollars we spend on their products and how many black employees and suppliers they have."

How to win votes and influence board members is a lesson in shareholder activism applied for years by religious groups, labor unions, and investor organizations. If members of your investment club are interested in attending a shareholders' meeting, simply contact the shareholders' relations department. You may submit a formal proposal or resolution as long as the group holds at least $1,000 worth of company stock.

You may not have the same strength and number of shares as institutional investors or mutual-fund managers, but companies don't dismiss your recommendations even though corporate bigwigs may not always implement them. By coming together, you can learn how to flex your financial muscle and wield clout in America's corporate boardrooms.

There is some controversy over whether big institutions increase the volatility and risk in the market when they trade large blocks of shares. One thing is certain: Time evens out the fluctuations. If you buy stock with the intention of holding it for at least three to five years, you're likely to find that your return will reflect the quality of the company and its business prospects.

Odinga says he wants to see African Americans take 10 percent of their $250 billion purchasing power and bring it to the marketplace every year and start purchasing major ownership in companies. He offers some handy advice: Investors should set a goal, over the next 10 years, of buying shares in at least 12 percent of the top 500 corporations in the world.

HOW THE MARKET'S PERFORMANCE AFFECTS YOUR CLUB'S PERFORMANCE

You probably have heard stories from your grandparents about the market crash of 1929 which initiated the Great Depression—a period that lasted until World War II—during which economic activity slowed tremendously and unemployment was very high.

Thousands of bank depositors were wiped out during the Depression. And, while the Federal Deposit Insurance Corporation (FDIC) was created in 1933 to guarantee bank deposits up to $100,000, Nana probably has been stashing some cash under her mattress ever since.

Market crashes precipitate a drop in stock prices and economic activity and are usually bought on by a loss in investor confidence followed by periods of high inflation. Many of us remember Black Monday—in October 1987—when the Dow plunged a record 508 points, reflecting investor anxiety about inflated stock prices, the federal budget and trade deficits, and foreign markets.

Despite the crashes of 1929 and 1987, stocks have outperformed all other investments, including corporate bonds. This may begin to sound like a broken record, but those people who make money in the stock market invest for the long term—five or more years.

The Center for Research in Security Prices at the University of Chicago has conducted studies of the stock market since 1926. Had an investor bought and sold any stock at random during a period between 1926 and 1960, that person would have made a profit 78 percent of the time.

The average return of the investment, assuming the person reinvested all dividends paid on the stock, would have been 9.8 percent a year. These are considered spectacular findings, given Americans did suffer through the Depression and a major world war during that period.

Even though the economic outlook may seem uncertain, the potential for above-average returns will always remain high in the stock market. There are many useful methods by which to estimate what kind of return a stock is likely to produce. These methods draw on a wide range of information, including economic data, the interest rate outlook, industry trends, and world events.

Many club members rely on the ratings and recommendations of analysts at investment firms and financial publications. Analysts devote a large segment of time looking at the past, present, and future performance of individual companies and their stock.

A GROWING ECONOMY AND INTEREST RATES

Why take you back to Economics 101? The more you understand about market cycles, inflation, interest rates, and economic indicators, the better decisions you can make regarding your club's investments.

We are familiar with the difference between the money we earn, our take-home pay, and the money we have left over after paying taxes—the tax collector is a dollar shrinker. There's also an invisible

tax collector and dollar shrinker—inflation. Prices have a tendency to rise over a period of time, and we call that *inflation*. If our wages are rising at about the same rate as prices, inflation isn't that big a deal. We are not really losing buying power.

Inflation *can* hurt when you are trying to save and invest, and the dollar you get back is no longer worth as much as the dollar you stashed away. If you have your money in a bank account earning 3 percent interest, but the inflation rate is 5 percent, you are losing money. You want to invest intelligently, so that you get a larger return on your money than the rate of inflation.

Stocks may not be the perfect inflation hedge at any one moment but, over the longer period of time, they have been quite effective in growing investors' dollars. Research by Roger G. Ibbotson, a nationally recognized authority on market returns, shows that over the past 70 years, common stocks have earned enough to outpace inflation (at a rate of 3.1%) by more than three times.

The ownership of common stock has been by far the most profitable of all major forms of capital investment. For instance, common stocks have been twice as profitable as high grade corporate bonds, with a total return of 10.9 percent, compared to 5.6 percent, and 3.8 percent for Treasury Bills.

A rapidly growing economy can be bad for stocks. The level of growth expected for the economy and interest rate forecasts influence the outlook for stock performance. In a growing economy—measured by such indicators as new housing starts, retail sales, and industrial production—corporate profits often rise. These increased profits, or expected increases in profits, push stock prices up.

If the economy grows too quickly and overheats, demand for money to fund expansion can shoot up and produce higher interest rates. The higher rates reduce corporate profits because of the higher cost of borrowing. In addition, higher interest rates can drive investors away from stocks and into money markets and other fixed-income investments.

A business cycle is like a roller-coaster ride—the economy is constantly moving up and down. Each peak *(recovery)* and dip *(recession)* can be measured by economic indicators, which also tell you how the economy is doing in terms of inflation, growth, and employment. On average, about two and one half years is when the nation's economy moves in and out of recession and recovery phases.

When businesses are operating at a good capacity, meaning their production of goods and services is up, running, and steadily humming

along—a business peak or economic boom is sure to occur. On the other hand, if business starts to slow down a bit and sales of goods and services drop, the market is likely to enter into the bust part of a business cycle and head for a recession.

What does all of this have to do with your club? In a recession, your club is bound to lose money, while in an expansion period, your club will make money. As long as your club practices the principle of dollar-cost averaging, your portfolio will balance out in these market cycles.

Truth be told, all investment clubs experience turbulent markets. Volatility happens when the stock market fluctuates up and down, but, like your faithful mailman, investment clubs don't veer from their course. They tend to stick with their buy-and-hold investment philosophy, hanging onto their stocks even amidst stormy weather when jittery investors are screaming "Sell!"

THE DOW AND OTHER INDEXES

The best way to determine how well your club's portfolio is performing is to use a benchmark. It is important to understand how your investments are judged. A *benchmark* measures the standard of performance reached by other investors. Sometimes, this is referred to as a *market average* or *index.*

If you were to take a bundle of stocks of all different types and lump them together, with a few financial formulas you would establish an average or an index. All these averages or indices give you an idea of where a stock is going.

Today, there are more than 20 major indices you can follow. The most popular stock index is the Dow Jones Industrial Average (DJIA), which comprises 30 companies that represent major industries, such as oil, retail, manufacturing, food, and technology.

The stocks in the Dow—often classified as blue chips—are widely held by individuals and institutional investors. These stocks represent about a fifth of the $8 trillion-plus market value of all U.S. stocks and about a fourth of the value of stocks listed on the New York Stock Exchange.

While there are always 30 stocks in the Dow, certain issues from time to time fall out of favor. Over the past couple of years, tech stocks—once considered volatile—have gained credibility as safe bets. In one of the biggest shake-ups in its 103-year history, the Dow

entered into the "digital age" in 1999 by dropping such time-honored companies as Good-year Tire and Sears Roebuck in favor of tech titans Microsoft and Intel. It also marked the first time stocks trading on NASDAQ joined the index.

The stocks in the Dow are often classified as blue chips (see Figure 10.1). These stocks represent 10 percent to 20 percent of the total market value of all stocks traded on the NYSE. Most of the blue chips are manufacturing companies, but a few service companies are included.

You can use the Dow as an aid in evaluating your stock's performance. If the Dow rose 20 percent one year and your stock rose only 10 percent, you know that your stock underperformed the market. You may want to consider selling your stock. Knowing how much the Dow goes up or down on any given day is less important than knowing what the trend is.

Market analysts have devised dozens of other stock indexes ranging from the Standard & Poor's 500 (see Figure 10.3), consisting of 500 stocks, to indexes that focus on just one sector, such as automobiles, utilities, or restaurants. For example, there is the Dow Jones 20 Transportation Stock Index, which follows such companies as TWA Corporation, Federal Express Company, and the Burlington Northern Railroad.

Many portfolio managers use the S&P 500, which is a better indicator of the market than the Dow, which is narrowly based. Both of these indexes are published daily in the business section of the newspaper.

The S&P 400 Midcap Index tracks the medium-sized stocks, and the Wilshire 5000 index tracks all major NYSE, AMEX, and NASDAQ stocks. The Russell 2000 Index and the Wilshire Small Cap Index both track the stock performance of smaller companies on all of the major exchanges.

These indexes exist as benchmarks against which you can compare your portfolio, depending on your investments. If you have any foreign investments, you might want to use the Morgan Stanley Capital International Europe Australia Far East (EAFE) Index.

RAGING BULLS AND MEANDERING BEARS

Believe it or not, there are bulls and bears on Wall Street. A *bull* in the financial markets is not unlike the fierce animal that stomps its hoof several times when it's about to charge full-steam ahead. If stock prices are rising and financial gurus are optimistic that the general direction of the financial markets will continue to move upward, they

are said to be *bullish.* A growing economy signals that investors are in for a long bull market.

Then there are *bears.* Not the ones named Yogi, in search of a picnic basket, but those huge and sometimes clumsy animals that meander through the wilderness hunting salmon in cold streams. They don't charge forward but, once they are on the move, you had better get out of their way. In financial markets, a bear brings stock prices down and a decline in growth. If financial naysayers think stock prices will continue on a downward spiral and predict doom and gloom about the general direction of the market, they are said to be *bearish.*

To determine what investments to make, you need to keep track of the direction in which the economy is moving, bullish (which is up) or bearish (which is down). Whether it is a bull or bear market, your club can make a profit. Remember, dollar-cost averaging.

Still, how do you go about checking out those companies that are in your industry or produce products and services that appeal to you? Once you discover that the company is traded publicly, simply call. Any company of substance will have a shareholder relations department, and annual and quarterly reports are free. If you're interested and willing to put in a little time, you can find out all about the company at very little cost.

Don't be afraid to ask questions of the folks in shareholder relations. If the company is currently unprofitable, you're allowed to inquire as to when the company expects to turn a profit, and how fast it projects sales will grow and who is its competition. Once you become a part-owner of a company, you will receive updates on how well the company is doing on a regular basis.

WHAT IT MEANS TO BE A SHAREHOLDER

Why do company founders relinquish control and profits by issuing stock to begin with? Simply put, to raise money. Although a company can borrow money to expand or for other reasons, loans may not be sufficient or cost effective at a given time. Rather, new shares of stock are issued to outsiders.

The most common way to participate in the stock market is by investing in common and preferred stock. When you buy shares of a company's common stock, the number of shares you own relative to the total number of shares the company has sold (shares outstanding), determines the extent of your ownership.

Common stock offers you the best opportunity to participate in the growth of a company, though it is riskier than bonds and preferred stock. As a common shareholder, you have certain rights, including the right to:

- Vote and elect directors of the company.
- Receive your share of profits in the form of dividends. If the company makes a profit, the board of directors can vote to pay you dividends in proportion to the number of shares you own.
- Receive a copy of the company's annual report.

Preferred doesn't necessarily mean better, but it does relate to having priority over common stockholders when it comes to the distribution of dividends and assets in the event of the breakup of a corporation. In essence, *preferred stock* is a cross between stocks and bonds—it has a dividend yield that is fixed and limited, but it has no maturity.

Shareholders with this type of stock are considered owners of the corporation, just like common shareholders, but preferred shareholders generally don't have voting rights. Many investors buy preferred stock for the steady income it offers and the hope that their principal will increase over the years.

Although growth possibilities with preferred stock are not as good as with common stocks, these stocks are usually an appropriate vehicle for protecting investors' original investment, except during severe inflationary periods.

LISTED AND UNLISTED STOCKS

The vast majority of corporations in the United States are private companies. Shares in private corporations are not sold on the stock market and can only be purchased from current stockholders—generally, a pretty small group of people. Private companies are like little private parties—you have to be invited.

However, as long as they pay an admission charge, anyone from the general public is invited to participate in a public corporation. Shares in a public corporation can be purchased by securities dealers and traded openly on a stock exchange.

There are two classifications of publicly held stock: the first is listed and the second one unlisted.

Listed Stocks

A stock that is *listed* trades on either the national or regional exchange. *Exchanges* are auctions where buyers and sellers come together to do business; a stock is worth only as much as someone is willing to pay for it. Exchanges operate Monday thru Friday from 9:30 A.M. to 4:00 P.M. (Eastern Standard Time).

The New York Stock Exchange (NYSE), also referred to as *the big board*, is located on Wall Street in New York and is the oldest and largest exchange. The NYSE lists over 1,600 stocks and provides a big meeting place for people to conduct trades. The American Stock Exchange (AMEX), also located in New York, lists and trades another 1,100 stocks.

There are also several local exchanges that list not only regional issues but many of the securities listed on the New York exchanges. They include the Philadelphia, Boston, Cincinnati, Intermountain (Salt Lake City), Pacific Stock Exchange (Los Angeles and San Francisco), and Midwest Stock Exchange (Chicago).

Unlisted Stocks

These stocks trade on the over-the-counter market (OTC), which is a marketplace where securities dealers buy and sell from their own accounts, for themselves. The OTC market refers to those times when some stocks were so small that they had to be purchased at the offices of brokers or banks, literally *over the counter.* There are currently more than 50,000 stocks trading in the OTC market, ranging from high-quality bank stocks to lower quality penny stocks.

The primary OTC market is known as the National Association of Securities Dealers Automated System, or NASDAQ. There is no great meeting place; stocks are traded by computers and telephone communications networks that connect brokers who represent buyers and sellers all over the country.

As a rule, smaller and newer firms are traded on the NASDAQ, although some big firms and a number of technology companies trade on NASDAQ as well. Once a new company's assets increase and it becomes a more popular company, it may apply to be listed on the NYSE.

Many companies that have enough assets to qualify for listing on the NYSE have chosen not to move up the big board and to remain

instead over the counter, as was the case with Apple Computer until recently.

IPOs

When a company goes public and offers its stocks and bonds to the general public for the first time, it is called an *initial public offering.* The IPO market consists of many new and relatively small companies with very limited track records. New issues of stock can soar three times its value in just one day because of all the hoopla surrounding the offering. But shortly after, the stock price of the IPO typically drops.

Had you been asked in 1996 to invest in the company that produced the season's computer-animated blockbuster *Toy Story,* wouldn't you have considered that a good pick? Certainly, and you would have been in good company. Many unsuspecting investors thought so and bought stock in Pixar, the film's producer, which issued a public offering at $22 a share around the time the movie was released. Within the first day of trading, Pixar rose to $49 and then dropped to $29. As initial Wall Street traders profited by cashing in their gains, latecomers where left holding the bag.

Today, Pixar is a $14 million enterprise whose stock is trading at $36 a share, slowly establishing a track record with other hits like *Toy Story 2* and *A Bug's Life.* While new issues can prove to be long-term winners, investing in IPOs can be risky. Until your club has been in the driver's seat for a while, avoid jumping on the latest IPO bandwagon.

By now, your club realizes that the stock market is indeed the best game in town. Keep in mind that regardless of what traders do day to day, investing over the long run is one of the biggest secrets to making money on Wall Street. While your club may not consist of the Warren Buffetts of the world—at least not yet—you can be assured that the more time club members have to wait out business cycles, the greater their financial rewards.

11

INVEST IN WHAT YOU KNOW: RESEARCHING STOCKS LIKE THE PROS

If you plant turnips, you will not harvest grapes.

—Akan proverb

If you keep your pockets full of coins, you will always have small change.

—Yoruba proverb

Few people can say they have gathered a lifetime's worth of investment advice.[1] Grafton J. Daniels, 88, can. Dubbed the "Godfather of Investment Clubs," by his fellow members, Daniels has helped to launch and counsel some 45 adult and two youth investment clubs in the Washington, DC, area over the past 35 years.

His latest effort is serving as founder and presiding partner of the St. George's Investment Club (SGIC), officially recognized as the number two club in the Washington, DC, metropolitan area by NAIC. The club owns 62 stocks, 40 of which are large-capitalization stocks, 10 midcap, and 12 small cap. Daniels says the club's biggest stakes are in Intel, 10 percent; Lucent Technologies, 10 percent; Safeway, 5 percent; and Time Warner, 5 percent.

A former Howard University student, Daniels was introduced to the stock market in 1959, while he was working for the U.S. Geological Survey, a branch of the Department of the Interior. A friend approached

him about selling mutual funds for the Hamilton Management Corp. He worked there part time from 1959 to 1970. Six months after starting the job, he was appointed assistant district manager, overseeing a 25-member sales force.

The group made cold calls to potential clients, selling mutual funds at a rate of $10 per month or for a lump sum of anywhere from $600 to $10,000 or more. Putting his money where his mouth was, Daniels himself eventually invested $50 a month in a Hamilton-sponsored mutual fund, earning $13,000 on an average return of about 10 percent over 11 years.

For a man who was totally green to the stock market, Daniels put in exceptional hours and effort to learn the tricks of the trade. In 1965, he took the National Association of Securities Dealers exam and gained a broker's license to sell stocks and bonds. He went on to work for a number of financial firms, including Consolidated Financial Services, in Silver Spring, Maryland.

The financial sage has taken some risks and has had his share of hard knocks. For instance, he lost a significant amount of money back in 1983—about $25,000—investing in diamonds while working as a district manager for San Diego-based International Diamond Corp. The company went belly up that year, and Daniels, who had been employed there since 1979, retired from the business. Despite this setback, he wisely remained invested in the stock market.

Daniels knows firsthand that often what looks like a safe bet on Wall Street requires much more scrutiny and investigation. Stocks should not be bought on the strength of rumor or popular opinion. When investing, the best research wins the greatest returns.

St. George's investment philosophy: 100 percent stocks, no bonds or mutual funds. In order to double your money every five years, clubs have to pick stocks that appreciate 15 percent per year, Daniels contends. St. George's members agree to sign a form indicating that they are committed to the club for a specific period of time. Since the median age of the club members is 60, that time frame is just three years. As a result, the club's securities committee, comprised of eight members of which Daniels is the head, tries to pick stocks that have the potential to return 30 percent annually.

"Initially, our main objective was to grow our portfolio every five years, now we are looking to double our money every three years," Daniels explains. "So, instead of choosing stocks with a growth rate of 15 percent or better, we must select stocks with the potential to grow

30 percent a year." The club's technology and Internet holdings have achieved similar high growth rates.

For example, the group purchased AOL at $40 per share in December 1996; it was trading at $122 as of June 1999. The club's other stocks in these sectors include Yahoo, Amazon.com, IBM, Compaq, Microsoft, Oracle, and Cisco Systems.

Finding stocks with high growth rates is an ambitious task, but the members of St. George's understand a key tenent: Your portfolio is only as good as the research that goes into it. For this reason, members rely heavily on financial publications and even frequent the SEC's library whenever they need additional information.

To picks stocks successfully, your club will need to be knowledgeable about the industries and the companies in which members wish to invest. This chapter offers some tips on finding and analyzing information to help members make informed stock-market decisions.

INVESTING: AN ART, NOT A SCIENCE

You don't have to be a rocket scientist to understand how to pick stocks. In fact, think of yourself as a fine artist. The art of investing encompasses the same basic ideas and actions as painting a portrait—you need perspective, depth, details, background, and range (to paraphrase NAIC experts).

Let's paint a picture of a company's performance. As does any artist, you first need the right tools: canvas, paint, brushes, thinner, and so forth. You should have at your disposal all possible information on any given company. Most of what you need to know can be found online or at the library, in publications such as the *Standard & Poor's Reports* and *Value Line Investment Surveys*. Other sources are stock tables, analysts' reports, and a company's annual and quarterly reports, as well as corporate press releases and announcements.

As with any artistic endeavor, you must first decide what your subject is going to be, in other words, what company are you going to research. Next, you must make a sketch or an outline, translation: What is it you like about this company in general? From there, you need to start adding color, details, and definition to your portrait, meaning you need to analyze figures pertaining to the company's sales, revenues, and potential growth rate.

Once you have completed your masterpiece, you want to step back and take a hard look at what you have done. Analyze what you see and make a decision as to whether you want to add this piece to your collection or portfolio (in this case). Now that you've got the basics of picking stocks, let's examine a little more closely some of the tools you need to paint that picture of a company's performance.[2]

READING THE STOCK TABLES

Everyone has seen the stock tables in the business section of their local newspaper. But if you have never really used them, these tables can seem overwhelming. You may feel like a secret agent attempting to decode some master spy's hidden message, but stock tables really contain simple shorthand on the status of stocks traded on the various market exchanges (see Figure 11.1).

There are stock tables for each of the three different exchanges. Once you familiarize yourself with the abbreviated names and ticker symbols of the companies you want to invest in, the rest of the information is a snap to get.

Stock tables tell you five key pieces of information: The 52-week high and low prices of the stock, dividend, present yield, volume, and price-to-earnings ratio (P/E).

High and Low Prices

The highest and lowest prices that an individual stock sold for over the previous weeks are reported daily. The range between these prices is a measure of the stock's volatility. Volatile stocks are riskier investments because of their potential to make or lose a great deal of money within a relatively short period of time. For example, a stock that has shifted in

Figure 11.1   A Sample Stock Table

| 52-Week | | | | Yld. | | Sales | | | | |
High	Low	Name	Div.	%	PE	100s	High	Low	Last	Chg.
$55\frac{3}{8}$	$31\frac{3}{8}$	WalMart	.20	.38	47	53,318	$52\frac{15}{16}$	$50\frac{3}{4}$	$52\frac{3}{8}$	$+1\frac{1}{16}$

price from 18⅞ to 47⅞ over 52 weeks (about 150 percent) would be considered volatile (because what quickly goes up often comes down).

Pay attention to codes following or preceding names. For instance, the letter *s* indicates the stock has split during the past 52 weeks or paid a stock dividend of at least 25 percent. As you can see in Figure 11.1, Wal-Mart did indeed split. Thus, owners of this leading discount store doubled the shares they owned when the company share price split.

You can use stock price patterns along with other fundamental measures to assess potential growth, says Pierre Dunagan, of DRI Financial Services in Chicago. Although he doesn't always advocate this approach, he comments, "What you want to ask is, did the stock make a new high and did it make that high on strong volume? If the stock is making new highs and its volume is more than usual, then it might be a good play." Essentially, you want to look for consistency and stability in a stock's price.

Dividend

Management's reward to the investor, a dividend is a steady stream of income that you can bank on. As you can see in Figure 11.1, the dividend column shows the actual cash amount of the dividend per share that is paid annually, which in this case was 20 cents. Check to see if a letter follows the sum shown. An *a* means the company paid the amount shown plus an extra dividend, while an *e* indicates there's no regular dividend but the amount shown was paid last year. If no figure appears then no dividend was paid.

Dividend Yield

Evaluating a stock's current value is important in determining future growth. The percent yield column on the financial pages tells you how much dividend is paid as a percentage of the current price. This figure is derived by dividing the dividend by the last or closing price per share at the end of the day. In Figure 11.1, the yield for Wal-Mart is 38 percent $[(.20 \div 52\frac{3}{8}) \times 100]$. This number also lets you compare the earnings of a stock with the earnings of other investments. However, it won't tell you the total return, which is the sum of dividends plus increases or decreases in stock price.

Volume

The market's interest in a particular stock can be measured by the volume of shares traded. This sales figure tells you how many shares were traded in that day. It is a composite of all the exchanges where that stock is traded. This figure is given in hundreds of shares unless the letter z appears after it, which denotes actual sales. An unusually large number of shares traded may mean that buyers and sellers are reacting to some new information, such as a shift in the market or a change in investor confidence in a particular security or industry.

P/E Ratio

This number tells if investors are getting their money's worth. A P/E measures the relationship between the company's stock price and earnings for the last four quarters. Multiple is another term used in exchange for P/E. To arrive at this figure, divide the current price of a stock by its earnings per share—this is the portion of a company's profit allocated to each outstanding share of common stock. For instance, a corporation that earned $10 million last year and has 10 million shares held by stockholders would report earnings of $1 per share.

You may have heard before that a certain stock was selling at a multiple of 15 or its P/E is 15. Translation: Investors were paying $15 for every $1 worth of company earnings. Note that the P/E ratio reports past, not future earnings, but it does indicate how people feel about a certain stock. Investors will pay more for a stock if they think the company has high growth potential, resulting in a high P/E.

The average P/E is about 13 to 14. Below that figure is considered low and above is high. Hot stocks are the ones with a high P/E ratio. For example, Netscape's P/E ratio was 50 when it came on the scene a few years back, which meant analysts had high expectations for the future earnings growth of the firm. The Internet company reached a high of $70 in 1999. Low P/E stocks tend to be in low-growth or mature industries or old, established blue-chip companies with a long record of stability and regular dividends.

It is not uncommon for a small, emerging company to have a high P/E and be an attractive investment, while a mature company could have a low P/E and be a bad investment. Two companies with a P/E of 12 may have two very different futures. One may be posting high earnings and the other heading for a loss.

The Future-Vest Investment Club in New York's club got its start around the 1987 stock market crash, snatching up company shares at bargain prices. The club purchased five stocks and four mutual funds using Citibank's brokerage account services.

"When we first started, we didn't want to get involved with very large companies," says Monica Noel, club president and regional NAIC council director. "We set a limit that the companies we invested in had to trade at $25 a share or less. We didn't specify industry, although some members said they didn't want to invest in tobacco companies."

Today, the club's portfolio is heavily weighted in blue-chip companies—about 60 percent, another 25 percent is invested in mid-sized companies, 10 percent in small companies, and the rest of their money is in cash and mutual funds. Future-Vest has some 35 active members who come from all walks of life, ranging in age from 25 to 75.

"A lot of the members are older and conservative; they want to stay with blue-chip stocks," says Noel, a former Citibank vice president and currently a financial planner. "Our younger members are interested in technology and Internet stocks, which tend to be more volatile."

Future-Vest's has more than $350,000 worth of stocks in its portfolio, averaging an annual rate of return of 16 percent. The club has positions in 20 companies, including Motorola, American Express, Abbott Labs, Hasbro, PepsiCo, Intel, Disney, IBM, and Lucent.

Scanning the financial pages of daily newspapers and financial publications and reading the stock tables of the different markets will help members keep abreast of market changes. Once they learn how to extract hard data on a company and examine it in a systematic way, each member will be able to paint a picture of a company and its prospects for future growth.

HOW THE PROS DO IT

The favorite adage on Wall Street is "buy low and sell high." Of course, this is nearly an impossible feat. How do you know when it's the right time to buy? Just as in shopping, says financial advisor Gail Perry-Mason. "If a company is down in value then look at it like it's on sale. It's a good time to buy, because you are getting it at a discount. If you see the company's earnings keep getting higher and higher, you want to buy it and hold onto it for the long term."

There are some money managers, including Perry-Mason, who like to purchase a stock when it's on sale—meaning everybody else is selling it. Rising stock prices are not always a good thing. Sometimes stock prices get too high, making it more than likely that the stock will do nothing but come down.

While there are several schools of thought when it comes to stock investing, the two most prevalent ones are *value* and *growth*. On Wall Street, the two represent opposing philosophies. Traditionally, *value investors* purchase companies that have fallen out of favor or discover overlooked firms selling at reasonable prices. Their rationale is that by buying stocks bought at bargain-basement prices, they will realize greater profits when other investors start to discover the true worth of those companies.

Growth investors, on the other hand, target companies with booming sales and profits. They want a company that can increase its sales or earnings per share faster than the overall market. Some money managers combine the best of both worlds. In the final analysis, they want growing companies with franchised products and superior management that are out of vogue and selling at a reasonable price.

There are two techniques that Wall Street professionals use to select value or growth stocks for their portfolios: *fundamental* analysis and *technical* analysis. You will need to have a grasp of both of these techniques to read and understand research reports published by major brokerage house analysts.

Fundamental Analysis

This is the most popular technique; it is based on investing in *undervalued stocks*—strong companies without debt problems that pay dividends and are lower priced than those of other companies in similar industries. Fundamental analysts focus on a company and its earnings—they look for stock with a low P/E.

If a company's P/E is lower than the current market average it is said to be *undervalued* and a good buy. If it is much higher, it is *overvalued* and usually the stock of a fast-growth company. Experts suggest that stocks that are in the neighborhood of 19 times earnings or a P/E of 19 are reasonable buys.

Fundamental analysts also look for companies whose shares are selling for less than the company is worth on paper. This figure is found

by comparing the current stock price with the book value—the company's assets minus its liabilities and that figure divided by the number of outstanding shares. If the current stock price is less than book value, it is considered undervalued. Experts suggest that you look for a price-to-book value of 4 or under. Price-to-book value figures can be found on the Web at such sites as Zacks Investment Research (www.zacks.com).[3]

Another figure investors use to separate cheap stocks from the duds is *return on equity* (ROE), which shows how efficient management is at putting their invested money to work. In general, money managers look for an ROE of 15 or better. A higher ROE shows that a corporation is working to get the most of the funds it has to invest in technology, new manufacturing processes, or key personnel.

Value investors measure a company's generosity to shareholders by its dividend yield. Currently, the S&P 500 stocks pay out an average yield of 1.2 percent annually, or 60 cents for every $50 share. Investment pros tend to like companies that payout roughly twice that amount, or 2.4 percent annually.

Technical Analysis

This method is used by analysts who follow the theory that stocks perform based on past history. They select stocks by plotting charts and graphs of market trends. They look for increases and decreases in the volume of a stock on a given day and whether or not the stock price is fluctuating more than usual *(volatility)*.

To measure market jitters, many money managers look at a stock's *beta,* which is a calculation of how much a company's stock price will go up and down relative to the S&P 500 stock index. Knowledge of a beta gives you a sense of what kinds of fluctuations your investment might undergo in the near future. A beta is the best indicator of how volatile the shares you own are, says Santo Famulare, an investment officer with AYCO, an Albany, New York-based money-management firm.

Just how do you determine a stock's beta? If stock prices of shares in the S&P 500 rises or drops 10 percent during a given time period, any stock that matches that movement will carry a beta of one. Stocks that move up or down in price 5 percent during the same time period will have a beta of .50; those that are likely to double in price, or 20 percent, will have a beta of two. Financial experts generally like stocks that have a beta between .90 and 1.10—meaning they are not more or less volatile than the overall market.

Typically, stocks in fast-moving industries, such as biotech, health care, and technology, carry high betas. "There are variable degrees of beta readings in the technology," says Famulare. "For example," he continues, "Intel is at the lower end at 1.15, and more commodity-driven semiconductors like Micron are at the high end at 1.65." Low beta stocks, he explains, are typically associated with more staid and stable industries, and points to such utilities as NYNEX (.80) and Texas Utilities (.70) as characteristic of this pattern.[4]

While betas usually aren't published in the newspaper, investors can find them in stock guides such as *Standard & Poor's Reports* and *Value Line Investment Surveys,* and on most online stock services. Also, check with your broker about your stock's beta.

The principals of Robert Van Securities, an African-American-owned investment firm in Oakland, California, are guided by a consensus as to where they think a stock's growth rate is heading down the road. A given company that makes the cut must have exhibited positive earnings momentum and a positive *alpha.* This is the measure of the amount of return based on the investment's inherent value over and above its relationship to the overall stock market, explains stock-picker and CEO Steven Singleton.[5]

A stock with an alpha of 1.25 is projected to rise in price by 25 percent in a year, on the strength of its inherent values such as growth in earnings per share, regardless of the performance of the market as a whole. Singleton seeks out opportunities in which his stock will go up despite the market cycles. By sticking with positive alphas, he never engages in bottom fishing.

EVALUATING ANNUAL REPORTS: HOW TO SEPARATE FACT FROM FLUFF

A man's best friend is his dog, but the investor's best buddy is the annual report. By reviewing this piece of literature, you can unearth a company's profitability, standards, new product and service offerings, and management team.[6]

A company uses its annual report to deliver mandatory and voluntary information to shareholders, as well as give an accurate picture of the company's performance over a 12-month period. If comprehensive, it can provide you with a window into the company's future.

The annual report is perhaps the most important document that companies produce for shareholders, says Kenneth Janke, president and

CEO of the Board of Trustees of the NAIC. "It is a vital tool in analyzing companies whose securities investors wish to buy, hold, or sell."

Your club should obtain a company's annual report before you ever invest, not after you become shareholders. In fact, it is recommended that you look at a company's annual reports from the last five years.

For nearly a decade, NAIC has given kudos to corporations with the best annual reports. The Nicholson Awards—named after George Nicholson, one of the organization's founders—are intended to help corporations improve the way they disseminate investment information and to make their annual reports more reader friendly. Companies go through a rating process in which forms are returned to participating corporations with comments from judges.

In 1999, investment club members evaluated more than 800 company reports. Just how are the documents rated? Companies are identified by industry—97 in total—although not every industry may have a winner. If there is a sufficient number of entries in a particular industry, the awards are further divided according to company size—from small caps to large companies.

"We think it is unfair for a company that has revenues under $100 million to have to compete with a company like IBM, which has billions of dollars in revenues," says Janke. "The smaller guys can't afford to spend the same kind of money preparing their annual reports."

"We instruct our judges not to judge the company but just the report itself," adds Janke. "We aren't saying whether a company is a good or bad investment. We are trying to find out if the information is there to help you make an educated investment decision."

Judges read the reports from cover to cover and award points for various types of information and content. Specifically, judges examine financial highlights, historical financial information, management discussion, other narrative comments, and report design and readability. Do the photos and charts actually supplement the written report or are they extraneous?

In general, an annual report is divided into ten sections: the CEO's letter to shareholders, company profile, operational overview, management's discussion and analysis, management report, auditor's report, list of board members and corporate officers, financial statements, footnotes, and shareholder information.

The CEO's letter to shareholders should spell out the company's past performance and its future prospects. Compare last year's letter

to this year's facts. In other words: Did the company meet its goals? Watch out for vague explanations or clichés.

Beware of a letter that fails to address any problems or areas of concern. Does it talk about increases or cutbacks in personnel, programs, product lines, inventory, and manufacturing plants? In general, increases are all positive signs. Are profits up or down? Is it due to industry price wars? Poor management? Product expansion? Cutbacks in expenses?

Moreover, do footnotes contain more detailed information about company operations? "Footnotes can clarify financial aspects," says Baunita Greer of Cromwell, Miller and Greer. "For example, they can give you more details on litigation or stock options. Beware of heavy markdowns of inventory, adverse government regulations, and other unusual events."

Janke points out that the judges of the Nicholson Awards really look to see if the companies are candid in their reporting. "Are they overly optimistic or are they talking about real problems as well as all of the successes they have had or expect?"

Janke believes annual reports are much more forthright today than they were 10 years ago, especially in providing complete financial information. The financial statements should examine the company's assets and liabilities, stockholder's equity, long-term debt, net earnings, and net revenues. "Basically, we look for fundamental information about earnings and pretax profit margins and a compounded growth rate (10 years, 5 years, or 3 years)," he explains.

Check all financial statements carefully. The company's balance sheet (see Figure 11.2) will paint a picture of the assets and liabilities at the end of the year compared with previous years. It will tell whether cash or liquid assets are diminishing and if accounts receivable, inventories, or total debts are rising.

The goal is to determine if the total assets are greater than the total liabilities. Divide the current assets by the current liabilities; a ratio of 2:1 or more is a good indicator that there are enough assets to cover immediate debts.

Ideally, you want a company that has a manageable amount of long-term debt. Whether it's manageable or not depends on the company's assets and sales. For example, $500,000 in long-term debt will be more manageable for a company with $10 million in sales, than one with only $100,000 in sales. The more debt a company has, the harder it will be for it to weather any financial storms.

Figure 11.2   Balance Sheet

(In millions, except per share amounts)	Motorola, Inc. and Consolidated Subsidiaries	
December 31	1996	1995
Assets		
Current assets		
Cash and cash equivalents	$ 1,513	$ 725
Short-term investments	298	350
Accounts receivable, less allowance for doubtful accounts (1996, $137; 1995, $123)	4,035	4,081
Inventories	3,220	3,528
Future income tax benefits	1,580	1,222
Other current assets	673	604
Total current assets	11,319	10,510
Property, plant and equipment, less accumulated depreciation (1996, $9,830; 1995, $8,110)	9,768	9,356
Other assets	2,989	2,872
Total assets	$24,076	$22,738
Liabilities and Stockholders' Equity		
Current liabilities		
Notes payable and current portion of long-term debt	$ 1,382	$ 1,605
Accounts payable	2,050	2,018
Accrued liabilities	4,563	4,170
Total current liabilities	7,995	7,793
Long-term debt	1,931	1,949
Deferred income taxes	1,108	968
Other liabilities	1,247	1,043
Stockholders' equity		
Common stock, $3 par value Authorized shares: 1996 and 1995, 1,400 Issued and outstanding shares: 1996, 593.4; 1995, 591.4	1,780	1,774
Preferred stock, $100 par value issuable in series Authorized shares: 0.5 (none issued)	–	–
Additional paid-in capital	1,672	1,750
Retained earnings	8,343	7,461
Total stockholders' equity	11,795	10,985
Total liabilities and stockholders' equity	$24,076	$22,738

See accompanying condensed notes to consolidated financial statements.

Eric Standifer, president of Robert Van Securities, says these numbers are all relative to the industry and the size of the company. "There are no absolutes when it comes to any financial computation," he explains. "They are tools that you can use to arrive at a decision as to whether a company represents good value or is a good investment."

Annual reports paint a rosy picture most of the time, but the numbers will tell the truth. You've heard it before: Look at the bottom line. Literally, the bottom line is a company's net income after taxes (see Figure 11.3). Net sales equals the amount of money collected for goods and services sold. If you were to take net sales and subtract the costs of goods and services sold plus operating expenses, you would know the net income (also synonymous with net earnings and net profit). Net income divided by net sales tells you the profit margin.

The net earnings of a company determine the value of the stock. Experts suggest that if this figure is lower than the year before, there may be a problem with the company. In most cases, a company's net

Figure 11.3   Statement of Consolidated Earnings

(In millions, except per share amounts)		Motorola, Inc. and Consolidated Subsidiaries	
Years ended December 31	1996	1995	1994
Net sales	$27,973	$27,037	$22,245
Costs and expenses			
Manufacturing and other costs of sales	18,990	17,545	13,760
Selling, general and administrative expenses	4,715	4,642	4,381
Depreciation expense	2,308	1,919	1,525
Interest expense, net	185	149	142
Total costs and expenses	26,198	24,255	19,808
Earnings before income taxes	1,775	2,782	2,437
Income taxes provided on earnings	621	1,001	877
Net earnings	$ 1,154	$ 1,781	$ 1,560
Fully diluted net earnings per common and common equivalent share[1,2]	$ 1.90	$ 2.93	$ 2.65
Fully diluted average common and common equivalent shares outstanding[1,2]	609.6	609.8	592.7

[1] Primary earnings per common and common equivalent share were the same as fully diluted for all years shown, except in 1994 when they were one cent higher than fully diluted. Average primary common and common equivalent shares outstanding for 1996, 1995 and 1994 were 609.0, 609.7 and 591.7, respectively (which includes the dilutive effects of the convertible zero coupon notes and the outstanding stock options).
[2] Includes adjustments for the 1994 two-for-one stock split effected in the form of a 100 percent stock dividend.

earnings should always be rising. If the profit margin is rising, that's a good indicator of the company's profitability.

Pay attention to trends over the past three years. If sales, earnings, dividends, and accounts receivable are continuously rising, this is a company worth investing in. You should also search for clues about company management, especially if key officers are constantly changing.

If biographies of top managers don't appear in the annual report, call the company and request them. You will want to know who is in charge of the company and what their credentials are. If the industry has no confidence in the company's leadership, its stock is likely to flounder.

Club members should review a company's annual report each year to assess the company's progress, especially as it relates to revenues and earnings per share (see Figure 11.4). For example, find out if a given company's earnings represent a percentage of investment capital (what has been invested in the company).

Don't use just the annual report to make investment decisions. Use advisory services and read analysts' reports. For the most part, the annual report gives you a feel for the company's management. It's essentially your chance to see what's on the mind of the CFO or CEO.

EXAMINING 10-K AND 10-Q REPORTS

In addition to the annual reports, you should also obtain quarterly reports. Public companies are required every year by the SEC to file a 10-K. This document provides information similar to the company's annual report, including financial statements and management's

analysis. The 10-K, however, is much longer and more in depth. In general, brokers and investment analysts use 10-K reports to look at such things as profitability, earnings momentum, and the technical aspects of a stock's performance.

If you don't want to wait for a yearly report to read up on a company, you can obtain quarterly information from the 10-Q, another mandatory document filed with the SEC. These reports provide financial statements and summarize corporate activities that took place over the course of the first, second, third, and fourth quarters. The easiest access to company 10-Qs is through the SEC's Web site (www.sec.gov).

While a company's 10-K report must be audited by an independent group of certified public accountants, the 10-Q does not have to

Figure 11.4   Annual Report

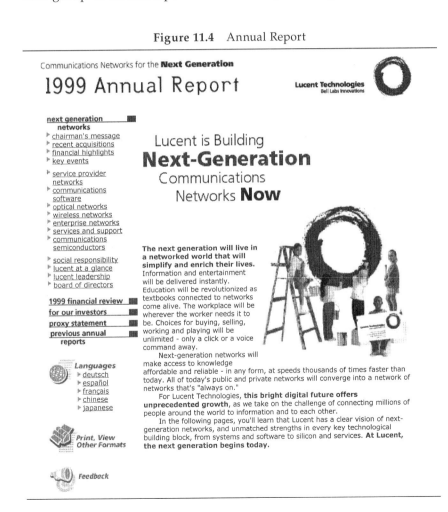

meet this requirement. As a result, information in the 10-Q is not as detailed as that of the 10-K.

Why bother with a company's 10-K or 10-Q to begin with? By studying these reports you can see what management does with investors' money. Are they putting money into research, product expansion, new factories, or buying more shares in their own company?

Don't overlook other key sources. For instance, many companies publish news bulletins whenever a major event occurs—like the introduction of a new product, management hirings or promotions, sale of a subsidiary or division, and the merger with or acquisition of another company.

Companies must file an 8-K report within 15 days of an event that could affect the value of the firm's securities. Changing accounting firms is usually considered serious enough to require filing an 8-K.

Any investor who acquires 5 percent of a company's stock must file a 13-D report with the SEC. This report also alerts management that someone may be trying to gain control of outstanding shares.

When you are researching a company, look for consistency. You are trying to formulate your own opinion and you are looking at a number of resources to see if they have the same commentary. In looking at various sources and analysts' reports, you may discover the start of a trend.

Once you establish a portfolio of well-researched securities, your club's objective each month is to determine whether to buy, sell, or hold on to shares owned. Too many clubs hold a stock for too long, says Future-Vest's Noel.

"If there's a potential problem with a company we'll get rid of it. If a stock meets or exceeds our expectations—doubled in growth—we may sell it. If we really like it then we will buy more shares. If you hold a stock once it has reached its projected growth potential, you won't be able to maximize your portfolio," she adds.

Future-Vest follows NAIC's *Challenge Tree* methodology, which allows members to compare the merits of one stock against another by using a five-year estimate of a stock's future price range (see Figure 11.5). This five-year estimate is based on a *rule of five*. This theory holds that out of every five stocks owned over a five-year period, one will encounter difficulty unforeseen by the investor, three will perform more or less according to expectations, and one will far exceed the standard set for it.

The Challenge Tree uses the upside-down ratio, which evaluates whether a stock is likely to fall or rise in price. As it relates to a stock's appreciation, a 3-to-1 ratio upside potential is the targeted mark. For

Figure 11.5 Challenge Tree Comparative Form

	COMPANY HELD	CHALLENGING COMPANY
	NATIONAL ASSOCIATION OF INVESTORS CORPORATION **NAIC** ® INVESTMENT EDUCATION FOR INDIVIDUALS AND CLUBS SINCE 1951	***Challenge Tree Comparative Form*** ® Date _____

	COMPANY HELD	CHALLENGING COMPANY
Current Price		
Estimated 5 Year High		
Estimated 5 Year Low		
Gain to 5 Year High		
Loss to 5 Year Low		
5 Year Upside-Downside Ratio		
Lower Price Range		
Middle Price Range		
Upper Price Range		
S & P Quality Rating		
Value Line Timeliness Rating		
6 to 18 Months Upside Action		
Earnings Advancing		
Business Cycle Upswing		
Industry Outlook		
Upside-Downside Outlook		
Growth Stock Potential		
Technical Base Forming		
New Products Coming In		

JUDGING MANAGEMENT	Good	Average	Poor	Good	Average	Poor
Driving Force:						
Rate of Sales Gain						
Rate of Earnings Per Share Gain						
Earned on Sales						
Earned on Equity						
Evaluating Price:						
High in 5 Years						
Low in 5 Years						
Upside-Downside Ratio						
Current Yield						
Total Return						
Other Considerations:						
Industry Potentials						
State of Business Cycle						
Stock Price Trends						
Quality of Stock						
Capitalization and Finance						

The Investor first prepares an NAIC Selection Guide and Report on the challenged and challenging companies. That information is then recorded above for comparison purposes.

© 1996. National Association of Investors Corporation; 711 West Thirteen Mile Road, Madison Hgts., Michigan 48071

Figure 11.5 *(Continued)*

Keeping Challenge Tree Records

Because the Challenge Tree may run for fifteen or twenty years, it is well to keep records on your performance. The table herewith keeps two records. One is on Tree Transactions and the other a Tree Dividend Record by years.

Record of Tree Transactions

Record Each Tree

	Price	Total
1. Company		
Bought		
Sold		
2. Company		
Bought		
Sold		
3. Company		
Bought		
Sold		
4. Company		
Bought		
Sold		
5. Company		
Bought		
Sold		

Record of Tree Dividends

Dividends Received

19__	Quarters				Year Total
19__					
19__					
19__					
19__					
19__					
19__					
19__					
19__					
19__					

example, let's say Value Line analysts project the high price for a certain stock is $50. The stock currently trades at $20.

First, subtract the present price from the projected price, which in this case equals $30. Now, take the present price and subtract it from the projected low price—which we will say is $15. This leaves you with

$5. Finally, divide the upside potential or $30 by the downside risk or $5. The upside-down ratio is 6:1. That particular stock is a good buy.

Here's how the Challenge Tree works: Suppose your club purchased a stock that it thought would double in value in five years. The stock realized 50 percent of its potential gain in the past six to eighteen months and its upside-down ratio dropped from 3:1, when it was purchased, to 1:1. The stock's upside appreciation declined from 100 percent to 50 percent. If your club could identify a stock in the same industry of equal or higher quality with a 3 to 1 upside-down ratio, and 100 percent appreciation, it would buy it—cashing out the old stock and using the money to replace it with the new stock.[7]

Although Future-Vest seeks to stay fully invested in the market, the group has taken profits on few stocks they have sold over the years, including Wal-Mart, Advanced Micro Devices, and Plygem (a home-building company). Members also once owned stock in companies that were bought out or consolidated, such as Suburu and Jaguar, which were acquired by other leading car companies.

NAIC's Ken Janke cautions that club members can't assume that because a company has doubled in value, it cannot continue to appreciate. Superior growth stocks can realize a 200 percent profit or more. He says members must look to see if a company has further potential to grow over the next several years by becoming thoroughly familiar with that company by reading corporate information and business publications.

PAYING HEED TO INVESTMENT TIP-OFFS

Looking for a scoop on what's going on in corporate boardrooms? You'll be surprised to know that company officials from Maine to Mexico are slipping investors inside information daily, literally clueing in everyone on how things are at corporate headquarters.[8]

No, I am not talking about the kind of stuff that got Michael Milken and Ivan Boesky outfitted in striped suits—and not the pin-striped ones either. High jinx of that kind—whereby you trade stocks based on company-specific information that isn't publicly available in order to amass huge profits—are not only strictly prohibited by the SEC, they'll indeed land you behind bars.

There are legal ways for you to get in on the action. Experts will tell you that companies tip investors off constantly. Know the signs,

they say, and you will know the many ways to profit in the stock market. There are at least four ways executives let you know business is good and company stocks may be headed upward. Insider stock buying, stock splits, buybacks, and dividend increases all send a message to the market, one that is often good to heed. And, to top it all off, the information is legal and readily available with a minimal amount of work—your intercom into a company's boardroom.

Tip-Off #1. Insider Buying and Selling

It is only logical that folks at headquarters will have a pretty good idea of what's going on at their company. They are exchanging memos daily. They are keeping an eye on the competitors. They are looking at sales and profit figures all day.

Within the limits of the law, those same officers and directors rely on much of that in-depth knowledge when they buy or sell company shares. If business is good, you are likely to see them snapping up their own stock. If things look rocky, or if their stock looks a little overpriced, it is not uncommon to see the same well-informed officials selling their shares.

The law allows top executives from the chairman down to buy or sell their company's stock all the time, by exercising options or swapping shares for cash on the open market, just as long as they tell the SEC what they are doing. The SEC requires corporate insiders, top officers, directors, and owners of more than 10 percent of a company's stock to report nearly all their stock trades. These same SEC records are available to the public. Follow management's trades and you will have a pretty good idea of what they know and where they think their stock is heading.

In fact, insider buying is such a strong signal that some money managers say they won't invest in a stock unless they see management actively investing in its own company's shares. While there can be any number of reasons insiders sell, in general there's only one reason they buy: They think the stock is headed up. They are not going to put their own money on the line unless they think they can do extremely well.

That is because bosses, even those raking in six- and seven-figure salaries, are strangely like the rest of us—they are not investing to lose money. Executives who are stocking up on their company's shares aren't merely looking for their investment to appreciate, they are in a

position to help it do so. So, when groups of insiders start purchasing more of their company's stock, it may be time to move with the group.

Some money managers like to see management ownership as high as 3 percent to 4 percent in large cap companies and 10 percent or more in smaller companies. Management has to think like owners, and concentrate on enhancing the company's value for all shareholders. Look at the market and you will see a number of stocks have moved up after their management purchased shares.

There are times when insider selling can raise a red flag, signaling to investors that a company's shares are in for some rough trekking. Don't rush to conclusions. Executives are often paid in stock options and can sell their shares for a myriad of financial planning reasons, say, to buy a new house, finance their children's education, or to buy a new Range Rover.

There can be a host of reasons that company top guns sell their shares, but if the CEO is selling interest in his own company, watch out! Tracking the sale and purchase of company shares by officers and large shareholders is sure to shed some light on a company's stock performance.

Tracking insider buying is easy since a company must list ownership in its 10-K report. When an official buys or sells shares, he or she is required to file a document called a Form 4 with the SEC. Form 4 filings and stories on insider activity are reported in *Barron's* and *Individual Investor*. The *Vickers Weekly Insider Report* (516-423-7710) reports on selected trades.

Tip-Off #2. Dividends

There's one catch to investing in stocks. You can hold shares through thick and thin, weather a crash, or rejoice over a bull market. However, no matter what happens, you typically don't get a dime until you actually sell your stake.

By offering a dividend, a company can put a little money in your hands and make its stock more like your trusty bank account. Dividends are essentially a company's agreement to pay you—usually each quarter—a sum of money for each share you own. As a source of steady, reliable income, dividends act almost like the interest a bank would pay you.

Here's an example: If you own 100 shares of Walt Disney, you would receive an annual dividend of 63 cents a share or a total of $63. Payments of $15.74 would be made every three months. In terms of *yield*—the percentage of the stock's price paid out in dividends calculated by dividing the annual dividend by the share price—Disney's payouts currently stand at 0.2 percent.

A dividend is more than a way for the CEO to share the wealth with shareholders. It also allows Wall Street a peek at a company's corporate health. A consistent, rising dividend shows several things. First, it is an indication that the company is generating enough cash to cover the quarterly payments to shareholders. It also is a sign that management is confident of future growth and knows that profits aren't about to dry up anytime soon.

"If you have a company that increases its dividend steadily and consistently, you can be sure it is enjoying great earnings growth," says Joseph Lisanti, senior editor of Standard & Poor's investment advisory newsletter, *The Outlook*. "Dividends are real. You can't fake them, and unless you have the earnings growth, you can't pay one."

There's another benefit to shareholders. Because dividend paying firms spread their profits around and generate regular income from shareholders, their shares are generally less volatile than those of companies that don't give dividends. They also tend to suffer less than other stocks during a market downturn.

It is not surprising that some of the biggest and most-established firms have a history of rising dividends. General Electric Co. has paid out an uninterrupted dividend for nearly a century. Its dividend is $1.20 a share, for a yield of 1.4 percent. Pfizer Inc. has paid a dividend every year since 1901. In 1999, it boosted its dividend for the 31st consecutive year. The company's dividend of 76 cents per share produces a yield of 0.7 percent. Abbott Laboratories is another company with a long history of rising dividends. Abbott Labs pays 60 cents per share in dividends, yielding 1.6 percent.

It is easy to get the impression that corporate generosity has all but dried up. Not so long ago, electric utilities, telephone companies, and other industrial giants paid yields of 4 percent to 6 percent annually. Because stocks have charged further upward over the past three years, dividends have lost much of their luster. The yield for the S&P 500 has slipped to around 1.4 percent. Historically, that figure has averaged about 4.5 percent, says Joseph Tigue, managing editor of *The Outlook*.

What does all this mean? Since yields are based on a fixed dividend, they are a good gauge of a stock's value. A high yield (a dividend that seems large in comparison to a stock's price) can indicate an undervalued stock—one investors haven't yet fully appreciated. A low yield can signal a stock's price has risen quite a bit. It might also mean that the stock is overvalued.

Tigue says many companies have opted for acquisitions and buybacks instead of dividend increases. Experts advise that if cash flow is good, look for large companies to pay dividends and mid-sized and smaller firms to reinvest in the business.

Tip-Off #3. Stock Splits

Another way companies can increase their share price is to declare a *stock split*—that is, give out a certain number of shares to holders for each share they currently own. Splits usually take place after a company's stock price reaches a certain level. Microsoft has had seven stock splits since it went public in March 1986, the latest being a two-for-one split in February 1999. Owners received one new Microsoft share for each one they owned. Microsoft's share price, meanwhile was halved.

Why all the fuss? Some advisors say splits aren't that big a deal, equating them with the cutting of a pie into sixteen slices instead of eight. You have the same peach cobbler, it is only divided into more pieces. A split doesn't necessarily throw any signs to shareholders that business is doing better or worse.

Still, share prices tend to shoot upward the minute a split is announced. One reason lies in *liquidity*—just how many holders are eager to buy or sell shares at any given time. Splits reduce share prices. In turn, that attracts many more small investors who might be reluctant to buy into a high-priced stock. The increase in demand relative to supply helps inch a stock's price upward.

For example, Cisco Systems, the computer networking company, announced a three-for-two split that went into effect in December 1998, when its shares were near $80 each. The stock, priced at $50 after the split, rose back to the $80 to $90 per share range.

Stock splits are often announced along with a dividend increase. In June 1998, Disney declared a three-for-one stock split, announced a buyback, and increased its dividend. Add that to the fact

that earnings were better than expected—Disney hit a 52-week high of over $128 a share.

Tip-Off #4. Corporate Buybacks

These are programs that companies set up to repurchase their own shares. These shares are *retired*—they are taken off of the market for good. A company that buys back its shares has less stock floating out on the market and that cuts supply relative to demand. With fewer shares outstanding and demand constant, the stock price pushes higher.

Experts are generally bullish on buybacks. A buyback is often a sign that a company's management thinks its stock is a bargain—in fact, it is so undervalued that management would rather use its profits to buy its own stock back rather than use the money for other reasons, such as an acquisition or product expansion. It is also a sign that business is good; management has confidence in the company and the industry.

According to Securities Data Co., a research firm in Newark, NJ, 549 transactions involving the repurchase of $76.7 billion worth of stock occurred during the first six months of 1998. Studies have shown that companies that repurchase their stock tend to see their shares outperform the market.

In June of that year, Campbell Soup Co. said it would buy back as much as $2 billion of its stock over three years, representing about 8 percent of its 451 million shares outstanding. The day the buyback was announced, the food maker's shares gained 2 percent. Buyback programs are announced in local papers and financial publications.

BUILDING A FINANCIAL HOUSE OF JOY

For members of TIF (tap into the future investment club), there's another key factor in its total evaluation of a security: Is the company socially responsible? "We have incorporated as part of our bylaws and our mission statement that we would be mindful of a corporation's past and present experience with African Americans and others of the African Diaspora," says Clara McDonald, presiding partner of the New York-based club.

For instance, several members liked and ate at Cracker Barrel. "But, when we were considering whether to purchase shares in the

chain restaurant, one of the members brought to the club's attention a pending discrimination lawsuit that had to do with the employment of gays." Notes McDonald, "Once we discovered that the incident had to do with only one particular restaurant and did not seem indicative of company policy overall, we decided to buy the stock. Also, we purchased 100 shares of Carver Bank. Growth rate aside, we felt that we had a responsibility to support those financial institutions that are vital to African-American communities."

TIF's portfolio is well diversified, with holdings in such sectors as pharmaceuticals, banking and insurance, technology and the Internet, food processing, restaurants, and retail. Together the group owns 15 stocks, including Quaker Oats, Abbott Labs, Microsoft, Bank of America, and Analog Devices.

McDonald says members use scientific and not-so-scientific methods to research stocks. They use NAIC's stock selection guides and other analytical tools. They also use members inside knowledge about stocks. For instance, they have a mother and daughter team from Atlanta. One has a Ph.D. in pharmaceutical engineering, so she is very familiar with the drug sector. She provided club members with a lot of the information on those companies that they currently invest in as well as those they are considering for future investment, such as Pfizer and Merck.

TIF relies on comparative analysis, examining different industries and how well companies in any given sector are performing. "Even though we recently purchased Microsoft, we continue to look at the performance of other stocks in that sector," says McDonald. "We look to see which stocks in a particular area have better prospects for growth. We will continue to hold a stock we own if it has better performance projections than competing companies, otherwise we will replace it."

McDonald is one of five members who organized the club in April 1997 with an initial investment of $1,000 each, monthly dues of $30, and an annual $500 assessment fee. The 18 partners who now fill the club roster are a relatively close knit group of sisters, family, extended family, and friends whose ties, in some cases, span more than 50 years.

In fact, the club's name is derived from the Tapawingo (a Native-American word meaning house of joy) Honor Society, a leadership training program of Camp Minisink, originally in Port Jervis, New York, in the Shanwangunk Mountains. Fourteen of the TIF members

are childhood friends who first met at the sleepaway summer camp, which has been in existence since 1929.

The median age of the partners is 55, although there are four associate members—all of whom are grandchildren of members—who range in age from 13 months to 10 years. "After the club was formed, we decided we wanted to educate younger children about investing, so, we decided to include associate members," says Brenda Jackson, TIF's recording partner. "They remain associates until the age of 21."

While associates are expected to pay monthly dues of $10 and can attend meetings, they have no voting rights. They are also taught how to research stocks. "A 10-year-old is now tracking Noodle Kidoodle, a company that makes educational toys for children and has about 41 retail stores across the country," adds Jackson.

Regular members now pay $70 in monthly dues, which was increased to encourage dollar-cost averaging as well as to spread the $500 annual special assessment fee over 12 months. Members also pay an additional $5 a month to the Harlem church where their monthly meetings are held. Jackson notes that initially, meetings were held in members' homes, but they were later moved to the church—a more central location.

TIF has had no problem beating the pros. The club was recognized by the NAIC for achieving earnings growth rates greater than the S&P 500. Over the 3-year life of the club, TIF had a compounded annual growth rate of 51.19 percent per year compared to the S&P's 33.63 percent.

The club's first purchase in July 1997 was 204 shares of Lucent Technologies at $18.69 per share. So far, Lucent has been the group's top performer with a total return of 239.02 percent and total value of $12,882 two years from when it was first bought. TIF owns a total of 15 stocks, all of which are DRIPs that they purchase online via Charles Schwab, and is worth close to $50,000 as of July 1999.

Although many members own individual stocks and mutual funds, by belonging to an investment club they can now ask more informed questions, says Jackson, who personally has been investing in the market for over 10 years. "I wanted to further educate myself. I wanted to join a group so that I could have a better grasp of what was going on with my own portfolio. We not only have a better understanding of what we own individually, but what is happening with the economy and Wall Street without having to rely on recommendations from a broker."

CONCLUSION

Insider trading, stock splits, and buybacks are a number of signs savvy investors can use to look into the minds of a company's head honchos. Your club will do just fine as long as members realize that successful investing is based on research, not rumors and hunches.

The bottom line is that you want to take your time and look before you leap by reviewing the figures of the companies in which you are interested. You want to project how high or low a company may sell in price over the next five years or market cycle. You want to gauge whether corporate management has what it takes to boost a stock in value by increasing sales or revenues.

The more details you have about a company, the better you will be in identifying trends. Your club's success will depend on members selection of which individual stocks to buy. You are literally risking your money on the actions and decisions of each other. A word to the wise: There are no guarantees. Even after following these general guidelines, not every stock pick will be a winner; your portfolio is bound to have few losers. Just remember, you're in it for the long haul.

12

TOOLS OF THE TRADE: USING THE NET AND NEWS TO FIND DATA

One's work may be finished someday, but one's education, never.
—Alexander Dumas the Elder

So, you want to invest in high-tech stocks but you don't know a microchip from a microphone. No need to panic. There are several ways that you can learn about an industry and stay on top of breaking news that could affect the market—all from the comfort of your PC.

You can supplement your own knowledge of a company by studying what Wall Street analysts read, including daily newspapers, trade publications, financial newsletters, company directories, and stock-and-bond guides. Analysts look for information that will ultimately lead to gains or losses in corporate profits.

For instance, announcements about executive appointments could signal a shift in how the company is run. New and improved products that ultimately could make fortunes for a company are written up in trade papers long before the average Joe hears about them. Rumors of corporate reorganizations and acquisitions appear regularly in these publications. When rumors become public knowledge, watch out: Stock prices can swiftly move up or down.

Some investors can even pick up clues about a company by paying attention to how often the company advertises. Increased advertising

is a good indicator that the company has a surplus of cash *or* desperately needs to generate cash.

Advertising cutbacks could signal that a particular product has fallen out of favor or other problems. If you are considering fashion stocks, *Women's Wear Daily* is the bible of the industry, and *Variety* and *The Hollywood Reporter* will give the low-down on entertainment news that won't show up in the market (or in stock prices) for months.

There are scores of financial publications available for subscriptions, ranging anywhere from $15 a year to several hundred dollars annually. However, if you have trashed, burned, or lost your library card, now is the time to get a new one. You can find many of these same publications free of charge at the library, along with directories that list various trade periodicals.

In addition to stock tables, your local newspaper will have a business section that covers corporate activities. This is a great place to find stories about corporations located right in your own backyard. To augment what you glean from the trade and local press, subscribe to newsletters. Mark Hulbert, whose *Hulbert Financial Digest* (703-750-9060) has tracked, profiled, and evaluated investment newsletters for nearly a decade, says these sources are particularly valuable because they provide consistent followup advice for every stock they recommend.

Investment newsletters are in no short supply. There are over 500 such publications, produced mostly by individuals who have registered with the SEC as advisors, though not all financial experts or all investment newsletters are registered. The *Hulbert Financial Digest* provides monthly appraisals of investment advice dispensed by financial advisors.

Hulbert cautions that picking a winning newsletter can be just as difficult as picking a winning stock. There's no easy answer as to what's a good newsletter. Many specialize in certain industries, while others chart technical market movements, rather than economic fundamentals or companies' performances. Still others track mutual funds instead of individual stocks.

If you ask nicely, most newsletters will send samples on request. Publishers frequently offer brief, introductory offers, making it possible for you to check out several newsletters at once. *Bull & Bear's Directory of Investment Advisory Newsletters* lists 445 newsletters in alphabetical order within each category, including international investments, mutual funds, new issues, and stocks. It also publishes addresses, phone numbers, descriptions, and subscription rates.

Big investment advisory companies such as Standard & Poor's Corp., Value Line Inc., and Nelson Investment Management, as well as individual stock pickers like Martin Zweig (*Zweig Forecast,* 800-535-9649) and Louis Naellier (*MPT Review,* 775-831-1396) have strong reputations for ferreting out undervalued investments.

Dozens of financial newspapers and magazines offer analyses of corporate management and industries, including the *Wall Street Journal, Barron's, Investor's Business Daily, FW* (formerly *Financial World* magazine), *Bloomberg,* and *Individual Investor.* There also are a host of television programs that cover the financial world, including *Wall Street Week* (PBS), which is hosted by Louis Rukeyser, where each week three guests quiz a special guest on a specific investment topic. *The Nightly Business Report* (PBS) summarizes the day's stock market results and presents interviews with market experts. Other daily television shows are *Money Talk* (CNBC), *Moneyline* (CNN), and *Your Portfolio* (CNBC). For radio listeners, there are *The Dolans* (syndicated) and *Sound Money* (Public Radio).

Do you recall the ideal painting you tried to create in Chapter 11? These are all the tools you need to add color and detail to your portrait of a stock. "We use *Value Line, Investor's Business Daily,* CNBC, and the Internet to research companies and keep up with financial news," says Kamau Odinga of the PULA Project Investment Club. "We look for things like profit margins, debt-to-equity ratio, price-to-earnings ratio, dividend yields, and return on equity, which are good indicators of how well management is running the company."

Since purchasing their first shares in such stocks as AT&T, DuPont, and Merck, PULA has watched its portfolio grow to a little over $200,000 from June 1996 to June 1999, with an average rate of return of 31.98 percent for that period. It seems fitting that the club's portfolio is growing with above average gains given that *pula* is the word for currency in Botswana; it also means "rain."

Odinga notes they are heavily invested in well-established large companies—roughly 90 percent, with the other 10 percent in smaller companies that don't fit the profile of a blue-chip company but have long-term growth potential. "We expect high growth rates—25 percent or more—for some, while others we project will remain steady (at around 15 percent)."

In evaluating a company, he adds, members look specifically to see if earnings for a given company have decreased or increased over the last three to five years. "What new products are coming out? Who are their competitors? Where does the company stand in the

marketplace and their respective industry? Is management changing with the times?"

GETTING A HANDLE ON NAIC STOCK SELECTION TOOLS

PULA is not unlike many clubs that bank on a number of resources created by NAIC to help club members evaluate a potential company's value and stay current on stocks that they own. The more popular of these are the Stock Check List (Figure 12.1) and the Stock Selection Guide (SSG) (Figure 12.2). These forms allow club members to plot financial figures and data in order to paint a detailed picture of a particular company. The objective is to evaluate past and present performance to make some predictions about a company's future.[1]

The Stock Check List records and reviews three numbers: a company's sales record, earnings per share, and price history. The Stock Selection Guide and Report, which is a little more sophisticated and shouldn't be used until your club is at least six months old, is broken down into five sections: visual analysis based on sales, earnings, and price performance over the last 10 years; evaluation of a company's management team; five-year comparison of price-to-earnings ratios, earnings per share, and dividend yield; evaluation of risk and reward based on a company's future price movement; and estimated growth potential or average annual rate of return over the next five years.

Remember, NAIC suggests that your club seek to double its money every five years. To accomplish that, the stocks in your club's portfolio must achieve a compounded annual growth rate of 14.9 percent, which translates into 20 percent a year—that would add up to 100 percent simple interest over five years.

With the data recorded in the Stock Check List, you can see if a stock meets the club's price range and projected growth rate by reviewing company's sales and growth record over the past five years or market cycle. You know from previous chapters that growing sales and earnings per share make a company increase in value and make its stock price go up.

As you can see in Figure 12.1, the Stock Check List calls for you to make judgments as to possible reasons for a company's past growth: a new product that proved successful, a cyclical business that experienced recovery, purchase of another company, product gained larger market share, or changes made by skilled management.

Figure 12.1 NAIC Stock Checklist

<table>
<tr><td>

NATIONAL ASSOCIATION
OF INVESTORS CORPORATION

NAIC®

INVESTMENT EDUCATION
FOR INDIVIDUALS AND CLUBS
SINCE 1951

</td><td>

Stock Check List ®

for Beginning Investors

</td><td>

Company _____

Prepared by _____

Date _____

See Chapter 7 of the NAIC Official Guide.

While Investors are learning to use NAIC's Stock Selection Guide, it is suggested the following Check List be used for each stock considered for investment.

</td></tr>
</table>

1 PAST SALES RECORD

Sales for most recent year were . . . . (1) $ _____

Sales for next most recent year were . . . . (2) $ _____

    Total of above (1 + 2) . . . . (3) $ _____

    Figure above divided by 2 . . . . (4) $ _____

Sales 5 years ago were . . . . (5) $ _____

Sales 6 years ago were . . . . (6) $ _____

    Total of above (5 + 6) . . . . (7) $ _____

    Figure above divided by 2 . . . . (8) $ _____

Increase in sales in above period (8 from 4) . . . . (9) $ _____

Percentage increase in sales (9 divided by 8) . . . . (10) _____ %

CONVERSION TABLE

This % Increase in Sales Gives →	27	33	46	61	76	93	112	129	148	205	271
This % Compounded Annual Growth Rate →	5	6	8	10	12	14	16	18	20	25	30

COMPOUND ANNUAL RATE OF SALES GROWTH WAS _____ %

Look for the percent increase that meets the objective you have set.

2 PAST EARNINGS PER SHARE RECORD

Earnings Per Share for most recent year were . . . . (1) $ _____

Earnings Per Share for next most recent year were . . . . (2) $ _____

    Total of above (1 + 2) . . . . (3) $ _____

    Figure above divided by 2 . . . . (4) $ _____

Earnings Per Share 5 years ago were . . . . (5) $ _____

Earnings Per Share 6 years ago were . . . . (6) $ _____

    Total of above (5 + 6) . . . . (7) $ _____

    Figure above divided by 2 . . . . (8) $ _____

Increase in Earnings Per Share in above period (8 from 4) . . . . (9) $ _____

Percentage increase in earnings (9 divided by 8) . . . . (10) _____ %

See **Conversion Table** above to determine ⟶

COMPOUND ANNUAL RATE OF EARNINGS PER SHARE GROWTH WAS _____ %

Earnings Per Share have increased _____ than sales in this period.
      (more)   (less)

Explain Apparent Reason for Difference in Sales and Earnings Per Share Growth: _____

_____

(continued)

Figure 12.1 *(Continued)*

Discuss Possible Reasons for Past Growth:

A new product was very successful_____ .

A cyclical business that experienced recovery_____ .

A research program has produced several new products or uses for older products_____ .

Purchase another company_____ .

Has taken larger share of business in its field _____ .

Skill of management _____ .

Will Factors Which Produced Past Growth Continue Effective

for the next five years _____ yes, _____ yes, but less effective, _____ no.

3 PRICE RECORD OF THE STOCK

Present Price $ _____ . Present Earnings Per Share_____ .

List Last 5 Years	High Price Each Year (A)	Low Price Each Year (B)	Earnings Per Share (C)	Price Earnings Ratio	
				at High (A ÷ C)	at Low (B ÷ C)
Totals					
Averages					
Average of High and Low Price Earnings Averages for the past five years.					

Present Price is ――――――――――― than high price five years ago.
　　　　　　　　(higher)　　　(lower)

Present Price is _____% higher than the high price 5 years ago. Compare this figure with the percent sales increase in 1 (10) and percent earnings per share increase in 2 (10).

The price change compares with sales growth and earnings per share growth ――――――――――― .
　　　　　　　　　　　　　　　　　　　　　　　　　　　　　(favorably or unfavorably)

This stock has sold as high as the current price in _____ of the last 5 years.

In the past five years the stock ――――――――――― sold at unusually ――――――― price earnings ratios.
　　　　　　　　　　　　　(has)　　　(has not)　　　　　　　(high)　(low)

The Present price earnings ratio is _____ .

In relation to past price earnings ratios the stock is currently

_____ selling at a higher ratio

_____ selling about the same

_____ selling lower

The average price earnings ratios of the past might be expected to continue _____ ,

or should be adjusted to_____ high, _____ low.

4 CONCLUSION

1. The past sales growth rate ――――――――――― meet our objective.
　　　　　　　　　　　　　(does)　　　(does not)

2. The past earnings per share growth rate――――――――――― meet our objective.
　　　　　　　　　　　　　　　　　　(does)　　　(does not)

3. Our conclusion has been that possible earnings per share growth rate――――――――――― meet our objective in the coming five years.
　　　　　　　　　　　　　　　　　　　　　　　　　(will)　　　(will not)

4. The price of the stock is currently ――――――――――― .
　　　　　　　　　　　　　　　(acceptable)　　　(too high)

This form is not meant to give you an adequate analysis of the stock, but is meant to help the beginner ask questions to indicate whether the company is likely to become more valuable and if it can be purchased reasonably. As Investors gain practice, a more thorough study of the stock is suggested using NAIC's Stock Selection Guide and Report as a guide.

ST-1040

Source: © 1998. Reprinted with permission. This material is copyrighted and taken from the NAIC's Official Guide to *Starting and Running a Profitable Investment Club.* Refer to that book for a full explanation of this material.

The Stock Selection Guide (see Figure 12.2) is designed to help you review a company's sales and earnings figures to determine how high or low a company's stock price will move over the next five years. It also lets you see if management is in fact doing a good job by recording two figures: pretax profit margins and percent earned on equity (or return on equity).

As you may recollect from Chapter 11, the percent earned on equity is important because it shows how effectively management used shareholders' money. The formula: EPS/Book value, or earnings per share divided by the company's net worth. The pretax profit margin is the amount of profit that a company makes on each dollar of sales before taxes. For example, a company's tax rate for 1999 was 37 percent. Subtract this number from 100 percent, leaving a 63 percent profit rate.[2]

The company's net profit or income is $115 million for 1999. Locate the profit rate from the net income. Now divide total sales by pretax income to arrive at the pretax profit on sales:

$$\frac{\$115M \text{ net income}}{.63} = \frac{\$182.50M \text{ pretax income}}{645 \text{ M total sales}} = 28.3\% \text{ pretax profit on sales}$$

Look at pretax profit margins for the past five years. What's the average? Pretax profit margins vary by industry. For instance, in the grocery business, this figure tends to be below 1 percent to 3 percent. By comparison, pretax profit margins in the broadcast industry range from 40 percent to 50 percent.

Standard & Poor's and Value Line publish reports on percent earned on equity and lists of companies' pretax profit margins sorted by industries. For the stocks you are researching, you want these two numbers to be above the average numbers of the competition.

A sore spot for many clubs is filling out the Stock Selection Guide. Unfortunately too many clubs move to the Stock Selection Guide before they fully understand and utilize the Stock Check List, and they become confused by all the numbers, says Cathleen Greer, vice president of the Windy City Investment Club.

The Stock Check List may be a basic tool, but it will certainly help get your club over the hump, she explains. "We decided to master the Stock Check List first. Later as an educational process, I took sections of the SSG and went over it during the regular monthly meetings. I did one section per club meeting. In fact, the group used the Stock Check List for one year to learn about management, sales, earnings, and other data needed to analyze a company."

Figure 12.2   NAIC Stock Selection Guide and Report

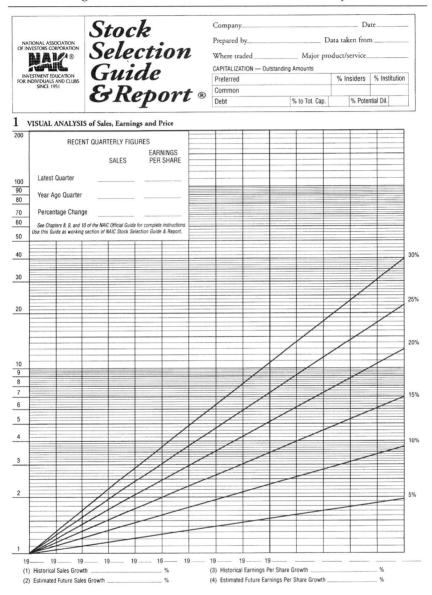

Figure 12.2 (Continued)

2 EVALUATING MANAGEMENT   Company _____

	19___	19___	19___	19___	19___	19___	19___	19___	19___	19___	LAST 5 YEAR AVG.	TREND UP	TREND DOWN
A % Pre-tax Profit on Sales (Net Before Taxes ÷ Sales)													
B % Earned on Equity (E/S ÷ Book Value)													

3 PRICE-EARNINGS HISTORY as an indicator of the future

This shows how stock prices have fluctuated with earnings and dividends. It is a building block for translating earnings into future stock prices.

PRESENT PRICE _____   HIGH THIS YEAR _____   LOW THIS YEAR _____

	A PRICE HIGH	B PRICE LOW	C Earnings Per Share	D Price Earnings Ratio HIGH A ÷ C	E Price Earnings Ratio LOW B ÷ C	F Dividend Per Share	G % Payout F ÷ C X 100	H % High Yield F ÷ B X 100
Year								
1								
2								
3								
4								
5								
6 TOTAL								
7 AVERAGE								
8 AVERAGE PRICE EARNINGS RATIO			9 CURRENT PRICE EARNINGS RATIO					

4 EVALUATING RISK and REWARD over the next 5 years

Assuming one recession and one business boom every 5 years, calculations are made of how **high** and how **low** the stock might sell. The upside-downside ratio is the key to evaluating risk and reward.

A HIGH PRICE — NEXT 5 YEARS
Avg. High P/E _____ (3D7 as adj.)   X Estimate High Earnings/Share _____   = Forecast High Price $ _____ (4A1)

B LOW PRICE — NEXT 5 YEARS
(a) Avg. Low P/E _____ (3E7 as adj.)   X Estimated Low Earnings/Share _____   = $ _____

(b) Avg. Low Price of Last 5 Years   = _____ (3B7)

(c) Recent Severe Market Low Price = _____

(d) Price Dividend Will Support $\frac{\text{Present Divd.}}{\text{High Yield (H)}}$ = _____ = _____

Selected Estimated Low Price _____   = $ _____ (4B1)

C ZONING

_____ High Forecast Price Minus _____ Low Forecast Price Equals _____ Range. 1/3 of Range = _____
(4A1)   (4B1)   (C)   (4CD)

(4C2) Lower 1/3 = (4B1) _____ to _____ (Buy)

(4C3) Middle 1/3 = _____ to _____ (Maybe)

(4C4) Upper 1/3 = _____ to _____ (4A1) (Sell)

Present Market Price of _____ is in the _____ (4C5) Range

D UP-SIDE DOWN-SIDE RATIO (Potential Gain vs. Risk of Loss)

$\dfrac{\text{High Price (4A1)} \_\_\_\_ \text{ Minus Present Price} \_\_\_\_}{\text{Present Price} \_\_\_\_ \text{ Minus Low Price (4B1)} \_\_\_\_}$ = _____ = _____ To 1
(4D)

E PRICE TARGET (Note: This shows the potential market price appreciation over the next five years in simple interest terms.)

$\dfrac{\text{High Price (4A1)} \_\_\_\_}{\text{Present Market Price} \_\_\_\_}$ = (_____) X 100 = (_____) − 100 = _____ % Appreciation (4E)

5 5-YEAR POTENTIAL   This combines price appreciation with dividend yield to get an estimate of total return. It provides a standard for comparing income and growth stocks.

Note: Results are expressed as a simple rate; use the table below to convert to a compound rate.

A $\dfrac{\text{Present Full Year's Dividend \$} \_\_\_\_}{\text{Present Price of Stock \$} \_\_\_\_}$ = _____ X 100 = _____ (5A) Present Yield or % Returned on Purchase Price

B AVERAGE YIELD OVER NEXT 5 YEARS
Avg. Earnings Per Share Next 5 Years _____ X Avg. % Payout (3G7) _____   = $\dfrac{\_\_\_\_}{\text{Present Price \$} \_\_\_\_}$ = _____ % (5B)

C ESTIMATED AVERAGE ANNUAL RETURN OVER NEXT FIVE YEARS
$\dfrac{\text{5 Year Appreciation Potential (4E)} \_\_\_\_}{5}$ = _____ %
Average Yield (5B) . . . . _____ %
Average Total Annual Return Over The Next 5 Years (5C) _____ %

Table to Convert From Simple to Compound Rate

Simple Rate 2 4 6 8 10 12 14 16 18 20 22 24 26 28 30 32 34 36 38 40

Compound Rate 2 4 6 8 10 12 14 16 18 20 22 24

The Stock Selection Guide and Report is indeed more in depth and number intensive, especially if club members opt to fill out the forms by hand instead of using NAIC software. Greer, along with club treasurer Ron Haskins, conducts Stock Check List classes. Held two to three times a month at Greer's home, the classes are limited to ten people and run about two-and-a-half hours, allowing for a question-and-answer period.

"We give an introduction on why you should be in the stock market; we give an overview on how to use Value Line; we analyze a company," says Greer, an account service representative at a local bank. "At the end of class, participants receive a blank Stock Check List form with the understanding that they should fill it in for a company they are interested in."

The classes are for not only members of the Windy City Club, but anyone who wants to learn about investing in the stock market (for a small donation), regardless if they belong to an investment club. Prospective Windy City Club members, however, are required to attend the class and to do a formal presentation on their stock of choice.

"The NAIC, through their publications, push the SGG," says Haskins, a research analyst at IBM. "When you are starting out with people who don't know anything about investing in the market, you have to help them comprehend sales and earnings and how that affects share price." He notes that once you start talking about pretax earnings and return on equity, you might as well be talking Greek to inexperienced club members.

After graduating to the Stock Selection Guide and Report, members can take advantage of other NAIC aids, such as the Stock Comparison Guide (see Figure 12.3), which helps you compare and contrast data on different companies you are considering. What happens when two members recommend a stock in the same industry and your club wants to choose the better performer of the two? Using the same figures plotted in the Stock Check List and Stock Selection Guide, this form guides members through three areas: sales and earnings growth, management, and price comparisons.

Once the club purchases a stock, you can't just sit on your laurels. You have to manage a stock once it is bought. You can't stay married to any one stock—today's winner could change drastically tomorrow for better or worse. This means you must review each stock monthly and annually to see if it is not meeting the club's expectation of doubling in value every five years or whatever your goal.

Figure 12.3 NAIC Stock Comparison Guide

NATIONAL ASSOCIATION OF INVESTORS CORPORATION **NAIC**® INVESTMENT EDUCATION FOR INDIVIDUALS AND CLUBS SINCE 1951	*Stock Comparison Guide*®	Prepared by _____ Date _____ See Chapter 11 of the NAIC Official Guide for complete instructions. **NAME OF COMPANY**				

GROWTH COMPARISONS
(From Section 1 of the NAIC Stock Selection Guide)

(1) Historical % of Sales Growth					
(2) Projected % of Sales Growth					
(3) Historical % of Earnings Per Share Growth					
(4) Projected % of Earnings Per Share Growth					

MANAGEMENT COMPARISONS
(From Section 2 of the NAIC Stock Selection Guide)

(5) % Profit Margin Before Taxes (Average for last 5 years) — (2A) Trend					
(6) % Earned on Equity (Average for last 5 years) — (2B) Trend					
(7) % of Common Owned by Management					

PRICE COMPARISONS
(See Sections 3-5 of the NAIC Stock Selection Guide)

(8) Estimated Total Earnings Per Share For Next 5 Years						
(9) Price Range Over Last 5 Years — High (3A) Low (3B)						
(10) Present Price						
Price Earnings Ratio Range Last 5 Years	(11) Highest — (3D)					
	(12) Average High — (3D7)					
	(13) Average — (3-8)					
	(14) Average Low — (3E7)					
	(15) Lowest — (3E)					
(16) Current Price Earnings Ratio — (3-9)						
Estimated Price Zones	(17) Lower-Buy — (4C2)					
	(18) Middle-Maybe — (4C3)					
	(19) Upper-Sell — (4C4)					
(20) Present Price Range — (4C5)						
(21) Upside Downside Ratio — (4D)						
(22) Current Yield — (5A)						
(23) Combined Estimated Yield — (5C)						

OTHER COMPARISONS

(24) Number of Common Shares Outstanding					
(25) Potential Dilution from Debentures, Warrants, Options					
(26) Percent Payout — (3G7)					
(27)					
(28)					
(29) Date of Source Material					
(30) Where Traded					

Source: © 1998. Reprinted with permission. This material is copyrighted and taken from the NAIC's Official Guide to *Starting and Running a Profitable Investment Club.* Refer to that book for a full explanation of this material.

Any work of art that is worth anything needs to be analyzed and appraised so that you know its value. Designed to help club members stay current on the stocks they already own are the Portfolio Management Guide and the Portfolio Evaluation Review Technique (PERT). The former is a chart that compares monthly P/E ratios. The latter comprises two worksheets that compare quarterly and annual changes in the same fundamentals you used to buy the stock in the first place.

PERT worksheet A (see Figure 12.4) examines earnings per share growth, pretax profit, sales, pretax profit as a percentage of sales, income tax rate and the income tax rate as a percentage of pretax profits. PERT worksheet B (see Figure 12.5) shows the stocks five- to 10-year history in terms of earnings per share, high and low stock prices, the current P/E ratio compared to past P/E ratios, upside-down potential, dividend payouts, and dividend yield.

Another tool available to all NAIC members free of charge is Investor's Information Reports (or Green Sheets, as they are nicknamed, because they are printed on green paper). These reports are prepared in the same format as the NAIC Stock Selection Guide and provide financial information on various companies. These reports, which are prepared by each participating company, include a corporate business profile, detailed financial information, and news of upcoming developments.

It takes four to six weeks to receive a full set of reports on over 100 companies, or reports on just those companies you indicate. Companies include The J.M. Smucker Co., Bell Atlantic, Maytag, Sprint Corp., La-Z-Boy Chair Co., and Texaco.

Of course, you don't have to stick with the NAIC's tools. Greer and Haskins have hammered out their own vehicle for analyzing the group's holdings—an industry chart. By culling information from other publications, lists of various industries, and the companies that fall within those areas, the duo highlights the industries in which the club is currently invested. In turn, they encourage members to study and select stocks in those sectors in which the club doesn't have any holdings.

"We use that chart to keep us focused. We are actively invested in 23 different industries," says Haskins. "Our very first stock purchase (in March 1997) was Philip Morris. Owning shares in that company not only put us into the tobacco business, but in the food-processing industry, because Philip Morris owns Kraft Foods."

Continues Haskins, "We are in the pharmaceutical sector because we own Pfizer, a major drug company for people (as well as animals). AFLAC put us into the insurance business. Clorox put us into

Figure 12.4 Portfolio Evaluation Review Technique

PERT Worksheet—A

NATIONAL ASSOCIATION
OF INVESTORS CORPORATION®

INVESTMENT EDUCATION
FOR INDIVIDUALS AND CLUBS
SINCE 1951

Company

PERIOD	QUARTERLY DATA															LAST 12 MONTHS DATA							
	EPS		PRE-TAX PROFIT			SALES		INCOME TAX RATE	EPS $	PRE-TAX PROFIT		SALES MIL	INCOME TAX		% CHANGE		
	$	% CHANGE	$ MIL	% SALES	% CHANGE	$ MIL	% CHANGE			$ MIL	% SALES		$ MIL	% RATE	EPS	PRE-TAX PROFIT	SALES
A	B	C	D	E	F	G	H	I	J	K	L	M	N	O	P	Q	R	S	T

Source: © 1998. Reprinted with permission. This material is copyrighted and taken from the NAIC's Official Guide to *Starting and Running a Profitable Investment Club.* Refer to that book for a full explanation of this material.

216

Figure 12.5 Portfolio Evaluation Review Technique

PERT Worksheet—B

Company _____ **Symbol** _____

		PRICE RANGE		P/E RATIO		5 YEAR AVERAGE P/E RATIO			DIV/ SHARE	% PAYOUT		% HIGH YIELD
										THIS YEAR	5 YEAR AVERAGE	
YEAR	EPS	HIGH	LOW	HIGH	LOW	HIGH	AVG	LOW				
A	B	C	D	E	F	G	H	I	J	K	L	M

chemicals and household products. Pep Boys threw us into the retail automotive aftermarket. Hilton Hotels puts us into the hotel business, but they also spun off a company called Park Place Entertainment which is in the gaming industry."

All together, the group has 14 holdings, including Disney; ADP, which provides software payroll and software solutions; Diebold, which produces ATM machines; and Carsons, the maker of Dark & Lovely hair care products. Adds Haskins, "We are probably rolling at about 80 percent of our funds invested in large cap, 15 percent in mid-cap, and 5 percent in small cap."

The only way you can learn is to become educated about the stock market and an active participant in your club, stresses Windy City's Greer. Meaning, "You have to attend workshops, study NAIC's tools, and read."

STOCK MARKET LITERATURE

By now, your head may be throbbing from all this talk of P/E ratios and pretax profit margins. Don't stress—there's plenty of relief. You don't have to do all the calculations yourself—analysts have already done them for you by examining each company's financial history, current health, and future prospects.

If you use a full-service broker, you will have access to the research reports written by the firm's analysts. These reports may be several pages long and conclude with a buy, hold, or sell recommendation. The major advantage is that they are free to customers, but you will want to scrutinize any of the firm's information. The costs will be absorbed by the commissions club members pay on their stock transactions.

Two of the most widely used tools by investment clubs are the *Value Line Investment Survey* and *Standard & Poor's Stock Reports.*

Value Line Investment Survey (800-833-0046)

These one-page reports (see Figure 12.6) cover 1,700 stocks and 97 industries. Updated weekly, each page is jam-packed with all the figures you need to pick stocks, including P/E ratio, earnings per share, beta, high and low stock prices, income tax rate, book value, and net profit. You can

Figure 12.6 Value Line Investment Survey Report

PEPSICO, INC. NYSE-PEP

RECENT PRICE	P/E RATIO		RELATIVE P/E RATIO	DIV'D YLD		VALUE LINE
34	27.2	(Trailing: 31.2 / Median: 20.0)	1.79	1.7%		1547

TIMELINESS	4	Lowered 10/23/98	High:	7.3	11.0	13.9	17.8	21.7	21.8	20.6	29.4	35.9	41.3	44.8	42.6
SAFETY	2	Lowered 11/13/98	Low:	5.0	6.3	9.0	11.8	15.3	17.3	14.6	16.9	27.3	28.3	27.6	30.1
TECHNICAL	4	Lowered 11/5/99													
BETA .90 (1.00 = Market)															

Target Price Range 2002 2003 2004

2002-04 PROJECTIONS

	Price	Gain	Ann'l Total Return
High	60	(+75%)	16%
Low	45	(+30%)	9%

LEGENDS
16.0 x "Cash Flow" p sh
···· Relative Price Strength
3-for-1 split 5/86
3-for-1 split 9/90
2-for-1 split 5/96
Options: Yes
Shaded area indicates recession

Insider Decisions

	D	J	F	M	A	M	J	J	A
to Buy	0	0	2	0	0	1	0	0	0
Options	0	1	1	0	0	1	0	0	1
to Sell	0	0	1	0	0	2	0	1	1

Institutional Decisions

	4Q1998	1Q1999	2Q1999
to Buy	484	480	428
to Sell	374	410	451
Hld's(000)	856468	875652	864504

Percent shares traded: 9.0 / 6.0 / 3.0

% TOT. RETURN 10/99

	THIS STOCK	VL ARITH. INDEX
1 yr.	4.3	13.4
3 yr.	32.3	49.9
5 yr.	131.2	107.3

1983	1984	1985	1986	1987	1988	1989	1990	1991	1992	1993	1994	1995	1996	1997	1998	1999	2000	© VALUE LINE PUB., INC.	02-04
4.69	4.55	5.10	5.95	7.35	8.25	9.63	11.29	12.42	13.75	15.66	18.02	19.30	20.48	13.93	15.19	13.00	14.35	Sales per sh	18.55
.32	.35	.45	.55	.74	.88	1.05	1.23	1.42	1.58	1.90	2.13	2.37	2.32	1.89	2.04	1.75	1.95	"Cash Flow" per sh	2.70
.17	.19	.25	.29	.37	.48	.56	.66	.75	.81	.98	1.11	1.24	1.17	1.10	1.16	1.22	1.37	Earnings per sh B	2.00
.09	.09	.10	.11	.11	.13	.16	.19	.23	.26	.31	.35	.39	.45	.49	.52	.54	.57	Div'ds Decl'd per sh C■	.72
.31	.34	.50	.57	.50	.46	.60	.75	.92	.97	1.24	1.43	1.34	1.48	1.00	.96	.75	.80	Cap'l Spending per sh	.85
1.07	1.10	1.16	1.32	1.61	2.00	2.46	3.11	3.51	3.35	3.97	4.34	4.64	4.29	4.62	4.35	5.00	4.85	Book Value per sh E	6.25
1684.1	1690.3	1578.7	1561.9	1562.5	1576.9	1582.1	1576.8	1578.2	1597.6	1597.6	1579.8	1576.0	1545.0	1502.0	1471.0	1425.0	1395.0	Common Shs Outst'g F	1305.0
11.9	11.8	12.6	16.3	15.5	12.6	15.7	17.8	20.4	22.8	20.0	15.9	18.5	26.5	32.5	32.4	*Bold figures are Value Line estimates*		Avg Ann'l P/E Ratio	26.0
1.01	1.10	1.02	1.11	1.04	1.05	1.19	1.32	1.30	1.38	1.18	1.04	1.24	1.66	1.87	1.69			Relative P/E Ratio	1.75
4.5%	4.1%	3.1%	2.2%	1.9%	2.2%	1.8%	1.6%	1.5%	1.4%	1.6%	2.0%	1.7%	1.4%	1.4%	1.4%			Avg Ann'l Div'd Yield	1.4%

CAPITAL STRUCTURE as of 6/12/99

Tot.Debt $5556.0 mill. Due in 5 Yrs $3000.0 mill.
LT Debt $2625.0 mill. LT Interest $160.0 mill.

(Total interest coverage: 10.0x) (27% of Cap'l)

Leases, Uncapitalized Annual rentals $356.0 mill.

Pension Liability None
Pfd Stock None

Common Stock 1,462,325,000 shs. (73% of Cap'l)
as of 7/9/99
MARKET CAP: $50 billion (Large Cap)

	1989	1990	1991	1992	1993	1994	1995	1996	1997	1998	1999	2000		02-04
Sales ($mill)	15242	17803	19608	21970	25021	28472	30421	31645	20917	22348	18600	20000		24200
Operating Margin	16.8%	16.6%	17.0%	16.3%	17.4%	16.8%	17.2%	16.1%	19.4%	18.4%	19.5%	19.5%		21.0%
Depreciation ($mill)	772.0	884.0	1034.5	1214.9	1444.2	1576.5	1740.0	1719.0	1106.0	1234.0	700	730		820
Net Profit ($mill)	886.4	1050.0	1200.2	1301.7	1587.9	1784.0	1990.0	1865.0	1730.0	1760.0	1815	1995		2735
Income Tax Rate	33.3%	33.0%	34.8%	31.4%	34.5%	33.0%	32.6%	35.0%	33.4%	31.0%	32.0%	32.0%		32.0%
Net Profit Margin	5.8%	5.9%	6.1%	5.9%	6.3%	6.3%	6.5%	5.9%	8.3%	7.9%	9.8%	10.0%		11.3%
Working Cap'l ($mill)	d141.0	d689.1	844.0	517.9	d1411	d198.2	316.0	- -	1994.0	d3552	220	d550		d100
Long-Term Debt ($mill)	5777.1	5600.1	7806.2	7964.8	7442.6	8840.5	8509.0	8439.0	4946.0	4028.0	2600	2700		2750
Shr. Equity ($mill)	3891.1	4904.2	5545.4	5355.7	6338.7	6856.1	7313.0	6623.0	6936.0	6401.0	7100	6800		8175
Return on Total Cap'l	11.8%	12.7%	11.3%	11.8%	12.9%	13.0%	14.3%	14.2%	16.6%	18.8%	20.5%	22.5%		26.5%
Return on Shr. Equity	22.8%	21.4%	21.6%	24.3%	25.1%	26.0%	27.2%	28.2%	24.9%	27.5%	25.5%	29.5%		33.5%
Retained to Com Eq	16.6%	15.4%	15.5%	16.9%	17.8%	18.1%	19.0%	18.0%	14.3%	15.7%	14.5%	17.5%		22.0%
All Div'ds to Net Prof	27%	28%	29%	30%	29%	30%	30%	36%	43%	43%	42%	40%		34%

CURRENT POSITION	1997	1998	9/4/99
(SMILL.)			
Cash Assets	2883.0	394.0	550.0
Receivables	2150.0	2453.0	--
Inventory (FIFO)	732.0	1016.0	--
Other	486.0	499.0	3047.0
Current Assets	6251.0	4362.0	3597.0
Accts Payable			
Debt Due	- -	3921.0	94.0
Other	4257.0	3993.0	3214.0
Current Liab.	4257.0	7914.0	3308.0

ANNUAL RATES	Past 10 Yrs.	Past 5 Yrs.	Est'd '98 to '02-04
of change (per sh)			
Sales	8.5%	3.5%	4.0%
"Cash Flow"	11.0%	5.0%	6.0%
Earnings	11.5%	6.0%	11.5%
Dividends	15.5%	13.0%	6.5%
Book Value	10.5%	4.0%	7.5%

Cal-endar	QUARTERLY SALES ($ mill.) A G				Full Year
	Mar.Per	Jun.Per	Sep.Per	Dec.Per	
1996	6554	7691	7867	9533	31645
1997	4213	5086	5362	6256	20917
1998	4353	5258	5544	7193	22348
1999	3884	4523	4579	5614	18600
2000	4175	4850	4925	6050	20000

Cal-endar	EARNINGS PER SHARE A B G				Full Year
	Mar.Per	Jun.Per	Sep.Per	Dec.Per	
1996	.01	.07	.00	.01	1.17
1997	.20	.26	.35	.29	1.10
1998	.24	.33	.37	.22	1.16
1999	.25	.31	.34	.32	1.22
2000	.28	.35	.38	.36	1.37

Cal-endar	QUARTERLY DIVIDENDS PAID C ■				Full Year
	Mar.31	Jun.30	Sep.30	Dec.31	
1995	.18D	.10	.10	--	.38
1996	.20D	.115	.115	--	.43
1997	.23D	.125	.125	--	.48
1998	.25	.13	.13	--	.51
1999	.26D	.135	.135		

BUSINESS: PepsiCo, Inc. operates two major businesses: Soft Drinks, about 35% of 1998 sales and 35% of operating profit; and Snack Foods, 49% and 64%. Also Tropicana, acquired 9/98, 3% and 1%. International business accounts for 31% of sales. Restaurant chains spun off, 10/97. Majority interest in Pepsi Bottling Group sold, 4/99. Major soft drink products: Pepsi-Cola, Diet Pepsi, and Mountain Dew. Specialty snack foods: Frito-Lay (major product offerings include Doritos, Ruffles, and Lay's), Walker Crisps, Smiths Crisps. Has about 142,000 employees, 207,000 stockholders. Insiders own less than 1% of common. Chrmn. & Chief Exec. Officer: Roger A. Enrico Inc.: NC. Add.: PepsiCo World Headquarters, Purchase, NY 10577. Tel.: 914-253-2000. Internet: www.pepsico.com.

PepsiCo is a well regarded growth company that has undergone a major transformation in the past several years. In the recent June quarter, it sold 65% of the Pepsi Bottling Group, its wholly owned bottling subsidiary, through a public offering, and also merged certain franchise territories in the U.S. and Central Europe with Whitman Corp. These moves followed the September 1998 acquisition of Tropicana (sales of over $2 billion) and the 1997 spinoff of the restaurant businesses (sales of $9.4 billion). For 1999, the bottling companies will no longer be consolidated, and the result is that PepsiCo's income statement and balance sheet data will be very different from what they had been. The funds generated from the bottling company transactions are being used to reduce debt outstanding and repurchase stock. At this point, it is still somewhat difficult to make detailed projections, but the numbers above are based on our best estimates for 1999, we believe that earnings will be just over $1.20 a share, up from $1.10 for 1998 (pro forma).
PepsiCo's snack food, soft drink, and fruit juice businesses all have large market shares and good growth prospects, and we look for steady earnings progress in the years out to 2002-2004. Frito-Lay North America is the dominant snack food company in the U.S. and is likely to continue to do very well. The Pepsi-Cola soft drink lineup has a strong #2 position in the U.S., and it has been gaining market share recently. We expect unit growth to average 2%-4% a year. Tropicana's volume is also likely to continue to increase. Growth prospects outside North America are particularly promising for Frito-Lay, which already is a major factor in many markets, and for Pepsi Cola, which is emphasizing expansion in fast-growing, third-world markets, notably China and India.
PepsiCo shares are not timely because of poor recent earnings comparisons, but we expect steady profit growth in the next 3 to 5 years. Snack foods (roughly 60% of sales of the newly configured PepsiCo), soft drink concentrates (25%), and juices (somewhat more than 10%) each have the potential for increasing earnings by 10% or more in the average year.
Stephen Sanborn, CFA November 12, 1999

(A) Quarters are 12, 12, 12 and 16 weeks. (B) Prim. earns. thru 1996; diluted thereafter. Ex. nonrecur. gain (losses): '85, 22c; '91, (7c); '92, (65c); '95, (24c); '96, (45c); '98, 15c. Next (A) earn. report due late Jan. (C) Next div. meeting about Jan. 20. Goes ex about Mar. 9. Pay. dates: about Jan. 2, March 31, June 30, Sept. 30. ■ Reinvest. plan avail. (D) Two divs. in qtr. (E) Incl. intang. In '98: $9.00 bil., $6.12/sh. (F) In millions; adj. for stock splits. (G) Reflects Restaurant spinoff in 1997 and sale of majority stake in Pepsi Bottling Group in 1999.

Company's Financial Strength	A+
Stock's Price Stability	75
Price Growth Persistence	80
Earnings Predictability	80

Reprinted with permission by Value Line Publishing Inc.

find information on a company's performance for the past 15 years and its projected performance for the next two or three years. *Value Line* also provides company rankings from one to five based on *timeliness*—a measure of its projected stock price performance—and *safety*—a measure of the volatility of its stock price. The lower the number, the better.

Value Line provides a summary of the company's major product lines; background of a company's business; current happenings in the company, such as recent acquisitions; information from its financial statements, such as net income and profits; and performance information, namely its stock track record.

The reports, which also include the name of the CEO, address, and telephone number of the corporate headquarters, are available through brokerage firms, the public library, or Value Line Publishing Inc.

Standard & Poor's Stock Reports (877-481-8724)

Commonly known as S&P sheets, S&P provides statistical data on 4,700 companies listed on all three major stock exchanges. The two-page reports are generated by analysts who give buy, hold, and sell recommendations in addition to analysis of management. Analysts compile data on the financial performance of the company, providing many of the same figures as *Value Line,* including debt-to-equity ratios, beta, earnings projections, 10-year history on a stock's price, P/E ratio, return on equity, and pretax profit margins. Just keep in mind that each source calculates figures differently, so you want to use the same report for each company that you review. The S&P stock sheets also include an industry overview for each company.

* * *

The figures and data you will need to review industries, evaluate companies, and compare stocks, bonds and mutual funds also are available in the following resource guides.

Value Line Mutual Fund Investment Survey

A one-page report that tracks the performance information of 2,000 mutual funds, including in-depth coverage of 1,500 equity and fixed-income mutual funds for subscribers. You can access their product information through www.valueline.com.

S&P's Stock Guide

This is a monthly pocket-sized book that provides one long line of data on thousands of public companies. It is easy to read and fun to flip through. It allows you to screen companies prior to sending away for financial information. Better still, many brokers pass it out to their customers as a freebie. This guide will tell you how strong a company is by answering such questions as how much cash does a company have in relationship to its long-term debt? There are six volumes with data for the most recent 15-month period on 12,000 companies.

S&P's Bond Guide

Analyzes the financial strength of bond issuers, both corporations and government bodies. Ratings range from AAA (highly unlikely to default) to D (in default).

S&P's The Outlook

Published weekly, it covers the status of the stock market. It lists stocks to buy and stocks to avoid, including highlights from the S&P's Master List of Recommended Stocks based on superior long-term total return.

S&P Industry Reports

This report provides a comprehensive look at 37 business sectors from aerospace to utilities, offering fundamental and investment forecasts by industry and buy and sell recommendations on individual stocks within sectors. It lists more than 800 companies by industry.

S&P Stock Market Encyclopedia

Published quarterly, it includes data on 750 companies—industries, utilities, transportation, and financial firms. A full-page report is included for every stock in the S&P 500.

S&P Register of Corporations, Directors, and Executives

Published annually in three volumes, Volume 1 lists 55,000 corporations with the address, telephone number, name, title, and function of some 500,000 officers, directors, and, other principals, along with a description of company products and services. Volume II offers listings of more than 70,000 individuals, officers, directors, trustees, and partners. Volume III consists of indexes.

Nelson's Directory of Investment Research (800-333-6357; www.nelnet.com)

This two-volume directory gives you a research edge on 24,000 stocks worldwide. It provides complete coverage from over 800 research firms and 10,000 security analysts. Company listings include business descriptions, five-year operating summary, addresses and phone numbers, and over 100,000 key executives' names.

Nelson's Catalog of Institutional Research Reports

This catalog of over 200,000 research reports is published by virtually every investment research firm worldwide. Reports are listed alphabetically by company and grouped by industry.

Nelson's Earnings Outlook

This is a compilation of estimated earnings per share based on figures supplied by security analysts who follow particular stocks and industries.

Investext (800-662-7878)

This resource offers over 700,000 analysts research reports produced by investment banks, research firms, and brokerage houses. It provides expert opinion, analysis, market trends, forecasts, and raw company data.

Hoover's Handbook on American Business (512-374-4500)

This two-volume set contains in-depth profiles of 750 large and influential companies, including giants like Coca-Cola, Exxon, General Motors, and Wal-Mart, plus a section on more than 50 of the largest privately owned companies. Examines the personalities, events, and strategies of the companies, along with 60 pages of business lists such as the Fortune 500 ranking of U.S. corporations, Computer Retail Week's Top 50 Computer Retailers, and the S&P 500 composite.

Hoover's Handbook on Emerging Companies

This handbook chronicles the rise of 300 of America's dynamic growth companies. It focuses on those firms with revenues between $20 million and $1 billion that have experienced sales of at least 25 percent annually over the past five years and have had positive net income for the last year. Two other Hoover titles are *The Guide to Computer Companies* and the *Master-list of Major U.S. Companies*.

Dow Jones Retrieval Service (800-522-3567)

This service includes current stock quotes, information from Dow Jones business news wires; can deliver company specific information.

Vickers Weekly Insider Report (516-423-7710)

While periodicals like the *Wall Street Journal* and *Barron's* magazine report selected trades, this is the most comprehensive source. It reports on corporate officers and directors who trade 500 or more shares within their companies at a price of $1 or more on the outside market. Vickers has a portfolio of current picks, based on particularly heavy insider purchases.

Barron's National Business and Financial Weekly (800-277-4136)

This publication provides news, commentary, advice, and analysis about a wide range of financial markets, stocks, and companies. Half the paper

is made up of articles and columns about current events—including interviews and hot news releases about companies—and the current state of the financial markets.

The other half consists of pages and pages of financial tables. There are also corporate reports for select companies each week. You'll find detailed statistical information at www.barrons.com.

Zacks Analyst Watch (www.zacks.com)

Big and small investing firms employ analysts whose job is to know an industry and to generate quarterly and annual growth projections for individual companies. This monthly publication offers quarterly, annual, and five-year earnings growth projections on 5,000 publicly traded companies. This earnings service is an ideal scorecard of the growth potential of a given company.

Investor's Business Daily (800-306-9744)

The daily financial newspaper provides in-depth stock information, tables and data. It gives complete market quotes and a variety of statistical information along with news stories. It also provides information on options, futures, and world markets.

Morningstar Mutual Funds (800-735-0700)

Published biweekly by Chicago-based Morningstar Inc., this is the most popular and comprehensive survey of mutual-fund performance. Each full-page report gives detailed information (e.g., total return, dividends, and net assets) and a bit of history on each load, low-load, and no-load fund. Morningstar not only tracks performance but assigns a special star-rating system to each fund. The rating is a measure of performance based on risk and gives investors a way to narrow the group of funds they want to look at in greater depth.

Mutual Fund Sourcebook

Morningstar's annual publication covers and rates the performance of some 1,800 equity and fixed-income funds. Don't overlook Morningstar's

site (www.morningstar.net) which is chockful of information, including financial columns and interviews with institutional investors.

Handbook for No-Load Fund Investors (SheldonJacobs.com)

A directory of more than 1,300 no-load stock and bond funds, plus 10-year performance figures on each fund and a section on how to pick and monitor funds. This handy guide is published annually by financial guru Sheldon Jacobs of the No-Load Fund Investor Advisory Service.

Moody's Investors Service (212-553-0300)

Moody's publishes several handbooks covering select NYSE and NASDAQ companies: *Industry Review,* updated semiannually, offers comparative financial and operational information on more than 5,000 corporation spanning 145 industries; *Emerging Companies,* profiles fast-growing small public companies; *Dividend Record Service* provides information on over 500 companies that have paid increasing dividends for the past decade; *Corporate Index,* published biannually, is a comprehensive list of 28,000 corporations; *Bond Rating Service* analyzes the financial strength of corporate and government issuers.

Better Investing (877-275-6242)

Published monthly by NAIC, this is the official magazine for investment clubs. *Better Investing* offers articles on stocks to study and undervalued stocks, along with helpful ideas for beginners and profiles of member investment clubs. It also offers tips on financial planning, stock, and mutual-fund markets.

SCANNING FOR INVESTMENT INFORMATION ON THE INTERNET

As you research potential stock picks before you go out and buy shares, cast the widest net. Where? On the Internet, of course. Much of

the data your club needs to analyze companies is at your fingertips or the click of a mouse. There are scores of online information—stock and mutual fund quotes, earnings per share and P/E ratio analyses, and industry data.

Before you start, your club will need the right kind of equipment. Robert Lancaster Jr., who researches stocks for Ebony Investors.com and who is president of New Freedom Investment Club, recommends using a computer with a Pentium microprocessor or higher; at least 32 MB of RAM and 2 gigabyte hard drive; and a 28.8 kbps or higher fax modem.

You will also need an Internet browser software program, such as Netscape Navigator or Internet Explorer, and an Internet Service Provider (ISP), such as America Online, AT&T Worldnet, MSN, or Earthlink. There are also many local ISPs. While services vary, the average price is $19.95 per month for unlimited access.

While many investment sites offer free access, others require a monthly fee, much like a subscription to a magazine. It should also be noted that stock quotes online are delayed at least 15 minutes. To get real-time quotes, you'll have to pay an extra $10 to $20 a month; you may want to think twice, given that on-the-spot quotes won't give you an edge worth paying for.

You will also want to examine market information—the ups and downs of the Dow Jones Industrial Average, for instance—as well as industry statistics, brokerage analysts' opinions, current news, and individual company data, such as financial statements and management decisions. Many let you input a portfolio of stocks you have bought and then allow you to track share prices over time.

Seek and You Shall Find

You can find everything you need if you know where to look. Check out free services first to get a sense of what you can get on the Web free. The NAIC sponsors an annual conference, Compufest, that emphasizes computerized investing and the Internet. For updated information, check NAIC's Web site (www.better-investing.org).

A great starting point is DBC Financial's site (www.dbc.com), which provides stock quotes, statistical ratios, and links to news sources and online trading companies. S&P's Web site (www.personal.wealth) provides information on investing in individual stocks with good

dividend records. Daily Stocks (www.dailystocks.com) offers quotes, analyses, and links to several sites. The Motley Fool (www.fool.com), a clever mix of humor and common sense, is a free online personal finance forum that aims to educate investors. The Financial Data Finder (www.cob.ohio-state.edu/dept/fin/osudata.htm) contains such sites as CNN Financial Network (www.cnnfn.com), so you can tap into late-breaking news affecting your stocks.

One comprehensive site is Stocksmart (www.stocksmart.com), where you can find hundreds of links to investment-related Web sites offering company information and stock analysis. You can access company and statistical information from Hoover's online database (www.hoovers.com), which covers more than 8,500 companies. Also, worth checking out is the Stock Research Group (www.stockgroup .com/). Another great place for getting company-specific information is the Securities and Exchange Commission (www.sec.gov), the government repository where public companies must file financial statements. For corporate filings, check out the SEC's Edgar database.

You can also find insider-trading data on several sites, including www.insidertrader.com. Search engine Yahoo! (www.yahoo.com) offers data provided by CDA/Investnet, a Rockville, Maryland, company that specializes in insider transactions. Also, take a look at Yahoo's split calendar (www.quote.yahoo.com); it details which companies are dividing up shares and when.

The Street (www.thestreet.com) features free content and premium-subscriber content services such as twice-daily financial news e-mail updates. You can scroll through listings of the S&P, Dow, and Nasdaq stock indexes.

Big Charts (www.bigcharts.com) is a great tool for getting quick analyses of companies. Type a company's stock symbol and select a time period (one month, two years, etc.). You'll get a chart of the company's performance and links to sites providing more detailed profiles.

Quicken (www.quicken.com) provides a full range of investment and finance information, including market highlights, breaking news, stock quotes, research, and portfolio evaluations. Bloomberg (www .bloomberg.com) offers free services, articles covering a wide range of money topics, domestic and international news, financial figures, and interviews with financial experts.

To help separate the dross from the gold, several financial Web sites have highly sophisticated stock screens with scores of filter criteria for identifying the companies with the credentials and performance

that inspire members to invest their money. The best way to picture stock screens is to remember old western flicks depicting crusty old prospectors panning mountain streams in search of gold. They would dip into the river's silt, swirl the mud and water around a bit, skim the contents, and collect the shiniest rocks.

A stock screen works much like the prospector's pan. It scoops up data on thousands of stocks that trade on the major stock exchanges and sifts through the numbers according to requirements that you plug in, discarding those companies that don't meet your criteria. For example, if you were looking for companies that were growing earnings at 20 percent or more a year, yet trading at a price-to-earnings ratio of 30 or less, a screen would ferret out a list of candidates for your researching pleasure.[3]

There's no shortage of readily available information online that can help club members keep their ears close to the ground. Whether or not members trade online, the Web needs to be an important part of their stock-picking efforts and in managing the club's portfolio. Members need to track the club's holdings on a regular basis (remember Key #6 in Chapter 7).

You can browse company sites via search engines such as Altavista (www.altavista.com), Infoseek (www.infoseek.com), or Excite (www.excite.com). While many companies release news on the Web, it's important to get your information from brokerage firms or other third-party sources. Company sites frequently offer information that is self-promoting.

CONCLUSION

Remember the key to researching a company is to look for consistency in sales and earnings growth. Examine a number of resources and analysts' reports to see if they offer the same commentary, then form your own opinion. Don't forget: You're not just looking for data, you're digging for dollars.

13

THINKING OUTSIDE THE BOX: INVESTING BEYOND THE STOCK MARKET

Do not follow the path. Go where there is no path to begin the trail.
—Ashanti proverb

Life has two rules: Number one, Never quit!; Number two, Always remember rule number one.

—Duke Ellington

Aunt Kizzy's Back Porch is the hot spot for some good old down-home cooking. Folks travel from miles around to get to Aunt Kizzy's place in Marina del Rey (just outside Los Angeles). Aunt Kizzy may not be a real person, but the restaurant that bears her name is like family to the largely African-American community it serves.

Restaurateur Adolf Dulan of Aunt Kizzy's Back Porch has reached out to the people in his hometown in other ways. In 1991, he cofounded the Millionaire Men's Investment Group. The club of professional black men uses a portion of its $100,000-plus investment portfolio to host several charitable events, including an annual Christmas toy drive and a quarterly soup night.

Philanthropy is only a portion of the Millionaire Men's Investment Group activities outside the purview of Wall Street. The group has invested heavily in real estate over the years, by taking rundown properties (single-family dwellings), renovating them, and putting

them back out on the market—generating an average rate of return of 25 percent, a percentage that more than holds its own against the strong stock-market performance of the past few years.

That's not to say that investment clubs can waltz into uncharted territory easily. "To branch out like this, you need someone in the group with a legal and/or financial background in this area," cautions the club's past president, Dr. Charles Loeb III. "We're lucky enough to have both."

The Millionaire Men's Club is not unlike a good number of clubs that look beyond traditional securities—stocks, bonds, and mutual funds—not only to invest gains they've made in the market, but as a means of giving back to their communities. Some clubs form with the intention of building personal wealth and investing money in their communities. For others, it's a point that they reach after they've been together for a while. To some it's a moral dilemma, for others a time of financial reckoning: Should we look beyond the stock market?[1]

While the men of Los Angeles are giving a new lease on life to the dilapidated buildings in their neighborhoods, the women of Washington, DC, are breathing life into local small businesses. Formed in 1987, the Washington Women's Investment Club (WWIC) debated before agreeing on how to invest their money. They decided to divvy up their investment portfolio between securities (about 65 percent in stocks and 25 percent in mutual funds) and 10 percent in cash, including funds set aside for small-business capitalization loans.

That way, they would be able to give fledgling African-American businesses a boost while garnering a return on their investment. This investment style seems to have worked: The group manages to average an annual rate of return of roughly 21 percent.

The group of 16 women follow strict rules to ensure that their ventures outside the market are a success. "We never take our money out of our securities to invest in outside ventures," says group president Irene Finch. "We maintain some liquidity at all times and use that money to invest in what we see as opportunities to maximize our returns. Our mission is to make money and to have fun doing it," explains Finch.

Altogether, WWIC has invested in 5 different entrepreneurial ventures, including a sports-management company and an art studio. WWIC has stayed together over the years by using committees to diversify their portfolio. They now characterize their dealings as investment opportunities pursued, missed opportunities, and opportunities rejected.

"You have to evaluate each project carefully, just as you would a stock investment," says club secretary Eloise Foster. "Will that project or business allow you to accomplish the club's investment objectives and the kind of return you want to see? We have a rate-of-return base for every venture that we invest in."

The principle of diversification means that you spread your investments and, therefore, your risk. Many clubs, such as WWIC, know that diversifying helps to balance a low-risk tolerance with a desire for maximum returns. By not concentrating strictly on equities, your club can achieve sheer capital growth over time.

WEALTH ACCUMULATION THROUGH REAL ESTATE INVESTMENTS

Making money by investing in real estate is by no means a new concept for the African-American community. Many people have achieved the American dream and made their wealth by starting a business or investing in real estate. Take, for example, *Fortune* and *Forbes* magazines' lists of billionaires and the 400 richest people in America. Most the individuals accumulated fortunes because real estate was a major portion of their investment portfolio.

Foreign investors, particularly Asians and Europeans, are well aware of the value of real estate, notes investment advisor and author Cheryl Broussard. "They consider real-estate prices in the United States bargains compared to prices in their own countries. They are steadily purchasing properties throughout the country, many of them located in the inner cities of Los Angeles, New York, and Chicago," she explains. These properties range from expensive high-rise office buildings to single-family homes in African-American, Latino, and Asian communities."

Broussard believes real-estate investing will continue as a major wealth builder and a much-sought-after commodity. "This increase in demand will cause substantial appreciation in real estate prices and provide those who invest in real estate with a viable means to make money."[2]

There are some benefits to including real estate in your club's investment portfolio:

- *Capital appreciation.* Real estate is an effective hedge against inflation because, when inflation increases, real estate prices generally rise.

- *Tax advantage.* Real estate can generate helpful interest and de-preciation deductions.
- *Income.* Real estate can produce income from renting and leasing property.
- *Leverage.* Real estate can be bought with a partial amount of the purchase price, sometimes less than 10 percent.

WWIC was formed at the peak of the Washington metropolitan area's real-estate boom. Consequently, the women sought to capitalize on this growth by establishing a real-estate committee to evaluate various residential and commercial investments. The committee has evaluated investments in single- and multifamily homes, as well as commercial and vacation properties. These properties were found using real-estate agents, by reviewing foreclosure notices, and by word of mouth.

Several years ago, WWIC's real-estate committee identified a house for sale in Baltimore's historic Bolton Hill area. The property, a three-story Victorian house with seven fireplaces, was listed for less than $20,000. While the basic structure of the house was sound, the property needed to be completely renovated in order to turn it into an attractive rental property or to resell it.

Although the group had sufficient funds in the treasury to purchase the house outright, some members were not comfortable using the majority of their funds for that purpose. On the other hand, if they obtained a loan (to cover the purchase price, renovation costs, or both) each member would have been required to assume full liability for the amount of the loan in the event of default. Again, members were not comfortable with the financing requirements.

"As we deliberated and debated how WWIC could buy and renovate the property, the house was purchased by another buyer who renovated and sold it within three months for $150,000," says Finch. Since that time, the property has been resold for an even higher price. In this case, WWIC was indecisive and risk averse; consequently, the group missed an opportunity to purchase their first piece of real estate.[3]

Investing in real estate does not require extraordinary knowledge or talent. It does take a willingness to learn the real-estate market. Becoming a successful real-estate investor entails building successful relationships with bankers, real-estate agents, and attorneys in your community, advises Broussard. "They can supply you with a wealth of information and lead you to profitable real-estate deals. You will need to keep abreast of the market—real-estate reacts

immediately to changes in the economy. If you are well-versed on the subject, you can react quickly to the changes that can yield you enormous real-estate profits."

In using a real-estate agent, you want someone who can work with a group of investors. "Not all agents are knowledgeable about or interested in working with groups, or know how to secure financing for group investors," cautions Finch.

She adds that arranging financing for a real-estate project may be difficult. "Your agent can put you in touch with lending institutions that are willing to make group loans. But you should recognize that it is much more difficult than purchasing property as an individual. Group purchases often require all investors to assume individual liability for the property."

To overcome this potential problem, you might use any of the following sources to pay for a real estate investment venture:

- *Make a cash call.* In this case, you can call on the membership to pay their dues all at once, a year in advance, or to put up money in addition to monthly dues to cover the down payment.

- *Build a reserve.* You may decide to set aside 15 percent of your club's portfolio to invest in real estate so that, when the time comes, you will have cash on hand. You may also opt to sell some of your securities to buy rental properties.

- *Raise the funds.* Members can sponsor special events, such as an art show or auction, and take a portion of the revenues to finance a prospective real-estate project.

- *Assume a mortgage.* Lenders usually require downpayments of 20 percent to 30 percent for rental properties because of the risk. Your club can try to get a fixed-rate mortgage from a commercial bank. Larry Lick, owner of 24 rental buildings and founder of Rental Housing On Line (www.rental-housing.com), a resource for small investors, suggests developing a relationship with a local banker. Another option is to seek out government loans through the Department of Housing and Urban Development (www.hud.gov).

The Millionaire Men's Club's Dr. Loeb says the group's tight-knit structure has been a boon when the club had trouble getting funding from banks and other financial institutions. "Each time we purchased

a property, an individual member had to apply, using his or her credit rating to get us through the purchasing process," he recalls.

A solid organizational structure helps as well. The seven-member club is set up as a general partnership; each charter member has an equal share. There are also at-large members. "What makes our group work is that we've known each other for over 15 years," adds Dr. Loeb, an obstetrician/gynecologist who has had his own private practice for the past 21 years. "While many of us invested on our own, we decided to form a group to invest in these kinds of ventures."

Scan the real-estate section of your local newspapers to learn of opportunities and to stay on top of market trends. Contact the National Association of Realtors in Washington, DC ,(202-383-1000) and the National Association of Real Estate Brokers in Oakland, CA, (510-568-4577). For out-of-state and foreign opportunities, contact the tourism board in that locale.

Request information about ownership and residency requirements, taxes, population, and pending changes in laws applicable to zoning ordinances and land development. Create and follow a timetable for completing specific tasks, collecting data, visiting sites, and obtaining financing.

There are various ways your club can invest in real estate. The most common and direct method is *hands-on real estate,* whereby you have the most control over the property and pay the lowest fees and commissions. Properties include single-family homes, multiple dwellings such as duplexes, office buildings, and raw land.

Go this route and you'll pay the highest cash outlay and spend the greatest amount of time to become a landlord. As direct owners, club members will assume all costs, such as liability insurance, and headaches, like tenants from hell, that go along with ownership. Then there's the risk that the investment property will not appreciate or produce the kind of income you expect.

The second method of investing is *hands-off;* you don't personally manage the property. You can invest in real-estate limited partnerships or real-estate investment trusts (REITs). These require a cash outlay of between $1,000 and $5,000. The method you choose will depend on the time, effort, and money the group is willing to commit.

"As new investors, if you want to manage your own property, consider residential rental real estate, particularly those properties with more than one rental unit, such as a duplex or larger," advises Broussard. "Purchase real estate close to home, making it easier to check on

the property. Location is a major factor in your club's profit potential—look for a well-maintained neighborhood close to schools, shopping malls, and mass transportation. Also, scout for fixer-uppers in desirable neighborhoods."

A word of caution: Don't buy the most expensive property in a rundown neighborhood hoping that the area will go through a gentrification. "Your investment may not pay off," warns Broussard. Investing in rental property unfortunately does not guarantee you positive cash flow. With high mortgage payments and property taxes, many properties have a negative cash flow.

"At one time this was great, when you were allowed to deduct your losses from your income taxes," explains Broussard. "Since the Tax Reform Act of 1986, the rules have changed. Negative cash-flow deductions are now limited and, therefore, it would be unprofitable for you to invest in this type of property."

Buying Commercial Real Estate: Limited Partnerships and REITs

Want to own commercial property like a shopping center or apartment complex without ever having to lift a finger? If club members have limited money and expertise, a real-estate limited partnership and REIT are viable alternatives. In a *limited partnership*, a small legion of investors band together to develop and directly own a particular property or several properties—apartments, office buildings, shopping centers, business parks, and mini-warehouses. The properties are usually professionally managed.

As discussed in Chapter 4, a *limited partner* is an investor and a *general partner* handles all management duties and assumes unlimited liability. As limited partners, club members would have limited liability—bearing responsibility for only the amount they contribute—and would enjoy the benefits of investing in real estate projects they ordinarily would not be able to afford.

A real-estate limited partnership that is offered to the public must be registered with the SEC. This means that partners must disclose every bit of information about the properties to potential investors. This disclosure document, called a *prospectus*, should be read from cover to cover by every single member of the club before plunking down any money.

Your club may not get to boast that it owns Trump Tower or the Twin Towers, however, registered limited partnerships are large offerings. They typically are in the $50 million or more range. The money is used to buy several properties that are expected to turn a profit.

Individual investors can get in usually for as little as $2,500 to $5,000. When selecting a registered limited partnership, look for one with a long-term track record in both rising and falling market tides. Check out *The Strange Register,* a publication that is available in most brokerage offices and some libraries, which rates registered limited partnerships.

Another type of limited partnership is made available through a private placement. In this case, a general partner can have up to 35 limited partners. Typically, the partners pool between $10,000 and $100,000 from each investor to buy or develop property.

The money your club invests can be paid in annual installments over five years or more. Since the SEC does not require the general partner to register the partnership, such a deal must be thoroughly scrutinized because of the high risk.

Before tax reform, private partnerships were used by the wealthy to obtain tax breaks. They were able to deduct twice the amount they invested from their income taxes. Since the Tax Reform Act of 1986, the amount that can be deducted is substantially lower.

The one major problem with investing in real estate is liquidity. You can't sell real estate as quickly as you can stocks or bonds. Once you fork over your share, you'll have to wait until the partnership sells the property to make a profit, which could take several years. If you are concerned about liquidity, consider buying shares of real-estate investment trusts (REITs).

REITs trade like stocks (you can buy and sell shares anytime) and work somewhat like mutual funds (in that they are pooled investments). An equity REIT invests in properties, like a limited partnership, that it thinks will produce a steady stream of income and/or appreciation. The required cash outlay for this type of investment can vary from $1,000 to $5,000.

REITs must pay their shareholders 95 percent of the rental and interest income they receive. The yield on REITs can range from 6 percent to 12 percent annually. Since REITs trade like stocks, their share prices rise and fall with the stock market. Keep your shares for at least three to five years, at which time managers are most likely to sell some properties and pay out the profits to shareholders.

There are more than 300 REITs publicly traded on the market. Find those invested in well-managed and in good locations. There are Web sites that provide listings of REITs as well as other useful information on property management and investing. One such site worth pursuing is www.realtymall.com.

WEALTH ACCUMULATION THROUGH ENTREPRENEURIAL VENTURES

Before your club ventures out, you need to focus on building up your stock portfolio. For the first eight years of operation, the Omega Diversified Investment Consortium invested strictly in stocks and mutual funds. Members concentrated on a small group of holdings: eight companies, including Oracle, AT&T, and Granite Broadcasting.

The Omegas also purchased shares in 10 mutual funds, staking out a claim in emerging and foreign markets by investing in the Calvert New Africa Fund and Templeton Developing Markets Fund. Investing with a conscience, the group also owns shares in Ariel Capital Funds, managed by Chicago-based Ariel Capital Management Inc.

Such socially responsible funds generally shy away from tobacco, alcohol, gambling, or defense industries. They also steer clear of industries that cause environmental problems. At the same time, they look for companies with good community relations or workplace diversity. Despite those stringent criteria, these funds often purchase stocks in the same trailblazing sectors—technology, healthcare, software, and the Internet—that other funds hold.

The group started out small—having just finished college together—investing $25 a month. Since that time, contributions have escalated every year. The minimum monthly dues are now up to $150. Some members toss in a little extra to sweeten the pot, contributing as much as $500. Today, the average age of the Omega men is about 35 and their professions cut across a wide spectrum, from bank executives to engineers.

The enterprising Omegas landed their first venture deal in 1989 when they purchased their first radio station, in Daytona Beach, Florida, changing the format from country-western to urban adult contemporary. It wasn't long before they purchased two other stations.

"We had considered a lot of different deals, but we found that communications is one of the areas in which African Americans are

still underrepresented," explains Hicks, a vehicle safety engineer with Ford Motor Company in Dearborn, Michigan.

"With three radio stations in hand, we rank within the top 20 percent of African Americans that hold positions in the communications market. This is significant because communications properties control how information is disseminated to our communities."

The members did a market analysis of each station and looked at the average rate of return on investment. As a group, "African Americans often don't look at these million-dollar radio stations as viable options because they can't always come up with the money," says Hicks, who notes that the investment club purchased its last station for over $1 million dollars, which is about the going rates these days. "Within one to five years, you can expect to see a return on your investment of about five million dollars." Radio stations make their money primarily three ways: through advertising, sponsorship, and the actual sale of the station for a profit.

Taking a hands-on approach, three of the club's partners left their corporate jobs to serve as general managers of the stations. "We had a member who was a physician, who rolled up his practice and uprooted his family. He has turned out to be our expert in the communications industry, working closely with our acquisitions for the past two years." Hicks is quick to point out though, "He had five years of on-the-job training before he actually quit his job. He spent that time doing research and learning as much as he could about the field."

Meanwhile, the club has done some outreach with local civic and social groups. "For example," says Hicks, "there was a church that wanted to deliver meals to college students, but they didn't have the funds to purchase stoves or vans. They couldn't get a traditional loan from the bank, so we made a short-term loan to them to get things up and running."

But the Omega men didn't just part with their money freely; they put the church group through the rigors of writing a business plan. "After we made them cross all of the t's and dot all of the i's, we loaned the money—$10,000, which they repaid in less than a year,"Hicks says. "By training them how to write a business plan and teaching them the steps needed to collateralize a loan, they were able to go out and secure a bigger loan from a commercial lender."

Currently, the group invests primarily through DRIPs. Hicks says the group's short-term plans are to change their investment mix by moving away from the capital ventures and moving toward some

extensive stock purchasing to shore up their holdings. Part of their long-term plan is to roll out an investment program that other college alumni organizations, fraternities, sororities, churches, and the like, can use to model their clubs after.

Right now, the members of the Omega Diversified Investment Club are working with the Coalition of Black Investors (COBI). In fact, Hicks serves as national VP of marketing for COBI and leads workshops throughout the Detroit area on how to start an investment club.

Much like Omega Diversified, the Washington Women's Investment Club started 12 years ago as a mechanism for making group investments. "At first, I thought people wouldn't welcome the idea and would be reluctant to put up the initial investment we were asking to join," recalls Sherri Blount, one of the club's founders.

Initially, members invested $500 each to start the club and paid monthly dues of $50 (dues now average about $70 a month). A pleasant surprise: Everyone who was invited to the first meeting not only showed up, but joined, according to Blount, who at the time was associate general council for Public Broadcasting Service (PBS). The careers of the 21 women represented ran the spectrum from an elementary-school teacher to a CEO of a Fortune 500 company subsidiary. The average age of a member was 38. What set WWIC apart from other clubs was a devotion to entrepreneurial ventures.[4]

Initially, WWIC established both an entrepreneurial ventures committee to investigate opportunities in new or existing businesses, and a franchise committee to explore franchise opportunities. The franchise committee evaluated the feasibility of acquiring a McDonald's, Krispy Kreme Doughnuts, and Diet Center outlet. After two years, the group concluded that they lacked the necessary resources to purchase any of the more popular franchises. Subsequently, the committee was merged with the entrepreneurial ventures committee.

Usually, the committee comes up with an idea for a specific business project and, if adopted, the members work as a group to implement it. Special projects will allow club members to become knowledgeable about business operations and to make the same kinds of decisions that small business owners and corporate executives make daily.

Business opportunities are usually found through personal contacts that club members have in the business world. Friends who are in management positions often know of successful businesses that are growing and need additional capital to expand.

Many members will already be affiliated with professional and political organizations, social clubs, civic groups, churches, or other

groups that sponsor banquets, picnics, bazaars, arts-and-crafts shows, or other events. Your club could contact these groups and offer to plan the event for free or arrange to handle a certain aspect, such as entertainment, for a percentage of the profits.

Also, talk to sororities, fraternities, and political organizations to determine what types of services they will need at their annual or regional convention. Submit a proposal to provide one of the services identified or offer to provide some other unique service or product.

Six months after WWIC was organized, it participated in a joint venture with the National Bar Association to sell convention souvenirs. Since one-third of the members were lawyers, it comes as no surprise that the legal community was the impetus for WWIC's first outside venture. In exchange for a free booth in the convention's exhibit hall, WWIC shared profits derived from the sale of the NBA memorabilia.

The women used money in their treasury to pay for the inventory. Rotating shifts, WWIC staffed the booth for 10 hours a day during the five-day event. The product mix included coffee mugs, athletic bags, and tee-shirts embossed with the bar association's logo. However, the hottest-selling item was ceramic dolls called Little Lawyers.

The dolls were individually designed, molded, baked, and creatively decorated by WWIC. Some of the figurines wore kente cloth shawls, others sported dashikis. The women crafted everything from female judges with short Afros to young clerks with dreadlocks. WWIC realized a modest profit from the venture.

In 1988, WWIC considered investing in artwork, and decided to sponsor an art sale. At the art affair, they exhibited and sold the works of approximately 20 local and national artists, including Gayle Fulton-Ross, Time Francis, Jacob Lawrence, Phoebe Beasley, and James Denmark. To cover overhead expenses, they charged a nominal fee.

WWIC sold the artists' work on a consignment basis, and divided the profits with the artist. A portion of the proceeds was donated to fund the creation of a mural in the women's dining room of a local homeless shelter and to fund a scholarship for a local graduating senior at the Duke Ellington High School of the Arts. WWIC netted a substantial profit from this project and decided to make it an annual event.

As the women became more experienced at judging the value of art, they increased the variety and the quality of the offerings. They became more knowledgeable about selecting, pricing, and delivering the pieces. Each year, they tried to improve the event by avoiding prior mistakes.

Hosting the annual art show has helped the women to develop skills that are useful in other investment ventures. In fact, members have learned about investing in art and many have acquired art work for investment purposes.

WWIC was approached by well-known African-American artist Gayle Fulton-Ross about investing in a direct-mail and marketing art studio that would promote her works as well as those of emerging artists. Since Fulton-Ross had participated in WWIC's art shows, members were familiar with her talents.

Her proposal called for the production of six lithographs of women, which she would sell via mail order. As the Fulton-Ross Collection expanded its stable of artists, their works would be promoted in the same manner. WWIC was impressed with this marketing strategy, because it had the potential to offer consumers easy access to high-quality, reasonably priced artwork. It also established a method for reaching consumers who lacked knowledge about art and might be intimidated by galleries, or who were located in areas far from galleries.

The agreement provided for WWIC's full investment to be returned, and for WWIC to receive a percentage of the business profits for a specified time. It also required that WWIC have one representative on the board of directors of the Fulton-Ross Collection.[5]

How to Evaluate Entrepreneurial Ventures as Potential Investments

As an alternative to approaching banks and venture capitalists, many fledgling entrepreneurs are raising expansion dollars through a *private placement,* whereby they offer stock in the business to a small pool of investors. Normally, a company will sell ownership of between 20 percent and 35 percent, and offer a return on investment that is greater than 20 percent.

Selling stock in a small enterprise is no different than selling stock on the New York Stock Exchange, in that price is determined by profit potential, not asset value. Typically, offerings are priced between $2 and $5 per share, with most companies requiring a minimum investment of between $500 and $1,000. Shares are offered as preferred stock, common stock, or debt securities (loans).

If your club is offered a private placement, there are two articles you will want to request:

- *Business plan.* All key elements must be present, including mission statement, product/service description, competitive analysis, market potential, management plan, income statement, balance sheet, three- to five-year projections on cash flow, and profit and loss.
- *Prospectus document.* Each investor should receive a copy of this memorandum, which must spell out how the stock is to be sold and how the money will be used to achieve the objectives of the business plan.

Not every marketing proposal and business plan that WWIC comes across is financed. Finch notes that there are several factors that the members analyze in the business plan before parting with a penny of the club's investment dollars:

- *Financial statements.* Review the financial status of the business to determine if it is currently operating at a profit or loss. Assess future financial needs to see whether the business will have a cash flow problem that could immediately eat up your investment or whether an investment of capital will ensure long-term growth. For new businesses, review the break-even analysis and the cash flow projections. This should help your club determine if the business has sufficient money to operate until a profit can be realized. Undercapitalization can be fatal. Your club does not want to invest in a company that is struggling to survive.
- *Management team.* Smart money invests in people. Meet with the principals of the business being considered to assess their experience, goals, and responsibilities. Examine their personal background, education, employment history, and industry experience. If expertise is lacking in certain areas, assess what the business needs to do to fill those gaps in the short and long run.
- *Market audience.* Identify and review their customer base. Look for a demographic profile, including age, sex, income, and size of the overall market, as well as a psychographic one, which includes values, lifestyles, interests, buying habits, and affinities of the target audience. Evaluate competition—does the company have a patent for a new product, proprietary technology, access to a scarce resource, greater distribution outlets, or a signature product/service?

- *Marketing plan.* Review the company's product, promotion, and distribution plans. Analyze data obtained from test marketing. Assess the product mix to determine its feasibility and marketability, and overall standing in the industry. Analyze the product's price, making sure it is high enough to cover expenses and make a profit, and that it is competitive and not out of line with what consumers are willing to pay. Evaluate the methods of promoting the product for cost effectiveness, and to ensure that advertisements and other promotional materials are reaching the right audience. Examine distribution methods to determine whether the product is easily obtainable or if it needs to be made available in additional outlets.

Never lose sight of the fact that your club's stake in an entrepreneurial venture or private placement will be highly speculative and risky. Such investments can generate high returns, so it is possible that club members could see a 100 percent return on their investment.

"But the reality," warns investment advisor Baunita Greer, "is that nine out of 10 times, investors never see their money again. If a person is comfortable with that possible loss, then fine. But I've seen too many investors fall prey to get-rich-quick schemes, thinking that they are going to take $2,000 and turn it into $20,000 overnight."

WWIC's Finch points out, "We built up our stock portfolio before we ever began investing in other areas. We quickly accumulated wealth because we got in the market on the Tuesday after Black Monday, when prices dropped. So, we were able to buy issues that we would have not been able to afford," including American Express, Toys 'R' Us, Reebok International, and Tiffany & Co.

CONCLUSION

Despite the adventurous nature of risk-takers like the Washington Women Investment Club, Omega Diversified Investment Club, and the Millionaire Men's Investment Group, the most active group in all three clubs remains their investment committee, which handles bond, stock, and mutual funds purchases. Securities continue to make up more than 50 percent of these club's total holdings.

Make no mistake about it: Investing beyond securities is risky business. It is true that by diversifying your portfolio your club is

minimizing the risks and maximizing possible gains. It is important for members to understand that it may take a while before they see a return on their investment. With real estate, it could take 10 to 15 years before your club realizes a profit. The same holds true for business ventures that might go completely bust after five years.

To play it safe, your club should try not to invest more than 15 percent of its portfolio in real estate, private placements, or any other highly speculative investments. It won't hurt to take a small percentage of your funds—about 3 percent—to sponsor community-related events, from toy drives to neighborhood block parties, or to give local youth college scholarships.

Just remember that when it comes to building wealth the primary tool for your club will be investing in securities. Your club can indeed reach that million-dollar mark by keeping its portfolio invested 100 percent in stocks over the long term.

14

NEVER TOO YOUNG TO INVEST: BUILDING YOUTH INVESTMENT CLUBS

Education is your passport to the future, for tomorrow belongs to the people who prepare for it today.

—El-Hajj Malik El-Shabazz (Malcolm X)

Generation Net is the latest label assigned to today's teens, presumably because they are lost souls in the technological world of the Internet and high-tech computer games. However, if you ask Amadi Anene and his friends "What's the dealie-yo?" they will tell you that they are part of a new power generation—teen investors.

The Detroit native is cofounder and vice president of the Young Investors Club, a group of eleven young men ranging in age from 12 to 15. The three-year-old club owns shares in three companies, entertainment titan Walt Disney, wireless communications firm Datalink, and fashion powerhouse Donna Karan International.

Like most of his peers, 13-year-old Anene spends much of his allowance and cash gifts on video games and sports gear—the young athlete is a power forward on his junior high school's basketball team. He also diligently sets aside at least 25 percent of his $15 two-week allowance to invest in the stock market.

Anene is following in the footsteps of his mother, Janet, who is cofounder of the Mainstream Investment Club. He wants to learn as

much as he can about the stock market, "I like investing and buying different stocks, because it's a good way to accumulate wealth and to put money back into your own pockets."[1]

The Young Investors Investment Club is one of dozens of youth-run investment clubs popping up across the country. In fact, about 10 percent of the membership of NAIC, which tracks investment club activity, is under the age of 30.

That's a marked change from past perceptions of teens as notoriously big spenders. A growing number of adolescents believe they should expend as much effort investing their money as they do throwing away wads of cash on a variety of consumer items.

By belonging to an investment club at an early age, a teen will have a better understanding of the value of money. It's a more effective and more real means for your teenager and his or her peers to learn about money, power, and respect.

Stocks influence several aspects of American life, including finance, politics, and entertainment. They show, for example, how the economy is becoming truly global. The Japanese company Nintendo, for example, is a perennial favorite of young American investors.

Starting out, a youth-run club may just be learning the benefits of owning a piece of America. But one day, junior investors may well put their financial savvy to use working in the halls of corporate America, trading on Wall Street, or running their own companies.

LEARNING THE FINANCIAL FACTS OF LIFE

If you think parents have dry mouths and sweaty palms when it's time to tell their children about the birds and the bees, try to get them to sit down and teach their kids the ABCs of money, and how it is spent and accumulated. It's a real chore.

Part of the problem is that most people, especially African Americans, didn't acquire financial knowledge when they were young and, by the time they are older, barriers stand between them and their money, which they tend to put in low-interest-bearing checking and savings accounts.

They never learned how to manage money instead of being managed by it—becoming overwhelmed with debt. And, of course, children learn by example. Experts say that it is important that parents discuss family finances with their children. Let them see you paying

monthly bills. Show them that they need to have a budget and learn to save to buy the things that they need and want.

The worst thing a parent can do is to shower their kids with expensive toys and clothes that carry a certain status, says financial advisor Cheryl Broussard. "This could have a detrimental effect by not developing an attitude of self-sufficiency and bringing about ungrateful kids who suffer from the instant-gratification syndrome."

As a result she adds, "They may not be willing to start out at the bottom and work their way up the career ladder or work for minimum wage. Instead, they may resort to illegal means of obtaining money—the underground economy—to obtain instant wealth."

Young people need to have an appreciation of the American economic system and better understand how capitalism works in order to get a headstart in the world of investments. Ideally, this financial education process should begin by age five, although even preschoolers know a quarter equals 25 cents and is worth more than a dime.

The springtime of one's life—adolescence—marks mental, physical, and social growth but also should include financial development. If your children are under 20 and you want them to have some skills, there are several lessons you need to teach them about money management:

- *Learn to respect money.* For most kids, pennies, nickels, and dimes are no longer considered real money. "That is one of my pet peeves with children, because they will throw a penny away without thinking twice. I have my kids put into a jar whatever loose change they find," says financial advisor Gail Perry-Mason, who has three boys aged 5, 8, and 14. "I asked them to do this every day and to tell me how much they have collected at the end of the month," she adds. You can do the same. You may find the end result astounding—a financial take of anywhere from $40 to $50 a month. That's not chump change.

- *Create a budget.* Budgeting begins with tracking expenses every month (school supplies, CDs, movies, snacks, clothing, and so forth). Your child should write down every single thing that he spends so that he has a complete picture of what items he bought and how much they cost. Review this information to see if there are ways you can help your child spend money more effectively and efficiently.

- *Save and invest money.* Every child should begin receiving an allowance somewhere between the ages of three and six. By age 12,

young people should be able to conduct their own transactions. If you haven't done it already, open up a savings and brokerage account for your child; see that they set aside at least 10 percent of the money earned from odd jobs, allowances, and received cash gifts. Encourage your child not to blow $100 on a new toy that will end up in the closet after a couple of weeks when the excitement has worn off. Also, encourage relatives to give the gift of stock certificates for holidays, birthdays, and other special occasions.

- *Read, read, read.* Encourage your child to scan the business and financial sections of the local newspaper and the *Wall Street Journal,* and to learn to read the stock tables—don't be afraid of the numbers, it's just dollars-and-cents. Have them subscribe to magazines and newsletters, such as *Family Money, Black Enterprise for Teens* and *Kidpreneur News,* and watch television business programs, such as CNN's *Moneyline,* CNBC's *Money Talk,* and PBS's *Wall Street Week,* to hear what the pros are saying about the market and the economy. Remember: Knowledge is power, and power creates wealth.

- *Create a financial plan.* Just like adults, children need to define financial goals: Looking to buy a car? Take a trip abroad? Or to finance a college education? They should write down their goals. Analyze the different paths they might take. Weigh the pros and cons of each. How much it will cost and how long it will take to accomplish their goals.

- *Use credit wisely.* Debt has become the American way of life, but it should be avoided. As soon as teens turn age 18 and start college, credit card companies will bombard them with offers. Don't believe the hype. Credit should be reserved for those special purchases and expenses whereby it makes economic sense, such as for a car, college tuition, or house, or for emergency purposes. There may be occasions when it's not as convenient to pay by cash, for instance, for Internet or catalogue purchases. Use a debit or check bank card instead.

BUYING GOODS AND SERVICES INTELLIGENTLY

Another important money-management skill is knowing how to get your money's worth from the things that you buy, says Jeffery Fox, a securities analyst and director of investment education at NAIC. Most experts say

that, by age 10, a child ought to understand comparison shopping and the value of merchandise, as well as the principles of banking and saving. By the time a teen lands that first job at Burger King, he or she should understand the basics of investing.

Today's youth have more money at their disposal in allowances and aftertax earnings than their parents did at the same age. According to Teenage Research Unlimited, a market research firm based in Northbrook, Illinois, by the end of 1998, teens had pumped a cool $141 billion into the economy through such purchases as soft drinks, CDs, fast food, clothes, computer games, movies, and athletic footwear.

Fox adds that the investing concept had never really been explained to teens before, but thanks to the efforts of clubs and other investment education groups, they now realize that they can put their money into securities that will grow over time, rather than into material goods that lose value. Instead of spending $10 to $20 per month on such items as soda, candy, and movies, these young investors are putting money into the stock market.

Fox is the editor of *Investing for Life,* a young investor's self-study course that covers general personal finance and investing. The course workbook exposes youth to a detailed strategy for selecting and buying common stock and investing using various stock-study tools. It also is designed to encourage adult–youth mentoring relationships.

The great thing about youth-run investment clubs is that it is a real adventure in learning how to obtain financial assets. For the first time in their lives, says Fox, many of these young people are experiencing that they are in control and that they have an important choice to make—they can either spend or invest their money.[2]

The advice Fox espouses: "Plan your purchases and avoid impulse buying; practice comparison shopping and check prices at different locations and develop the art of creative purchasing, which means buying generic brands, wholesale, bulk, or secondhand goods."

REAPING THE BENEFITS OF INVESTING

Learning the basics of investing will give you extra credit in the classroom. For instance, stock prices are reported as fractions, an important math concept for grade-schoolers. But, since basic math is anathema to most kids, how can you get them excited about stock splits, P/E ratios, and betas? What's the big payoff?

Getting your young comrades interested in stocks pays dividends—literally. Consider this: $10,000 invested 16 years ago in McDonald's—a favorite among small-fry investors—would be worth $75,000 today. Put another way: That original $10,000 would have been enough to fund four years of tuition at many colleges.

Belonging to an investment club not only helps you accumulate wealth as a group, it can help you fill your own treasure chest with stocks. Perry-Mason's oldest son, Brandon, who is 14 and the director of research for the Young Investors Investment Club, has a stock portfolio worth more than $25,000.

Brandon, who plans to use the money to help pay for college, owns shares in over 20 companies, including Donna Karan, Rain Forest Café, Disney, Forest Glade, Hasbro, Board Kids Entertainment, Viacom, Campbell Soup, and Colgate-Palmolive. Brandon's bedroom walls—as well as those of his younger brothers—are covered with framed stock certificates of each company—a reminder that he is a company owner.

In addition, researching companies by following developments in the newspaper and magazines improves reading and communications skills. For older children, learning how stock prices relate to corporate performance means grasping a range of complex economic principles.

INVESTING FROM A CONSUMER PERSPECTIVE

Aside from their youthful exuberance for the stock market, young investment clubs tend to hook into one of the key tenets of wealth accumulation—invest in companies with familiar products. Most are shareholders of the very same businesses of which they are big consumers, including fast-food giants, like McDonald's; footwear companies, such as Nike; and high-tech companies, such as Microsoft.

Each month, members of the Young Investors Investment Club meet and report on their stock of choice. Anene had been eyeing three: Wendy's International, Sara Lee, and Coca-Cola. After examining the stocks' fundamental data—their price and earnings history—he settled on Coca-Cola, but not for the club's portfolio; instead, he decided to purchase shares in the soft drink maker to help jump start his own personal portfolio.

"I had been following Coke for a while," the junior high school student explains. "We buy a lot of Coke for the house. The company

also puts out a lot of other products that we buy. So I felt it was a good stock to buy." Every time he sees someone tilt their head and gulp down a can of Coke, Anene knows that he's getting paid.

While stock-picking teens like Anene may not be in the same league as financial guru Warren Buffett, they are well on their way. Teens tend to use more common sense when investing than adults, says Gail Perry-Mason, who acts as the Young Investors' broker and counselor.

She cites, for example, the NBA Players Association strike, which affected the 1998 basketball season. The club wanted to buy shares in Nike, because they felt that, once the strike was over, there would be an increase in product demand for the number one athletic shoemaker. "Adults tend to track a stock for two to three months, looking only at P/E ratios and earnings per share," says Perry-Mason. "Sometimes they take so long researching a stock that they miss the boat."

Younger investors tend to be more aggressive. But that's no worry, says NAIC's Jeff Fox. "They have half a century to invest their money and wait out market cycles; that means mistakes are often swept away with time."

Don't be misled into thinking that the stock market is kid stuff. The S.G. Junior Investment Club (SGJIC), a group made up mainly of boys and girls belonging to St. George's Episcopal church in northwest Washington, DC, is busy dissecting annual reports and investigating trends whenever members aren't busy with Bible studies or prayer meetings.

Currently, 30 industrious kids, from 11 to 18 years of age, belong to SGJIC. Besides the currently active members, 11 alumni who've graduated from high school and moved on to college are still enthusiastic enough to send in dues each month, as does SGJIC's cofounder and former president, a 19-year-old college junior named Michele Campbell, and her twin sister, Renee, who was the club's vice president.

SGJIC started in January 1996 with an initial investment of $750, pooled from a $50 initial investment put up by its 15 original members. The concepts of investing may have been very elementary, but members learned to do fundamental and technical research. They engaged in learning to select and analyze stocks using basic tools of the trade.

These faithful investors met once a month in the basement of the church, paying $5 in monthly dues. Through the process of investing regular amounts of money in a group of diversified growth stock companies, along with reinvesting all dividends, the club watched its

investments grow to just short of $10,000 the first year (see Figure 14.1). Since its start-up—thanks to a roaring bull market—the club has built a portfolio valued at over $25,000, with holdings in 14 companies including Nike, Coca-Cola, America Online, Staples, and Reebok.

Just like SGJIC, any youth club will want to carefully research companies that have favorable investment characteristics. Members will have to learn the key components of assessing a company and its product. Things to consider: Is the product the top of the line? How many units are they likely to sell? Does the product have good marketing behind it? Does the product have longevity?

SGJIC also has five adult sponsors who serve as advisors, a common practice of teen clubs. Grownups from a church congregation, coaches, teachers, or group counselors can help youngsters form an investment club. Consult the NAIC about locating local adult investment clubs.

Fox notes that it is important that investment club members take time to teach the next generation of investors. In turn, youth clubs can help one another to build the foundation of investment knowledge.

Forming a Youth-Run Club

Why are youth investment clubs so popular? For one, they're quite easy to set up. They're organized and run the same way as any other club. They must choose members, select officers, set a date for meetings, and collect monthly dues. They have to open a brokerage and bank account, write bylaws, and form a legal partnership.

The only real difference is that parents have to sign custodial agreements with the partnership, since members are too young to buy stocks on their own. This way, junior members don't end up actually owning shares until they turn age 18.

As with adult clubs, the first place to begin is by recruiting other youth who want to own a piece of America. Teens can talk to fellow students. If they sing in a choir or attend Sunday school, they can solicit younger church members. They can call on sports teammates to start an investment club. Also, they shouldn't overlook social and civic organizations, such as the Boy Scouts and Girl Scouts. These members may "be prepared" to invest their money wisely in the stock market.

When it comes to setting up a club, older investors tend to make things more complicated, notes Perry-Mason. "Young people run their

Figure 14.1   St. George's Junior Investment Club of Washington, DC

| | | | | December 19, 1997 | | | |
Company	Shares Held	Average Cost per Share	Total Cost	Market Price per Share	Total Value	Percent of Total	Total Gain (Loss)
America Online	10	$30.00	$ 300	82.625	$ 826	9.0%	$526
Bet Holdings	14	33.00	462	53.250	745	8.1	283
Callaway Golf Co.	5	43.50	217	27.500	138	1.5	(79)
The Coca-Cola Co.	5	60.40	302	65.500	328	3.5	26
Coca-Cola Enterp.	12	20.67	248	33.125	397	4.3	149
GreenTree Finance	10	37.47	375	25.000	250	2.7	(125)
Kmart Corporation	20	17.53	351	11.000	220	2.4	(131)
McDonald's Corp.	14	55.57	778	46.000	644	7.0	(134)
Mills Corporation	10	28.75	287	24.000	240	2.6	(47)
NIKE, Inc. "B"	13	65.66	854	40.125	522	5.7	(332)
Reebok International	10	36.60	366	28.625	286	3.1	(80)
Staples, Inc.	10	22.90	229	26.000	260	2.8	31
Cash			4,358		4,358	47.3	—
Total			$9,127		$9,214	100.0%	$ 87

meetings with the same parliamentary proceedings but they don't have as many committees as adult clubs."

Just as their elder counterparts do, younger club members put a high price on individual participation. Dues for the Young Investors group are $7 a month, but anyone who fails to come up with his share gets hit with an extra $2 late fee.

Members of club's like SCJIC and Young Investors take what they do very seriously. In general, young investors will want to adhere to the same key objectives outlined by these clubs to:

- Realize an annual average rate of return of 15 percent or better on their investments.
- Teach others about the principles of economics and money management.
- Pick up a basic understanding of the stock market and modes of investing.
- Engage in fund-raising activities to help grow the club's assets.
- Invest long term and require members to stick with the group at least until they graduate from high school.

The Detroit Ladies of Wall Street managed to raise $500 by selling 50 copies of a poetry book (at $10 apiece) donated by a local writer. Formed in the summer of 1999, the group has 15 members—all girls. The investment club is divided, practically in half, between seven to 12-year-olds, who pay $7 in monthly dues, and 13- to 17-year-old members, who contribute $10 each month.

"In order to join the club, we required members to research a stock. We gave them a time limit to come back and present their findings before the group," says Lloryn Ruth Love, the club's president and cofounder. Members also were asked to hand in autobiographies and to give a speech on what special talents they had to bring to the group.

Love sees herself as a natural leader, with credentials such as having been a member of the National Honor Society, Student Council, Students Against Drunk Driving, and the Voices of Union Choir. The 17-year-old high school senior also is a graduate of Junior Statesmen of America associated with Northwestern Illinois University, and the HOBY leadership team sponsored by Eastern Michigan University.

Financial leaders of tomorrow, the Detroit Ladies review each stock for six months. "We look at whether the stock has gone up or down in price," says Love. "If it has remained in a positive position, we will consider it further as a stock buy." The group's first purchase was shares of Sara Lee Corporation. Other holdings include McDonald's and fashion maven Tommy Hilfiger.

The young sages learned early that "if you use a certain product, you need to buy shares in that company. It doesn't benefit you to just buy the product," explains Love. "If you are an owner in the company, you can take advantage of discounts and other perks. Companies make money from us, so why can't we make money from them."

Bitten by investors' fever, Love has begun to build her own stock portfolio. In addition to using the money to contribute toward college tuition and other costs, she is concerned about her long-term financial well-being. "I know social security won't be available when I get older. Also, I may have to take care of my parents one day," adds Love, who will attend Howard University in the fall of 2000, majoring in corporate law with a minor in business.

Learning about the stock market could open doors to a host of highly paid occupations, from Wall Street and beyond. A bit of financial knowledge can go a long way. Understanding how companies work and earn profits gives teens insight into many career opportunities

beyond the investment field, including such areas as accounting, business management, and law.

When one is young, it is difficult not to follow the crowd and give in to the pressure to buy now and pay later. It takes self-discipline to resist the temptation of immediate gratification. It takes an independent spirit to see through the advertising images of the good life and testimonials by celebrities, athletes, and music artists sporting platinum and ice one day and crying bankrupt the next. It's important that you teach your children to believe in themselves—their ability to plan and manage their lives.

STOCKS 'R' US: PLAYING WALL STREET'S STOCK MARKET GAMES

As part of a national drive to make young Americans more proficient in economics and finance, a number of investment-education programs are surfacing. At least a half-dozen stock games are being played nationwide today. Better still, more African-American finance pros are sponsoring programs of their own, steering youth to the stock market.

This gives young people a leg up on money management. No one knows this better than stock specialist Alan Bond, president and chief investment officer of New York City-based Bond, Procope Capital Management. "When I was 10 years old, my family went to Disney World," he recalls. "When we got back, my parents said, 'We've got $5,000 to put in the stock market; what should we buy?'"

"I said I thought we should invest in Walt Disney, because it was so much fun; Delta Airlines, because it flew us there; and GM (General Motors Corp.) because we had rented one of their cars." Good thing his parents listened: Over the next decade, those three stocks soared and helped pay for Bond's four years at Dartmouth College.

Today, Bond shares his market smarts with inner-city youngsters. For 12 years, he has sponsored "A Day on Wall Street," a program that includes a visit to the floor of the New York Stock Exchange and lunch in its ornate, *beaux-arts* boardroom, and helps teach youngsters that the products they use can open the door to investments and profits.

Based on his own childhood experience, Bond, now 37, encourages kids to invest in brand-name companies, but his young charges don't place bets on a whim. Under Bond's program, students from New York City public schools buy imaginary stock after they have done careful research.[3]

If your children want to learn about the market and test their stock-picking prowess before investing any real money, they should check out national stock-market programs.

The Stock Market Game™ *(212-618-0519)*. The nation's first effort to bring Wall Street into the classroom was the Stock Market Game, launched in 1977 by the Securities Industry Association (SIA). Today, the 10-week simulation program helps boost morale for hundreds of thousands of kids from coast to coast by giving them confidence in their ability to invest money. Grades four through college compete against one another during the fall and spring semesters. Players start out with an imaginary $100,000, which they can invest in any stock listed on the American Stock Exchange, New York Stock Exchange, or the over-the-counter markets tracked by Nasdaq. They can borrow another $100,000 in a margin account, and they can short the stocks if they expect them to fall in price.

NAIC Trustee Robert Wynn is working in conjunction with the National Council on Economic Education to establish the Wisconsin Economic Education Partnership, which consists of four components to:

1. Promote the participation in the Stock Market Game to central-city youth.
2. Provide intensive economics training to urban middle school and high-school teachers (eight-week program hosted by the University of Wisconsin each winter).
3. Offer a summer youth enterprise academy. Each June, this economics day camp targets 25 to 30 urban high-school students—mostly tenth graders—teaching them basic principles on business and stock ownership, as well as leadership skills.
4. Create enterprise youth investment clubs, taking the top five performers from the summer camp. Funded by grants from foundations and private donors, the first two clubs received $10,000 each to invest over a course of three years. The money, which is held in a trust, will be dispersed in equal shares to the students upon their graduation. The catch: They must attend college.

Also worth looking into is the CNBC Student Stock Tournament (http://sst.cnbc.com). Broadcast on CNBC and sponsored by Knight/Trimark Group Inc., the tournament is held during the fall and spring terms and is open to elementary and high school students. Teams

consist of three students and one parent or teacher advisor. The team whose portfolio has the greatest total return wins awards and prizes.

Over 600 colleges and universities nationwide use the Virtual Stock Exchange (virtualstockexchange.com), a simulated securities broker that provides mock trading of all securities listed on the major U.S. exchanges. Cornell and Stand University alumni founded it in 1997; they believed that hands-on experience would help students to better understand and appreciate both the practical and theoretical sides of investing.

To win these games means taking big risks. The most successful students trade actively—a strategy that is practically *de rigeur* to win a game that lasts only a few weeks or months. Of course, such an investment philosophy is not synonymous with the principles practiced by NAIC-affiliated investment clubs. Conventional wisdom says that the best way to make money in stocks is to purchase the securities of sound, well-managed companies and hold them for years, oblivious to the day-to-day market volatility of common stocks.

There are certain risks these young investors will take with fake money that they wouldn't dare embark on if they had to part with their own hard-earned cash, but there does come a time when avid investors will want to swap phony money for the real thing.

Andre Brooks was a senior at Howard University in the nation's capitol when he participated in the AT&T Collegiate Investment Challenge in 1993 (the program has since been discontinued). He soon found more satisfaction investing through his Mo' Money Investment Club, which was founded in the fall of 1992. Playing the Challenge gave Brooks and his buddies more confidence to purchase real company stock. He notes: "Investing is a hands-on thing."[4]

Obviously, teens don't have to play one of these organized stock market games to learn about investing. Ideally, they should begin to amass some real money. Sometimes it pays to follow the lead of Nike's slogan: "Just Do It."

15

THE NEXT FRONTIER: LEARNING TO INVEST ON YOUR OWN

It takes a deep commitment to change and an even deeper commitment to grow.

—Ralph Ellison

Decide that you want it, more than you are afraid of it.

—Bill Cosby

Wipe the sweat from your brow, take a deep breath, and let out a sigh of relief. You have just navigated safely through the "mind" field of investment education. Your head didn't explode from information overload. To the contrary, you and your comrades should feel fired up—well on your way to running a successful investment club.

As you master this learn-by-doing approach to accumulating wealth as a group, you should start to build individual investment portfolios. While it is great to invest together, at some point, you will have to cut the umbilical cord and venture out on your own. One of the main purposes of setting up an investment club program is to encourage individual members to become self-reliant investors.

INVESTING STRATEGIES DIFFER AT DIFFERENT STAGES IN LIFE

Where do you begin? For every stage in life there are different financial strategies. You'll want to outline an investment plan for all seasons. For many people in their twenties, summer madness starts to take affect after college. Armed with a freshly minted degree, so-called Generation Nexters stake out their claim in the real world—not the one on MTV but in corporate America. That first real paycheck comes and the limits on credit cards rise.

Sounds like you? Your first notion probably is to go out and live the life you always dreamed of—phat crib, fly car, and designer clothes. But instead of living above and beyond your financial means, create a budget. Define the kind of lifestyle you want and measure that against your fiscal capacity to support that lifestyle. Anyone who is bringing home $1,500 a month but whose expenditures are $2,500 a month ought to know that something is wrong.

A common condition among people in their late twenties and early thirties is finding themselves in debt from their college days and early working years. They accumulated thousands of dollars of debt on their credit cards and spent more than they brought home in their paychecks. Now they feel as if they are going to spend the rest of their lives saddled with student loans and other high-interest payments. Don't fret it. If you are 35 or under, you are in your asset-building years. You have plenty of time to drive down your debt and ride out wide fluctuations in the stock market.

Financial challenges are sure to arise for those between the ages of 35 and 45. Changing family situations, such as marriage or remarriage, six-figure college educations for children, aging parents' needs, or career moves are dramatically putting the squeeze on finances. At the same rate, "Squeezers" are discovering their earning power is at the highest level it has ever been.

They are also taking notes from the lessons of Baby Boomers. Experience has taught them that their forties and fifties are no time to coast. It's now or never for them to get their financial houses in order. This not only refers to having a sound investment portfolio but adequate health coverage, life insurance, and estate plans.

The best way to deal with change is to prepare for it. So, if you are in the autumn of your life, start squirreling away as much money as you can. Work on reducing your income taxes. Look for tax-free or

tax-deferred vehicles (e.g., annuities, municipal bonds, and treasuries) to store your money. If you haven't done so already, participate in employer-sponsored salary-reduction plans (e.g., 401K, 403b, or cash balance account) or contribute to an Individual Retirement Account (IRA).Your strategy should be to improve the rate of return on your investments and overall net worth.

Get an early start on saving and investing in the springtime of your life (which was discussed in Chapter 14 on youth investment clubs) and you'll have the money you need when you retire. Unfortunately, too many retirees are encountering winters of discontent, simply because they didn't do a good job of planning ahead or they didn't bother to plan at all. They relied on other retirement sources that are quickly fading into the realm of nonexistence—company pensions and Social Security.

Life after salary doesn't have to be turbulent. You can rejoice at the thought of saying farewell to a long sentence of hard labor and hello to golden-year cruises and summer resorts. It just takes time and effort to become financially independent. Once you hit age 60, your investment strategy is to preserve capital.

When it comes to saving and investing, you might ask yourself, "How much money would it take to act my age?" There is a general rule of thumb that says subtract your age from 100 percent (see Figure 15.1). This will determine how much money you should invest in equities, says Eric McKissack of investment management firm, Ariel Capital Management, in Chicago.

Following this guideline: If you're 40, you should have 60 percent invested in stocks, while a 60-year-old should have 40 percent of his or her money invested in stocks. The idea is that your portfolio should become more conservative as you get closer to retirement age, because you will need to have access to your money much sooner.

If you start investing in your twenties, you'll end up with more money—and perhaps be able to retire earlier—than your older counterparts, advises Simone Thompson of New York-based Edward Jones Investments. Investing $100 a month, beginning at age 25, at an assumed rate of return of 12 percent, will grow to more than $1 million by age 65, says Thompson. If you wait until age 30, that $100 per month will only amount to $649,000 at age 65. So, you would need to invest $200 per month to reach the $1 million mark.

Omega Diversified Investment Club Chairman Charles Hicks hopes to be a millionaire within the next seven years. "There is a Bell

Figure 15.1   A Lifetime of Asset Allocation

The following asset allocation models are for six distinct types of investors.

Teen (Age 15)
Stocks 85%
Bond Funds 10%
Money Market Funds, CDs 5%

GenXer (Age 25)
Growth Stocks and Mutual Funds 75%
Municipal Bonds and Bond Funds 20%
Money Market Funds, CDs 5%

Thirty-Something (Age 30+)
Stocks 65%
International Stock Funds 15%
Municipal Bonds and Bond Funds 20%
Money Market Funds, CDs 10%

Mid-Lifer (Age 45)
Stocks 55%
International Stock Funds 5%
Municipal Bonds and Corporate Bonds 30%
Money Market Funds, CDs 10%

Baby Boomer (Age 55)
Stocks 45%
International Stock Funds 5%
High-Yield Corporate Bonds 30%
Money Market Funds, CDs 20%

Retiree (Age 65)
Stocks 35%
Bonds 20%
International Bond Funds 10%
Money Market Funds, CDs 35%

helicopter that I want to buy that costs $6 million," jokes Hicks, explaining why he has an aggressive stock portfolio that is heavily weighted in automotive and high-tech industries. He currently owns shares in such companies as AOL and Ford Motor Co., which stands to reason for the Ford employee of some 14 years.

Company stock is a popular offering in retirement plans. Hicks isn't unlike 41 percent of the 24 million Americans who are covered by 401K plans; he invests a good chunk of his nest egg in company shares. The crash-safety engineer and team leader is in good company—Ford is a blue-chip stock. You may work for an industry titan or at a technology firm whose shares are rocketing upward. Still, experts advise, put no more than 10 percent in one stock option, including company stock.

Hicks, who is 37, notes, "I didn't start investing on my own until after I joined the investment club. By being part of a club and working closely with COBI (Coalition of Black Investors), I have boned up a lot on investing over the years." To help him achieve his goals, Hicks is working closely with a broker and financial planner.

It's important that you seek out professional financial experts in such areas as tax, estate, and retirement planning. These moneywise gurus can be brokers, financial planners, certified pubic accountants, and/or registered financial consultants.

CLIMBING THE STAIRWAY TO A FINANCIAL HAVEN

Once you take your age and lifestyle into account, then what? To help you with your life's journey—whether you are in your twenties or sixties—here are ten steps to reaching financial wealth.

Step One: Assess Your Short-Term and Long-Term Financial Goals

Do you want to build wealth to start a business of your own? Fund Junior's college education—or your own? Buy that dream home or car? Pay off your student loans? Reduce your burden of credit-card debt? Secure a financially comfortable retirement lifestyle?

Use the financial planning worksheet (Figure 15.2) to list your financial goals, the amount needed to achieve them, and the time frame it will take for each. You want to end up with a financial plan that includes at least four components: (1) realistic monthly budget, (2) investment program, (3) tax and estate plan, and (4) retirement plan. Should you need professional help drafting a financial blueprint, seek out a financial planner. Get references from family, friends, or colleagues, or contact the Financial Planning Association at 303-759-4900.

Figure 15.2 Financial Planning Worksheet

<<< financialplanningworksheet >>>

Our first worksheet is designed to give you an overview of your
financial state, pointing out both strengths and weaknesses.

STEP 1: List your financial goals.

	Goal	Amount Needed	Time Frame
1	_____	$ _____	_____
2	_____	$ _____	_____
3	_____	$ _____	_____

For example, buying a house, paying off school loans, saving for additional educational expenses, paying off credit card debt, investing for retirement, etc.

STEP 2: Take stock of your net worth.

Your Assets		Your Debts	
Checking accounts	$ _____	Credit card balances	$ _____
Savings accounts	$ _____	School loans	$ _____
Money market account	$ _____	Car loans	$ _____
Cash value of life insurance	$ _____	Mortgage	$ _____
Bank CDs	$ _____	Other	$ _____
Mutual funds	$ _____		
Stocks	$ _____		
Bonds	$ _____		
IRA	$ _____		
401(k)	$ _____		
Other	$ _____		
TOTAL	$ _____	TOTAL	$ _____

Your Assets minus Your Debts = Your Net Worth

You could, of course, have more debts than assets, particularly if you have recently graduated and have yet to achieve your full earning potential. The amount of your net worth, positive or negative, is less important than the fact that you actually complete this worksheet and know where you stand. Taking stock of your finances is a critical tool to nudge you forward as a saver and investor. Finally, it also pays to remember that this Net Worth Worksheet captures your financial standing at one particular moment in time. Consequently, it is a good idea to figure out your net worth every six months or so to make sure that you are still on track.

STEP 3: Determine how much you need to save in order to meet your goals.

Obviously, the amount you need to save and invest is approximately the difference between what you want (your financial goals) and what you have (your net worth).

Total Amount of Your Goal minus Net Worth = Amount You Need to Save and Invest

STEP 4: Determine how much you need to save each month to meet your goals given the time frame that you outlined in Step 1.

STEP 5: Figure out where your earnings are going and where you may be able to adjust in order to meet your financial goals.

Your Total Monthly Income:

Your monthly salary or wages	$ _____
Dividends and interest	$ _____
TOTAL INCOME	$ _____

Your Total Monthly Expenses:

Rent or mortgage payment	$ _____
Utilities	$ _____
Telephone	$ _____
Cable	$ _____
Household maintenance	$ _____
Transportation/car payments	$ _____
Car maintenance	$ _____
Credit cards	$ _____
School loan payments	$ _____
Insurance	$ _____
Food	$ _____
Entertainment	$ _____
Medical	$ _____
Tuition/education	$ _____
Restaurants	$ _____
Dry cleaning	$ _____
Club memberships	$ _____
Vacations	$ _____
Other	$ _____
Savings and investments:	
IRA	$ _____
401(k)	$ _____
Other	$ _____
TOTAL EXPENSES	$ _____

Total Income minus Total Expenses = Net Monthly Cash Flow

Step Two: Take a Financial Snapshot of Your Life

First, tally your assets and debts, then subtract your debts from your assets to find out your net worth. Whether your net worth is positive isn't as important as the fact that you have a financial picture of where you stand. Over the years, you can retrace this simple sketch of your assets and its measure of your cash flow to determine just how far you've gone and how much farther remains.

Step Three: Reduce Your Credit-Card Debt

Pay yourself first by striving to have good cash flow and no debt. Don't send every penny you earn to credit-card companies. Develop the habit of saving every month while still paying your bills. You probably already have heard that it's a must to pay off credit cards and other high-interest lenders.

Let's say you have a household income of $70,000 and $16,000 in credit-card balances. It would take about one-third of your annual aftertax income to pay off that debt. If the balance isn't paid off, the interest will continue to accrue at about $3,000 per year.

If you have a credit card with an interest rate of 18 percent, paying off that loan is the equivalent of earning 18 percent after taxes, since the interest on a credit-card loan isn't deductible. If you can't pay off the debt completely, try to reduce it as much as you can. Other obligations, such as student loans bearing a 7 percent to 8 percent interest rate, should be paid off on schedule.

Step Four: Build a Cash Reserve

It's critical that you have an emergency fund in case a financial crisis arises. You or your partner might get downsized out of a job, or decide to stay home and raise a family. Financial planners suggest you save and invest a minimum of 10 percent of your income, although 25 percent or higher is a better figure to aim for. That may be more than you have at your disposal if you are strapped by student loan payments and a car note to boot. Stay calm. Start with whatever amount you can and increase it each year. Meanwhile, where do you stash your cash?

There's no getting around it: Your local bank has its sights on things other than giving you the highest possible interest rate. Forget a bank account with a wee 3 percent interest rate; open up a money-market mutual fund.

Money-market funds are designed to keep your principal—the amount that you have put into the fund—intact, and in essence function as a souped-up checking account. They pay a healthy amount of interest—currently as high as 5.8 percent—and allow you to draw on your savings by check, if the need arises. That kind of liquidity separates this type of account from CDs, which assess heavy penalties for withdrawals prior to maturity. You can start by tapping into larger fund families that offer money market accounts such as Vanguard (800-662-2739), Strong (800-368-3863), and Fidelity (800-544-3902).

Step Five: Practice Dollar-Cost Averaging

Sound familiar? It should; it's one of the key tenants of investment clubs. Remember, you want to save money on a regular basis, setting aside the same amount each month. Don't have your money invested in funds and just sitting there—although the return is compounding. Put a set amount into a money-market account or mutual fund on a regular basis, even if it is as little as $25 per month per fund. Again, you buy fewer shares when prices are down and more shares when prices are up.

Step Six: Develop an Asset-Allocation Mix

Make sure your asset allocation is structured properly. Whether it's saving to buy a home or fund your retirement, the safest and fastest route to your financial destination is dividing your money among several asset groups (e.g., cash, stocks, bonds, and real estate).

Independent studies have shown that a portfolio's returns stem from the decision to target myriad investments. Asset allocation will help you ride out shifts in the economy as well as hedge against market swings. Your asset-allocation strategy will vary according to your age, income, and lifestyle. The asset-allocation worksheet will help you to shape a model portfolio (Figure 15.3). Start by listing whatever securities you currently own. Next, you will be able to determine roughly how much you should allocate to each class using the formula provided.

Figure 15.3   Asset-Allocation Worksheet

<<< assetallocationworksheet >>>

This, our third worksheet in the Investing series, is designed to help you shape your model portfolio and then take steps to reconfigure your current holdings to fit.

STEP 1

WHERE YOU CURRENTLY STAND
List your portfolio's holdings and the amount presently invested in whatever stocks and stock mutual funds as well as bonds that you own.

STOCKS/STOCK FUNDS   **BONDS**

_____   _____
_____   _____
_____   _____
_____   _____
_____   _____

TOTAL PORTFOLIO: _____

STEP 2

DIVVYING IT ALL UP
Calculate how your assets are divided up.

STOCKS_____   **BONDS** _____

STOCKS/TOTAL PORTFOLIO _____ (percentage invested in stocks)

BONDS/TOTAL PORTFOLIO _____ (percentage invested in bonds)

STEP 3

SUGGESTED WEIGHTINGS
Calculate roughly how much you should have invested in each asset class. Example: A 50-year-old should look to have roughly half of his or her investment portfolio in bonds, and 100 minus his or her age, or 50% of the portfolio, in stocks.

AGE   Your optimal bond weighting as   100 minus your bond weighting
          percentage of portfolio (the per-   (suggested stock weighting as
          centage here equals your age)   percentage of portfolio)

_____ _____   _____

We'd suggest that you consider your profile as an investor from worksheet two for the next part of Step Three, tailoring your weighting to fit your style. Example: You're a 50-year-old playing catch-up. You feel the need to invest aggressively in the market, and decide that a 50% weighting in bonds should be lowered to 40% for the time being. Or conversely, if you're risk-averse and feel comfortable with the amount you've saved, you might opt to stick to 50% in bonds or even up your fixed-income weighting to 55% or 60%.

Aggressive investors: You can stomach extra risk, and you're prepared to endure whatever gyrations the stock market has to offer. Add 10%, but no more than 15%, to your stock weighting if you're a daredevil.

Moderately aggressive investors: Add 5%, but no more than 10%, to your stock weighting.

Moderately conservative investors: You want to be in the market but are a bit nervous about having too much tied up in stocks. Add 5% to your bond weighting.

Arch conservative investors: You get a bad case of the jitters the minute you go to the newspaper's stock listings. You're willing to forgo the extra punch stocks add to your portfolio. Add 10% to your bond weighting.

Step Seven: Invest in Stocks and Mutual Funds

You know by now that the stock market, for the past 20 years, has been the best place to be. One of the best ways to play the market as an individual investor is to look at mutual funds, which spread your money across a well-diversified portfolio of 30 to 50 stocks. Kamau Odinga, and his wife, Tamanika, are preparing for retirement, having amassed more than $600,000 worth of stocks. The members of the PULA Project Investment Club have been investing on their own for the past 12 years. More recently, they have begun to give shares of stock to their children and relatives as birthday, graduation, and Kwanza gifts.

There's an initial hurdle to mutual funds: Most require that you ante up $1,000 to $2,500 or even more to start. Of the 10,000 funds listed in the Principia Pro Plus database compiled by Morningstar, Inc., the Chicago firm that tracks fund performance, some 5,500 have an initial minimum outlay of $1,000 or more.

Consider dividing your equity portfolio into four segments:

1. Large-company value stocks or funds—value stocks are those that look underpriced relative to the rest of the market.
2. Large-company growth stocks, which have outstanding prospects for increasing earnings, or moderate-growth funds, which focus on established blue chips.
3. Small-company stocks or aggressive growth funds, which emphasize promising young companies.
4. Foreign stock funds, which invest in both U.S. companies with international divisions or subsidiaries, and those companies that are based overseas.

A mutual fund is only as good as its fund manager, who acts as a stockpicker. Your money is handed over to that portfolio manager, who decides what to buy and when to sell. With that in mind, the fund manager should have a solid long-term track record of at least three years for that specific fund—better still, five years—so that you can see how he or she fared in good years and bad. Did the person at the helm beat the market? (See Figure 15.4 to check exactly what to look for.)

Morningstar's Web site (www.morningstar.com) provides a synopsis of a given fund's prospectus, plus an overview and summary of

Figure 15.4 Checklist: Picking the Right Mutual Fund

With nearly 9,000 funds in the market, how's an investor to pick and choose without suffering migraine headache? Well, you get some relief by trying to get a good mix of different mutual fund asset classes. A good middle-of-the-road portfolio mix is to invest 25 percent each in a stock fund, balanced fund, bond fund, and an international or global fund, advises Charles Ross, an Atlanta-based certified financial planner and nationally syndicated radio talk show host. If you only have $1,500 to invest, the above formula doesn't give you much leeway, since most funds require an initial ante of $1,000. But there's no shame in building your financial edifice one brick at a time. In picking the right fund or funds, here are a few things to look for to help you lay that foundation. Much of the information you need can be found in the prospectus:

1. *Investment Objective.* How much risk are you willing to take? Are you looking for growth or somewhere safe to stash your money? Let's say you're saving for your child's college education or retirement. Then you can afford to invest in aggressive growth funds because you'll have time to recover from market swings. The closer you are to retirement, the more you will want to stock up on growth and income, and bond funds.
2. *Performance.* Total returns—dividends, interest, capital gains and changes in share price—are the best indicators of performance. Study annualized returns for various time periods, usually one, three, and five years. Look for consistency; long-term performance is most important. Compare the fund you're interested in with other funds in the same category.
3. *Sales Charges.* Since expenses eat away at your returns, hefty sales charges can turn a winning fund into a mediocre one. First you need to know the difference between a load fund—one with an upfront sales charge ranging from 4 percent to 8 percent—and no load funds that are purchased directly from the fund company. Sales charges reduce the amount of money you initially invest. Besides, there is no correlation between how much a fund costs and how well it performs, at least according to Sheldon Jacobs, publisher of the Irvington, New York-based *No-Load Fund Investor Newsletter* (www.sheldonjacobs.com).

   Watch out for back-end loads, which even the most enticing no-load funds have. If you pull out early, you may get hit with a fee—usually 5 percent for the first year and then it falls one percentage point for each year you stay in the fund. Most funds have a management fee, usually 0.5 percent to 1 percent of the fund's annual assets, which is what a company pays an advisor to manage a portfolio. If your balance falls below a certain minimum, you may get hit with a maintenance fee—usually $10 to $50 annually. Some funds also add a charge for marketing and advertising, known as 12(b) fees. This expense can cost as much as 2 percent of your assets.

(continued)

Figure 15.4   *(Continued)*

4. *Expense Ratio.* This is an indication of how high or low a fund's fees are. It is the percentage deducted each year from the fund assets to pay for bills. According to fund tracker, Morningstar Inc., in Chicago, the average U.S. stock fund has an expense ratio of about 1.42 percent, which means you pay $14.20 per every $1,000 invested.

5. *Management Style.* Most analysts would agree that a mutual fund is only as good as its manager, the person picking the stocks for that fund's portfolio. The funds you choose within a certain category have different investment strategies. Some fund families have pretty much the same investment philosophy for all their funds. Then there are those run independently of the company, meaning that each fund's portfolio manager has his or her own approach—some are value picker and others look for growth. A good indicator of a manager's style is the fund's turnover rate—a measure of how many times the manager sells and buys stocks in a course of a year. A fund with a turnover of 300 percent changes its holdings three times a year. A lot of buying and selling pushes up the fund's transactions costs. On top of that, if the manager is selling winning stocks, those short-term capital gains are taxed as part of your income.

---

its performance. You'll see a list of the stocks and other investments the manger has bought into and you'll also get a sense of what strategies are being used to invest the fund's money.

Step Eight: Contribute to Your Company's 401K, 403(b), and the Like

Enroll in an employer-sponsored savings plans. If you don't know if such a plan is available where you work, go to your benefits or human resources department first thing in the morning. Many plans allow you to enroll only at certain times during the year. Most employees are eligible after being on the job for six months to a year.

You want to contribute the maximum amount of money you can to the plan each year. Typically, this is 15 percent of your gross annual earnings. The money you contribute will be deducted from your taxable income; your company may match all or some of your contributions. You can take money out at any time, but, if you are younger than 59½, you will be hit with a 10 percent penalty plus pay income taxes. However, you are allowed to borrow against the funds, usually up to 50 percent of the total amount, to pay for school, buy a house, or other reasons.

Step Nine: Invest in Tax-Deferred and Tax-Free Investments

If your company doesn't sponsor a 401K plan, consider putting $2,000 per year into a traditional IRA (Individual Retirement Account) or Roth IRA. You can contribute $2,000 a year to an IRA, lowering your tax bill. Say you are in the 28 percent tax bracket, your $2,000 contribution is really only $1,440, saving you $560. The money you put in your IRA grows tax-deferred (meaning you don't have to pay taxes on it until you withdraw it—after age 59½, otherwise you'll have to pay a 10 percent tax penalty). Depending on how much you earn, your IRA contributions may be fully tax deductible. You can deduct annual contributions on your taxes if your adjusted gross income (AGI) is $30,000 or less ($50,000 for married couples).

You have the option of contributing $2,000 a year to a Roth IRA if you earn less than $100,000. While your contributions aren't tax deductible, your money grows tax-free while in the account. The good news about Roth IRAs is that for educational purposes, you can take out the money you put in a Roth IRA before you reach age 59½ free of penalty charges (this doesn't apply to capital gains, dividends, or interest earned on your savings). However, you have to wait five years from the day you open a Roth IRA before you can withdraw your earnings.

It's simple to open an IRA. It's just a matter of filling out an application and having a set amount automatically withdrawn from your checking account on a regular basis. Most mutual-fund companies offer such accounts, usually for less than the required initial minimum—$250 compared to $2,500—knowing that you will continuously and faithfully add money to your IRA.

Step Ten: Don't Overlook Fixed-Income Investments

It's okay to bond with your investments. In essence, bonds work as loans—be they to the federal, state, or local government. Your promise to let those entities borrow a set amount of money from you is twofold: you'll get your principal or original investment back at a certain maturity date, and you'll receive regular interest payments. The downside is that when interest rates rise, a bond's principal decreases, making the bond worthless.

Historically, 30-year U.S. treasuries have been the yardstick used to judge the bond universe. These government securities average a 5 percent annual return. A $5,000 30-year treasury bond will mature in the year 2027. If it pays 6 percent annual interest (or yield), you will garner $150 in interest every six months. You should turn right around and reinvest in another bond, stock, or mutual fund.

Another angle, especially if you are in the 31 percent or higher tax bracket, is munis (municipal bonds). What makes munis attractive is their tax-free status on the local, state, and federal levels. Don't let munis low yield fool you. A municipal yielding 4 percent actually earns more in tax-adjusted terms. If your tax rate is 31 percent, for instance, your tax-adjusted yield on a 4 percent muni amounts to about 5.8 percent (divide the muni's yield by 1 minus your tax rate to get this figure).

A word of caution about corporate bonds. While corporate bonds are issued by a wide variety of companies, buying individual corporate issues can be expensive. Individual treasury bonds guarantee your principal should you hold until maturity; corporate bonds can't make the same promise—they are only as solid as the company that issues them.

The advantage of investing in bond funds is that the portfolios are managed by full-time professionals and are diversified—the typical fund owns hundreds of different issues. What's more, you generally can't buy an individual bond for less than $1,000, but you can buy into a bond fund with an initial investment as little as $500.

GETTING YOUR FINANCIAL HOUSE IN ORDER[1]

Getting your finances together to invest on your own and as part of a group may seem like a lot to ask. Why not just tell you to put your head in a vise and squeeze away? But it can be done—building a team and individual portfolio. The sooner you start, the better.

Kimberly Felder knows she has time on her side. Over the past three years, the 29-year-old teacher has been investing in stocks, mutual funds, and a tax-deferred annuity plan that seeks maximum capital gains. "People always say they don't have money to invest in the stock market," she maintains. "But the money is there. It just depends on your priorities. I know that the stock market is going to give me a greater return on my money than any other vehicle."

Felder is not above investing in riskier securities to gain her reward. She's cofounder of a year-old investment club composed of

seven under-30 professional women. Dubbed ISIS (Independent Sisters Investing and Saving), the club has developed an aggressive approach, scooping up shares in small-cap, high-tech, and emerging growth companies.

"I don't mind investing in volatile stocks, like technology and pharmaceuticals, or aggressive growth funds, because I can afford to take more risks at my age," she explains. "This is money that I have put aside for the long term and don't plan to touch for another 25 to 30 years."

As members of the NAIC, ISIS is using NAIC's formula to evaluate stocks within certain industries, particularly technology. However, most of the companies it invested in have been overpriced. Now, the club members are reviewing other sectors for value buys.

The members of ISIS are considering an investment vehicle often overlooked by most new and experienced investors alike—a *unit investment trust* (UIT). A UIT is similar to a mutual fund, but invests in fixed-income securities, such as corporate bonds and preferred company stock. This vehicle serves as a good way for ISIS to limit its risk and not overpay for equities.

A UIT may invest in as many as 20 companies (based on outstanding performance), and the portfolio generally represents the top companies in select industries. Sticking with its aggressive approach, ISIS can take advantage of a UIT that specializes in technology. As a result, the club puts its money to work in a range of companies—those that produce hardware, software, or servers as well as the much-ballyhooed dot coms.

Members contribute $30 a month, having amassed a few thousand dollars in their portfolio, most of which is sitting in cash as the group continues to search for stocks that are growing at a rate of 15 percent or more, but with relatively low price-to-earnings ratios. ISIS purchased its first stock in 1999, Indicare, a growth company that produces wheelchairs, safety banisters, and other medical products and devices used in nursing homes. Today, they also own shares in the Cheesecake Factory, Chiron, Elan, and Pfizer.

Felder has invested about $1,000 of her own money in the direct-investment stock plans of electronics manufacturer Kopin, digital photofinisher Seattle Filmworks, and mortgage banker Fannie Mae as part of her personal portfolio. As a result, she has become an avid reader of financial publications. She, along with members of ISIS, use online research to explore investment opportunities.

"It's important for me to do the research myself rather than having to rely solely on a financial planner or broker," Felder says. "When considering stocks to invest in, I look at the history of the company, the types of products they are producing, and management's earnings expectations. With mutual funds, I thoroughly read the prospectus and look at which companies are in the fund's portfolio, what management is doing, and the returns for the past 5 and 10 years."

While the Gen-X investor is on the right road, she was slightly sidetracked. She decided to pursue a master's degree in public administration at Baruch College in New York City. To pay for her education, she had to dip into her cash reserve for roughly $1,500, and reduce monthly contributions to her savings from $300 to $100.

"I decided to pay outright for classes instead of taking out a student loan and being burdened with debt," says Felder, who is debt free, with the exception of the $50 a month that goes toward paying off an undergraduate student loan. "I made sure I eliminated all of my credit-card debt before I seriously began investing a few years ago, because I know that whenever you have credit-card debt or loans, whatever return you are making on your investments is canceled out by the interest due on your account balances."

As with most people when they reach their early to mid-thirties, Felder hopes to purchase her first home within the next five years, borrowing money from her teacher's tax-deferred annuity to make the down payment, without being penalized for withdrawal before the age of 59½. Once Felder is ready to purchase her home, she will need about $20,000 for a down payment.

Felder, whose take-home salary is a little over $20,000, has more than $50,000 stashed away for retirement thus far. This includes her stock investments; two mutual funds, which invest in small caps and mid-sized companies; and the annuity. She is currently contributing the maximum amount to the annuity—25 percent of her salary. In addition, she has a traditional pension, one in which she will not become fully vested until she has taught for 30 years.

Essentially, most people's retirement funds will come from three sources: personal savings, employer-sponsored plans, and Social Security. In the work environment of the new millennium, employees—whether they are teachers or high-powered corporate executives—can expect to foot the biggest chunk of their postcareer cash.

That said: It's imperative that you take time to craft a sound retirement strategy by developing a formula that helps you determine

Figure 15.5 Retirement Planning Worksheet

<<< retirementplanningworksheet >>>

Want to know when you'll be able to retire? How much you need to save each year to get there? Use our Retirement Worksheet. (State Street Research & Management Co., a Boston-based money management and mutual fund sponsor, helped in the development.)

1 Current annual income (you and your spouse combined)

_____ **$80,000**

2 Desired retirement income

_____ **$60,000**

3 Estimated Social Security and pension income

_____ **$20,000**

4 Income needed from personal savings (includes tax-deferred plans and portfolio investments)

Subtract (3) from (2) _____ **$40,000**

5 Desired retirement age (Make note of the income multiple that fits your wishes)

Retirement Age	Income Multiple
50-54	**26**
55-59	**23**
60-64	**20**
65 & over	**17**

(For our model, we'll use **20**)

6 Necessary personal savings

Multiply (5) by (4) _____ **$800,000**

Number (6) is your retirement savings goal. Now, determine how to get there:

7 Total personal savings now

_____ **$250,000**

(Your IRA, annuities, insurance policies, etc.)

8 Approximate years until retirement

Years	Growth Multiple to Retirement
8	2
12	3
16	4
20	5
24	6

(We'll use **8** for a multiple of **2** in our model)

9 Estimated value of current personal savings at retirement

Multiply (8) by (7) _____ **$500,000**

10 Savings shortfall

Subtract (9) from (6) _____ **$300,000**

11 Approximate years until retirement

	Savings Factor
8	.100
12	.070
16	.045
20	.032
24	.025

(We'll assume **8**—a factor of **.100** in our model)

_____ **.100**

12 Annual savings necessary

Multiply (11) by (10) _____ **$30,000**

when you can afford to stop punching the clock. The retirement planning worksheet will show you how much you need to save each year to reach your goal (Figure 15.5).

CONCLUSION

You'll do just great investing on your own as long as you bear in mind that becoming prosperous involves more than stockpiling cash in your bank account. It requires that you change your lifestyle—spending habits—and that you invest in the stock market on a regular basis. Whether you earn $25,000 or $250,000 a year, you can strike it rich by following the money strategies outlined in this chapter—and throughout this book. Good luck!

EPILOGUE

Congratulations! If you have made it through this book and faithfully followed the information outlined in each chapter, your club should be up and running. You have all the tools you need to build a prosperous portfolio.

Here are some final words on managing your investment club. Keep in mind that your club may get off to a shaky start during the first year of operation. By the second year, you probably will have weeded out the slackers, and your club will be left with a core group of people who aren't afraid to roll up their sleeves and do some serious work.

As members become more comfortable and confident about their stock-picking abilities, the amount of money your club has under management will grow significantly. In time, your club will discover what thousands of clubs have known for years: Good research and regular deposits are all it takes to invest and make money like the pros.

The good news about belonging to an investment club is that not only are you helping to enhance the group's cash reserves, but you are learning personal wealth building for the enrichment of your family, children, and the next generation. It's important that individual club members apply their knowledge and experience to a wide range of investments, if they truly want to become the "millionaires next-door."

What better incentive do you and fellow club members need other than knowing that more and more regular folks are proving that anyone, young or old, can accumulate wealth. Take Mattel "Mat" Dawson, a 78-year-old rigger who runs a forklift for Ford Motor Co. By putting aside $25 a week, he has managed to build a small fortune, in addition to giving away more than $1 million to churches and colleges.

To attain a measure of success, power, and wealth, individual members must commit to the principles outlined in this book and

participate fully in the capital markets. They must embrace a mission that stresses preparation, education, and fortitude.

Stay focused. This is a life-long project, not a get-rich-quick scheme. Don't allow external or internal forces to keep your club from reaching its investment goals. You'll do fine if you stick to the universal club motto: *We have to be in it to win it for the long haul.*

NOTES

Chapter 1: Think, Save and Grow Rich: Getting Started

1. Thomas E. O'Hara and Kenneth S. Janke, Sr., *The Official Guide from The National Association of Investors Corporation: Starting and Running a Profitable Investment Club* (Times Business, 1998). Facts about Frederick C. Russell and the Mutual Investment Club are taken from this book.
2. Carolyn M. Brown, *Test Your Investment Club IQ*, Women's Wire (www .women.com), 1998.
3. NAIC Membership Guide, *Where Wall Street and Main Street Meet*, 4th ed.
4. Karen Brelsford, "Unlikely Investors Own a 'Pebble' of America," *Better Investing* (April 1998), pp. 19 and 89. Facts about the Divas and Dons Investment Club are from this article.

Chapter 2: All for One, One for All: Recruiting Members

1. Sections of the a call to members are from The Washington Women's Investment Club, *How to Start an Investment Club* (WWicked Publications, 1993). Reprinted with permission.
2. *Ibid.*

Chapter 5: Rules to Live By: Designing Operating Procedures

1. Carolyn M. Brown, "Designing Operating Procedures," *Black Enterprise* (November 1996), p. 49.
2. Sections about members' responsibilities are taken from The Washington Women's Investment Club, *How to Start an Investment Club* (WWicked Publications, 1993). Reprinted with permission.

Chapter 6: Meeting of the Minds: Running Meetings Smoothly and Effectively

1. Carolyn M. Brown, "5 Ways to Make Your Investment Club Prosper," Black Enterprise (February 1998), pp. 180 and 182.
2. James A. Anderson, "Read All About It," *Black Enterprise* (January 1998), p. 36.

Chapter 7: Seven Keys to a Profitable Club: Following the Right Path to Investing

1. Carolyn M. Brown, "Seven Keys to a Profitable Investment Club," *Black Enterprise* (February 1999), pp. 157–164.
2. Laura Washington, "How Much Is Enough?," *Black Enterprise* (October 1997), p. 50.

Chapter 8: Sweat the Small Stuff: Recordkeeping and Other Taxing Issues

1. "Doing Your Club's Tax Return," instructions mailed with the *NAIC Accounting Manual.* Facts about partnership tax forms are taken from this material.
2. Carolyn M. Brown, "Giving Uncle Sam His Dues," *Black Enterprise* (September 1998), p. 48.

Chapter 9: Do You Need a Broker? Buying and Selling Securities

1. Ivan Cintron, "Direct Investing," *Black Enterprise* (August 1999), p. 48.
2. NAIC Membership Guide, *Where Wall Street and Main Street Meet,* 4th ed.

Chapter 10: Grab the Bull by the Horns: Investing in the Stock Market

1. C. Frederic Weigold, *The Wall Street Journal Lifetime Money Guide* (Hyperion, 1997).
2. Carolyn M. Brown, "Make Your Money Talk," *Black Enterprise* (February 1999), p. 66.

Chapter 11: Invest in What You Know: Researching Stocks Like the Pros

1. Gale Carter and Tanisha Ann Sykes, "A Lifetime of Investing," *Black Enterprise* (October, 1999), pp. 149–150. Sections about Grafton J. Daniels are taken from this article.
2. *Stock Selection Guide & Report: Painting the Perfect Picture,* Video From NAIC.
3. Cheryl D. Broussard, *The Black Woman's Guide to Financial Independence* (Penguin Books, 1996).
4. James A. Anderson, "A Measure for Market Jitters," *Black Enterprise* (February 1997), p. 52.
5. Lynette Khalfani, "High-Tech Investing," *Black Enterprise* (March 1999), p. 51.
6. Carolyn M. Brown, "Evaluating Annual Reports," *Black Enterprise* (June 1999), p. 74.
7. Thomas E. O'Hara and Kenneth S. Janke, Sr., *The Official Guide from The National Association of Investors Corporation: Starting and Running a Profitable Investment Club* (Times Business, 1998). Facts about the Challenge Tree are taken from this book.
8. Laura Egodigwe, "Investment Tip-Offs from Management," *Black Enterprise* (September 1998), pp. 105–110.

Chapter 12: Tools of the Trade: Using the Net and News to Find Data

1. Thomas E. O'Hara and Kenneth S. Janke, Sr., *The Official Guide from The National Association of Investors Corporation: Starting and Running a Profitable Investment Club* (Times Business, 1998). Facts and data about the Stock Check List, Stock Selection Guide and Report, and the Stock Comparison Guide are taken from this book.
2. Explanation of pretax profit margin is from *Investing for Life,* self-study course published by the NAIC.
3. James A. Anderson, "Screening for Investment Gold," *Black Enterprise* (October 1998), p. 94.

Chapter 13: Thinking Outside the Box: Investing beyond the Stock Market

1. Carolyn M. Brown, "Investing Philanthropically," *Black Enterprise* (March 1998), p. 42.
2. Cheryl D. Broussard, *The Black Woman's Guide to Financial Independence* (Penguin Books, 1996). Sections about real estate investing are taken from this book.
3. Sections about WWIC investing in real estate and entrepreneurial ventures are taken from The Washington Women's Investment Club, *How to Start an Investment Club* (WWicked Publications, 1993). Reprinted with permission.
4. Carolyn M. Brown, "How to Start an Investment Club," *Black Enterprise* (April 1993), pp. 49–54. Facts about WWIC are taken from this article.
5. Sections about Little Lawyers project and the Art Affair are taken from the Washington Women's Investment Club, *How to Start an Investment Club* (WWicked Publications, 1993). Reprinted with permission.

Chapter 14: Never Too Young to Invest: Building Youth Investment Clubs

1. Carolyn M. Brown, "Headstart," *Black Enterprise* (October 1999), pp. 105–108.
2. Carolyn M. Brown, "You're Never Too Young," *Black Enterprise* (December 1998), p. 49.
3. Timothy Middleton, "Stocks 'R' Us," *Black Enterprise* (May 1993), p. 56.
4. *Ibid.*

Chapter 15: The Next Frontier: Learning to Invest on Your Own

1. Carolyn M. Brown, "School Daze," *Black Enterprise* (June 1999), p. 76.

INDEX

ABTE. *See* Alliance of Black Telecommunications Employees (ABTE) (New Jersey)

Account(s), cash *vs.* margin, 135

Accounting. *See* Investment club(s): recordkeeping

Activism, shareholder, 165–167. *See also* Social consciousness/activism

Advertising cutbacks/ups, 203–204

A.G. Edwards (full-service broker), 128

Allen, Arletha, 147, 148

Allen Investment Ministries (AIM) (New York), 21, 26, 27, 28

Alliance of Black Telecommunications Employees (ABTE) (New Jersey), 55–56

Alliance Investment Group (AIG), 56, 71, 72, 74, 80, 128

Alliance Kids Investment Club, 72

Alpha, 185

Altavista (Web site), 227

American Stock Exchange (AMEX), 136, 171, 174

Ameritrade Securities (deep discounter), 130

Analysis, professional, 182–185

Anderson, Ewan D., 21–22, 26–27, 28

Anene, Amadi, 244, 249, 250

Anene, Janet, 244

Annual reports. *See* Corporation(s), data on

Annuities, 259

Ariel Capital Funds, 236, 259

Artists, 239, 240

Asset allocation, 125, 260, 264–265, 266
  age brackets, models for (Figure 15.1), 260
  equity portfolio, four segments, 266
  worksheet (Figure 15.3), 265
  youth, model for, 260

AT&T Collegiate Challenge (stock market program, simulated trading activity), 256

AT&T employees' forming employment. *See* Alliance Investment Group (AIG)

Balance sheet (Figure 11.2), 188

Bank accounts, 34

Barron's, 196, 205, 222–223

B.BIG (Black Business Investment Group, LLC) (Oakland, California), 40–41, 51–52

Benchmark, 170

Beta, 184, 185

Better Investing magazine, 8, 102, 224

Big Charts, 226

Black Business Investment Group, 145

Black colleges/universities, 70

Black Enterprise (magazine), 3–4, 93

Black Enterprise for Teens, 247

Black Lawyers Association, 8

Black Monday, 155–156, 168, 242

Black Women Investment
    Corporation (BWIC) (Raleigh,
    North Carolina), 71, 87–89, 90
*Black Women's Guide to Financial
    Independence*, 101
Bloomberg, 205, 226
Blount, Sherri, 238
Blue chip common stocks, 35,
    170–171
Bond, Alan, 254
Bonds, 32, 34, 35, 224, 259, 260,
    269–270
    convertible, 35
    corporate, 35, 260, 270
    funds, 35, 260, 270
    international funds, 260
    municipal, 32, 35, 259, 260, 270
    rating service (Moody's), 224
Bookkeeping. *See* Investment club(s):
    recordkeeping
Bossette, Eddy and Pat, 17–18
Boston, Calvin, 8
Boyd, Patricia, 119
Brokers/brokerage firms, 129–136
    accounts (two basic types), 135
    cash accounts, 135
    confirmation statement, 137
    deep-discount brokers, 130–132
    discount brokers, 129–130
    fees, 131–132
    full-service brokers, 129
    margin accounts, 135
    shopping for, 132–135
Brooks, Andre, 256
Broussard, Cheryl D., 101, 161, 230,
    231, 233, 234, 246
Brown & Co. (deep discounter), 130,
    131
Bryant, John, 166
*Bull & Bear Directory of Investment
    Advisory Newsletters*, 204
Business cycle, 169–170
Business plan (entrepreneurial
    venture), 241
Buybacks, corporate, 199
Bylaws. *See* Investment club(s):
    operating procedures (bylaws)

Calvert New Africa Fund, 236
Campbell, Michele, 250
Campbell, Renee, 250

Carlson, Chuck, 139
Carter, Rod, 40, 51, 146
CD, 32, 34, 264
CDA/Investnet, 226
Challenge Tree methodology,
    191–194
Chapman, Nate, 15–16
Chapman Company, 15–16
Charles Schwab (discount broker),
    129, 130, 134, 147, 148–149, 156,
    201
Chicago: Windy City Investment
    Club, 71, 118, 209, 212, 217
Citibank brokerage account services,
    182
City National Bank of New Jersey,
    74
Clark, Walter L., 39, 117, 119, 134
CMG Investment Club (Wall Street
    professionals), 97, 98, 119
CNN Financial Network (Web site),
    226
Coalition of Black Investors (COBI),
    8, 97, 157, 238, 261
Coles, Gerald, 94, 96–97, 98, 123,
    124
Collectibles, 35
Collegiate Challenge (stock market
    program, simulated trading
    activity), 256
Collier, Jerrilyn O., 105
Commercial real estate. *See* Real
    estate
Committees, 77–78
Common/preferred stock, 169,
    172–173. *See also* Stock(s)
Compound interest, power of, 10–11,
    13
Compufest (NAIC annual
    conference), 225
Consumerism, intelligent, 247–248
Consumer perspective, investing
    from, 249–254
Corporate bonds, 35, 260, 270. *See
    also* Bonds
Corporate buybacks, 199
Corporate Index (Moody's), 224
Corporation(s), data on:
    annual reports, 185–189
    researching (*see* Stock picking:
        research)

S&P Register of Corporations, Directors, and Executives, 221
Corporation(s), legal structures, 41
Corporation, operating club as, 41, 54–61
  double tax whammy, 56
  fees, 61
  income tax return (Form 1120) (Figure 4.3), 57–60
  maximum of 75 shareholders, 55
  naming, 61
  online corporation kit, 61
  registering, 56–61
Cost(s)/fees:
  Handbook for No Load Fund Investors, 224
  loads, 267
  maintenance/organizational, 41
  transaction, 61, 89, 131–132, 267, 268
Cost averaging. *See* Dollar-cost averaging
Cost cutters, stock buying/selling, 137–145
  direct stock purchase (DSP), 140, 141
  DRIPs (dividend reinvestment plans), 137–140
  NAIC's low-cost investment plan, 140–145
  optional cash purchases, 140
Crashes, market, 155–156, 168, 182
Cultural traditions for pooling money, 9–10
Cyclical industries, 163

Daily Stocks (Web site), 225
Daniels, Grafton J., 75, 176–178
Dawson, Mattel "Mat," 275
Day order, 136
DBC Financial (Web site), 225
Debt instruments, 32
Deep-discount brokers, 130–132
Defensive industries, 163
Delinquent contributions (club bylaws), 72
Detroit Ladies of Wall Street, 253
Direct stock purchase (DSP), 140
Discount brokers, 129–130

Divas and Dons Club (Baltimore), 15, 16
Diversification, 96, 120, 242–243. *See also* Asset allocation
Dividend(s), 97–98, 137, 180, 184, 196–198, 224
  Record Service (Moody's), 224
  reinvesting (key principle), 97–98 (*see also* Dividend reinvestment plans (DRIPs))
  yield, 180, 184
Dividend reinvestment plans (DRIPs), 137–140, 164, 165, 201, 237
Dollar-cost averaging, 93–95, 170, 264
Dow Jones Industrial Average, 154, 170, 225
Dow Jones Retrieval Service, 222
Dow Jones 20 Transportation Stock Index, 171
Dreyfus (deep discounter), 131
DRIP Central (Web site), 140
DRIP Investor, 139
Dulan, Adolf, 228
Dunagan, Pierre, 161, 180

Earnings Distribution Statement, 111
Earnings per share (EPS), 121, 209
Ebony Investor.com, 90, 225
Ebony Prospectors Investment Club, New Jersey, 100
Economic fundamentals: growth and interest rates, 168–170
Education committee, 77
Edward Jones Investments, 259
Ellis, Victoria, 15
Ely, Randall, 101
Emerging Companies (Moody's), 224
Employer-sponsored savings plans, 259, 268
Enterprising Minority Investors (EMI) (Hartford, Connecticut), 29–30, 33
Entrepreneurial ventures, 236–242
  business plan, 241
  evaluating as potential investments, 240–242
  financial statements, 241
  management team, 241
  market audience, 241

Entrepreneurial ventures *(Continued)*
  marketing plan, 242
  private placement, 240
  prospectus document, 241
Entrepreneurial ventures committee,
    78
Environmental problems, industries,
    236
Equity investing. *See* Stock(s)
Evans family (founders, Family 7
    Inc., Linden, New Jersey), 3
Excite search engine, 227
Executive committee, 77

Family Money newsletter, 247
Family 7 Inc. (investment club,
    Linden, New Jersey), 3
Famulare, Santo, 184, 185
Federal Deposit Insurance Corp., 167
Fees. *See* Cost(s)/fees
Felder, Kimberly, 270–272
Fidelity, 130, 160, 264
Field trips, 89–90
Financial Data Finder (Web site), 226
Financial plan, four components:
  investment program, 261 *(see also*
      Investing/investment)
  monthly budget, 261
  retirement plan, 261 *(see also*
      Retirement)
  tax/estate plan, 261
Financial Planning Association, 261
Financial planning worksheet
    (Figure 15.2), 262
Financial security, ten steps to,
    261–270
  assessing short/long term
      financial goals, 261
  asset allocation mix, 264–265
  cash reserve, 263–264
  credit-card debt reduction, 263
  dollar-cost averaging, 264
  employer-sponsored savings plans,
      268
  financial snapshot, 263
  fixed-income investments, 269–270
  mutual funds of stocks, 266–268
  stock investments, 266–268
  tax-deferred and tax-free
      investments, 269
Financial stages of life, 258–261

Financial statements, 185–189, 241
Finch, Irene, 229, 231, 232, 242
Flake, D. Floyd A., 21
Ford, Joan, 155
Foster, Eloise, 230
Fox, Jeffery, 247, 248, 250, 251
Franchises, 238
Full-service brokers, 129. *See also*
    Brokers/brokerage firms
Fundamental analysis, 183–184
Futures/commodities, 35
Future-Vest Investment Club (New
    York), 72, 74–75, 77, 182, 191, 194

Games, stock market, 254–256
  "A Day on Wall Street," 254
  AT&T Collegiate Challenge, 256
  Stock Market Game, 255
General partnership, 41. *See also*
    Legal structures: alternatives for
    investment clubs
Gold/silver, 35
Goodwin, Keysha, 15
Green Sheets, 214
Greer, Baunita, 97, 98, 102, 164, 187,
    242
Greer, Cathleen, 209, 212, 214, 217
Growth, economic; and interest
    rates, 168–170
Growth, industry groups' annual
    rate of (1960-1995) (Figure 8.6),
    122
Growth potential, performance
    measurement by stock's,
    124–125
Growth stocks/investing, 32, 95, 163,
    183, 266, 268

Hall, Michael, 134
Hamilton Management Corporation,
    75, 177
Handbook for No Load Fund Investors,
    224
Hartford, Connecticut: Enterprising
    Minority Investors (EMI),
    29–30, 33
Haskins, Ron, 212, 214, 217
Healthy Start, 15
Heard, Lillian, 155, 156, 164, 165
Hicks, Charles, 61, 70, 71, 237, 238,
    259, 260, 261

Hoover's:
  database, 226
  Handbook on American Business, 222
  Handbook on Emerging Companies,
    222
Hulbert, Mark, 204
Hulbert Financial Digest, 204

Income and Expense Statement, 111
Independent Sisters Investing and
    Saving (ISIS), 271
Index(es), 170–171, 184, 224, 226
  Dow Jones 20 Transportation
    Stock, 171
  Morgan Stanley Capital
    International Europe
    Australia Far East (EAFE), 171
  Russell 2000, 171
  S&P 400 Midcap, 171
  S&P 500, 171, 184
  on the Web, 226
  Wilshire 5000, 171
  Wilshire Small Cap, 171
Individual Investor, 196, 205
Individual Retirement Account
    (IRA), 259, 269
Industry/sectors/groups:
  cyclical, 163
  defensive, 163
  diversification, 96
  Dow Jones Industrial Average, 30
    stocks in (Figure 10.1), 154
  environmental problems, 236
  fast-moving/trailblazing sectors,
    185, 236
  growth rates, 121–122
  Industry Review (Moody's), 224
  NAIC formula to evaluate stocks
    within, 271
  performance measurement by,
    120–122
  S&P Industry Reports, 95, 220
Inflation, 169
Infoseek (search engine), 227
Insider buying/selling, 195–196
Insidertrader.com, 226
Institutional investors, 136
International bond/stock funds, 260
Internet:
  browser software, 225
  equipment, 225

financial Web sites, 225–227
research resource, 224–227
search engines, 227
service providers, 225
stocks, 36, 100
trading, 128, 145–146
Investext, 221
Investing/investment:
  advisory companies, 205
  art of (*vs.* science), 178–179
  asset allocation (*see* Asset
    allocation)
  bonds (*see* Bonds)
  brokers (*see* Brokers/brokerage
    firms)
  clubs (*see* Investment club(s))
  knowledge, test of (Figure 1.1),
    11–12
  vs. lottery, 6–7
  low-cost/low-risk, 15–16
  real estate (*see* Real estate)
  rewards of, 10–15
  vs. saving, 10
  stocks, 153–175, 266–268 (*see also*
    Stock(s))
  stocks, other than, 228–243 (*see
    also* Entrepreneurial ventures;
    Real estate)
  and taxes (*see* Tax(es))
Investing/investment: individual,
    257–274
  assessing short/long-term
    financial goals, 261
  asset allocation mix, 264–265
  asset allocation models for five
    distinct age brackets (Figure
    15.1), 260
  dollar-cost averaging, 264
  employer-sponsored savings plans,
    268
  financial snapshot, 263
  fixed-income investments,
    269–270
  getting your financial house in
    order, 269–274
  life stage and investing strategies,
    258–261
  mutual funds of stocks, investing,
    266–268
  steps (ten) to financial security
    (haven), 261–270

Investing/investment: individual
        (*Continued*)
    stocks, 266–268
    tax-deferred and tax-free
        investments, 269
Investing/investment: principles
        (seven key), 93–99
    diversification, 96
    dollar-cost averaging, 93–95
    growth investing, 95
    patience and long-term stance,
        99
    portfolio evaluation, 98–99
    reinvesting earnings/dividends,
        97–98
    study teams, 96–97
Investing/investment: reasons for
        (five key), 13–14
    building lifetime of financial
        success, 14
    earning money, 13–14
    having fun, 14–15
    owning piece of corporate
        America, 14
    time is on your side, 14
Investing/investment: strategy,
        29–39, 258–261
    differing with stage of life,
        258–261
    factors affecting risk tolerance,
        30–31
    investor profiling, 36–38
    mission statement, 38–39
    pyramid investment model,
        riskiness of investments,
        33–36
    risk, four basic categories of
        investments/risk, 32–33
    risk-takers, three classes of people,
        30–36
Investing for Life, 248
Investment club(s): defined, 4
    advantages of, 275
    average club age, 100
    average portfolio size, 100
    first, 8–9
    "Godfather of," 176
    legal structure (*see* Legal
        structures: alternatives for
        investment clubs)
    maximum size allowed by SEC, 21

    total membership/assets (United
        States), 4
    track record *vs.* S&P 500, 9
Investment club(s): getting started,
        6–16, 17–28
    first meeting, 22–25
    introductory meeting, 19–22
    invitations to introductory
        meeting, 19–22
    mission statement, 38–39
    recruiting members, 17–28
    steps after have at least five
        interested people, 25–28
    surviving shaky start, 275
Investment club(s): meetings, 19–25,
        26, 71, 81–91
    first, 22–25
    frequency (in bylaws), 71
    member's responsibility to
        attend/participate, 69, 78–79
    recruiting/introductory, 19–22
    setting regular date, 26
Investment club(s): meetings
        (general guidelines), 82–87
    agenda, setting, 82–83
    calling for next meeting, 86–87
    encouraging member
        participation, 83
    field trips, 90
    guest speakers, 87
    keeping interest high, 87
    sample agenda (Figure 6.2), 83
    sample minutes (Figure 6.3),
        84–85
    sample notice (Figure 6.1), 82
    securities reports/
        recommendations, 86
    socializing, 89–91
    starting on time, 82
    voting on securities, 86
Investment club(s): member
        recruitment, 17–28
    age, 19
    application form (Figure 2.1), 20
    compatibility, 22
    coworkers, 18
    criteria for selection/admission,
        22
    forming multiple clubs, 21
    maximum size allowed by SEC,
        21

questionnaire for potential
    members (Figure 2.2), 23–24
shared investment outlook, 22
teamwork, 22
Investment club(s): member
    responsibilities, 78–80
attending meetings, 78–79
participating in meetings, 79
researching investments, 79
selecting officers, 79
voting on investments, 79
Investment club(s): member testing,
    23–25, 36–38
member's investor profile (Figure
    3.2), 37
questionnaire for potential
    members (Figure 2.2), 23–24
Investment club(s): member
    withdrawals/terminations, 39,
    49–50, 72–73, 87, 89, 118
bylaws, 72–73
full/partial withdrawals, 73
replacement waiting list, 87
termination of partner's interest,
    or partner's death, 49–50
withdrawal of partner, 49
Investment club(s): operating
    procedures (bylaws), 28, 69–80
committees, 77–78
decision-making process, 71
delinquent contributions, 72
meetings, how often, 71
member's leaving club, 72–73
member's personal difficulty, 74
member's sharing in
    profits/losses, 71–72
money handling, 74–75
new members, allowing to join,
    72–73
officers, 75–78
preliminary decisions, 70
purpose of group, 70
registration of stock, 74
termination of partnership, 75
withdrawals, partial/full,
    allowing for, 73
Investment club(s): recordkeeping,
    104–126
available help, 106
bookkeeping, 105–108
evaluating club's earnings, 125–126

filing partnership and individual
    tax returns, 107–117 (*see also*
    Tax(es))
paying members in cash or stock,
    118
performance measurement by
    company size, 122–124
performance measurement by
    industry, 120–122
performance measurement by
    stock's growth potential,
    124–125
portfolio review, table for each
    stock holding, 125–126
surveying club's results, 120
tax-selling, end of year, 118–120
valuation statement, sample
    (Figure 8.1), 107
valuation statement for meetings,
    106
Investor's Business Daily, 205, 223
Investor's profile: testing attitudes,
    36–38
Investors 2000 Plus (Richmond,
    Virginia), 157–158
IPOs (Initial public offerings), 27, 39,
    175
IRS. *See* Tax(es)

Jackson, Brenda, 201
Jacobs, Sheldon, 224, 267
Janke, Kenneth S., Sr., 120, 121, 126,
    185–186, 187, 194
January effect, 119
Jett, André and Medina, 29–30, 33
Joyner, Ann, 100
Junk bonds, 35

King, Gary D., 73

Lancaster, Robert, 90, 225
Legal structures: alternatives for
    investment clubs, 40–68
corporation, 41, 54–61 (*see also*
    Corporation, operating club as)
limited liability company (LLC),
    41, 67
limited partnership, 41, 67–68
partnership, 41, 42–54, 108 (*see also*
    Partnership, operating club
    as)

Legal structures: alternatives for investment clubs *(Continued)*
  S-corporation, 41, 61–62 *(see also* S-corporation, operating club as)
Legal structures: alternatives not appropriate for investment clubs:
  closely held corporation, 41
  professional corporation (PC), 41
  sole proprietorship, 41
Legal structures: issues to address in selecting, 41
Liability protection, 41, 54, 67
Lick, Larry, 232
Limited liability company (LLC), 41, 51, 67
Limited partnership, operating club as, 41, 67–68
Limited partnership, real estate, 233, 234–236
Limit order, 135–136
Liquidity, 198
Lisanti, Joseph, 197
Loeb, Dr. Charles, III, 229, 232, 233
Lottery *vs.* investment, 6–7
Love, Lloryn Ruth, 253
Lynch, Peter, 8, 160

Madison Area Investment Club (Wisconsin), 8, 95
Mainstream Investment Club (Detroit), 244
Maldonado, Isreal, 128
Management ownership (legal tip-off), 195–196
Management style, mutual funds, 268
Management team (entrepreneurial venture), 241
Margin accounts, 135
Market audience (entrepreneurial venture), 241
Marketing plan (entrepreneurial venture), 242
Market order, 135
McDonald, Clara, 199
McKissack, Eric, 259
Measuring performance. *See* Performance measurement
Merrill Lynch, 129

Millionaire Men's Investment Group (Los Angeles), 228, 232, 242
Minority Empowerment for Tomorrow (Columbia, South Carolina), 161
Mission statement, 38–39
MMS Securities Inc., 143, 147
M.O.D.E.L. Club (Managing Our Dollars, Earnings and Learning) in Sacramento, California, 73
Money handling (in club bylaws), 74–75
Money management. *See* Youth/teenagers, money management training
Money-market accounts/funds, 35, 260, 264
Moody's Investors Service, 224
Morgan Stanley Capital International Europe Australia Far East (EAFE) Index, 171
Morgan Stanley Dean Witter, 129
Morningstar, 102, 223, 266
Motley Fool, 226
MPT Review, 205
Municipal bonds, 32, 35, 259, 260, 270
Mutual funds, 35, 100, 119, 223–224, 266, 267–268
  checklist for picking (Figure 15.4), 267–268
  expense ratio, 268
  manager, 266
  Sourcebook, 223–224
Mutual Investment Club (Detroit) (first investment club), 8–9

Naellier, Louis, 205
NAIC (National Association of Investors Corporation):
  Advisory Service, 15
  annual conference (Compufest), 225
  Investment Club Earnings Survey, 126
  Investor's Information Reports (Green Sheets), 214
  membership age, 245
  Nicholson Awards, 186
  number of local chapters/councils, 8

offerings, 8, 15, 106, 156, 224
official magazine (*Better Investing*),
    8, 224
Portfolio Evaluation Review
    Technique (PERT), 214, 215,
    216
principles of investing, 93
regional council meetings, 102
regional council reps as guest
    speakers, 87
Rule 3.0610 (transfer of securities),
    52
Top 100 listing, 157
training, 8, 28, 77, 102, 247
Web site, 8, 225
NAIC (National Association of
    Investors Corporation): stock
    selection tools, 88, 134, 206–217
    Challenge Tree methodology,
        191–194
    Stock Checklist (Figure 12.1),
        207–208
    Stock Comparison Guide (Figure
        12.3), 213
    Stock Selection Guide, 95, 156,
        210–211
NAIC (National Association of
    Investors Corporation): stock
    service (low-cost investment
    plan), 140–145
    companies featured in (Figure
        9.4), 144
    platinum/gold/silver plan options
        (Figure 9.4), 144
    stock bought the most by, 141
NASDAQ (National Association of
    Securities Dealers Automated
    System), 136, 171, 174–175
National Association of Real Estate
    Brokers, 233
National Association of Realtors, 233
National Association of Securities
    Dealers (NASD), 132, 177. *See
    also* NASDAQ (National
    Association of Securities
    Dealers Automated System)
National Bar Association, 239
Nelson Investment Management,
    205, 221
    *Catalog of Institutional Research
        Reports,* 221

Directory of Investment Research, 221
Earnings Outlook, 221
Netstock Direct, 140, 141
New Freedom Investment Club
    (Durham, North Carolina), 90,
    162, 225
New York Stock Exchange (NYSE),
    136, 138, 170, 171, 174, 175, 254
Nicholson, George, 186
Nicholson Awards, 187
Noel, Monica, 74, 182, 191
No-load funds, 224, 267
NYNEX, 185

Oakland, California: B.BIG (Black
    Business Investment Group,
    LLC) (Oakland, California),
    40–41, 51–52
OCP. *See* Optional cash payment
    (OCP)
Odd lot, 136
Odinga, Kamau, 165–166, 167, 205,
    266
Odinga, Tamanika, 266
Officers, club, 75–79
O'Hara, Thomas E., 81, 100, 105, 108,
    120, 131
Omega Diversified Investment
    Club/Consortium (Detroit),
    61–62, 70, 236, 237, 238, 242, 259
Online resources/trading. *See*
    Internet
Option(s), 33, 35
Optional cash payment (OCP), 139,
    140
Optional cash purchases, 140
Orders, kinds of, 135–136
Organizational costs, and legal
    structure, 41
Organization Investment Club
    (Beaumont, Texas), 17–18, 38
Outlook, The, 197, 220
Over-the-counter markets, 136, 174.
    See also NASDAQ (National
    Association of Securities
    Dealers Automated System)

Parker, Reginald L., 161
Partnership, operating club as, 28,
    42–54
    agreement, 42, 43–51

Partnership, operating club as
    (*Continued*)
  vs. incorporating, 28
  primary advantage, 42
  registering, 52
  taxes, 42
  termination, 49–50, 75
Partnership agreement, sample
    (Articles 1–20; Figure 4.1), 43–51
  accounting and audits, 48
  amendment, 50
  arbitration, 50
  bank of the partnership, 43
  capital contributions, 45–46
  compensation, 47
  dissolution, 50
  investments, 46
  liability of partners, 48
  loans, 46–47
  management, 45
  meetings, 44
  membership, 43
  name, character of business and
      term of partnership, 43
  notices, 50
  profits and losses, 47
  termination of partner's interest,
      or partner's death, 49–50
  title to partnership property, 47
  voting, 44–45
  withdrawal of a partner, 49
Performance measurement, 120–126
  by company size, 122–124
  by industry, 120–122
  by stock's growth potential,
      124–125
  surveying club's results, 120,
      125–126
  table for each stock holding,
      125–126
Perry-Mason, Brandon, 249
Perry-Mason, Gail, 36, 163, 164, 166,
    182–183, 246, 249, 250, 251
Philanthropy, 228–229. *See also* Social
    consciousness/activism
Pooling money, cultural traditions
    for, 9–10
Portfolio, evaluating/reviewing
    club's, 98–99, 120
Portfolio Evaluation Review
    Technique (PERT), 214

Portfolio Management Guide, 214
Precious metals, 35
Preferred/common stock, 172–173.
    See also Stock(s)
Price(s), high/low (in stock tables),
    179–180
Price/earnings (P/E) ratio, 181–182,
    183
Price-to-book values figures can be
    found, 184
Principia Plus database, 266
Private companies, 173
Private placement, raising expansion
    money through, 240
Professional corporation (PC), 41
Progressive 20 Investment Club, 75
Prospectus (entrepreneurial
    venture), 234, 241
Proxy, 166
Prudential Securities, 129
PULA Project Investment Club
    (Luling, Louisiana), 165, 205,
    266
Pyramid model, 33–36

Quicken (Web site), 226
Quick & Reilly (discount broker), 130

Raleigh, North Carolina: Black
    Women Investment Corporation,
    71, 87–89, 90
Real estate, 35, 52, 54, 78, 80, 156,
    230–236
  benefits, 230–231
  capital appreciation, 230
  cash for, 232
  commercial, 54, 234–236
  committee, 78
  development, 80
  hands-on/hands-off, 233
  income, 231
  leverage, 231
  limited partnerships, 233, 234–236
  mortgages, 232
  REIT (real-estate investment
      trust), 156, 233, 234–236
  sources of money for investing in,
      232
  tax advantages, 231
Recordkeeping. *See* Investment
    club(s): recordkeeping, 104–126

Recovery/recession, 169–170
Regional stock exchanges, 174
Registration:
    legal structure of club, 52, 56–61
    stock, 74
Reinvesting earnings/dividends,
    97–98. *See also* Dividend
    reinvestment plans (DRIPs)
REIT (real-estate investment trust),
    156, 233, 234–236. *See also* Real
    estate
Rental Housing On Line, 232
Retired shares (corporate buybacks),
    199
Retirement, 259, 261, 269, 272–274
    component of financial planning,
        261
    Individual Retirement Account
        (IRA), 259, 269
    planning worksheet (Figure 15.5),
        273
    sources of funds (three), 272
Retreats, annual, 89
Return on equity (ROE), 184
Risk(s), 30–36
    aggressive growth, 32
    categories of, 32
    growth, 32
    income, 32
    safety of principal, 32
Risk pyramid model (levels of
    investment risk), 33–36
Risk tolerance, 30–31, 35–36, 123,
    125
    assessment test (Figure 3.2), 37
    classes of people (three), 35–36
    and diversification, 96, 123 (*see also*
        Asset allocation)
    factors, 30–31
    high roller, 36
    investment objective, 30
    moderate, 36
    rate of return, 31
    staunch conservative, 35
    time, 30
Robert Van Securities, 185, 188
Roth IRA, 269
Round lot, 136
Rukeyser, Louis, 205
Rule of 5, 191
Rule of 72 (Figure 1.3), 14

Russell, Frederick C., 8–9
Russell 2000 Index, 171

Saving *vs.* investing, 10
Schwab (discount broker), 129, 130,
    134, 147, 148–149, 156, 201
S-corporation, operating club as, 41,
    61–62, 67
    income tax return (Form 1120S)
        (Figure 4.4), 63–66
    vs. limited liability company, 67
    requirements, 62
Securities, buying/selling, 127–149
    with brokers (*see* Brokers/
        brokerage firms)
    direct stock purchase (DSP), 140
    DRIPs (dividend reinvestment
        plans), 137–140
    NAIC's low-cost investment plan,
        140–145
    online trading, 145–146
    optional cash purchases, 140
    orders, kinds of, 135–136
    process, 135–137
    stocks (*see* Stock market)
    transfer of securities, 41, 52, 118
Securities, buying/selling: cost
        cutters, 137–145
    direct stock purchase (DSP), 140
    DRIPs (dividend reinvestment
        plans), 137–140
    NAIC's low-cost investment plan,
        140–145
    optional cash purchases, 140
Securities & Exchange Commission
    (SEC), 21, 54, 55, 90, 102, 166,
    190–191, 204, 226, 234, 235
    reports required by, 190–191
    Web site, 226
Securities Industry Association, 255
Securities Transfer Association, 52
Selling, tax (end of year), 118–120
S.G. Junior Investment Club (SGJIC)
    (Washington, DC), 250, 251, 252
Shareholder(s):
    activism, 165–167
    maximum number of, 55
    receiving annual reports, 185–189
    what it means to be, 171–173
Singleton, Steven, 185
Small-business loans, 52

Smith, Greg, 29–30
Social consciousness/activism, 28, 165–167, 182, 228–229, 236
Socializing at meetings, 89–91
Sole proprietorship, 41
Specialist, 136
Splits, stock, 198, 226
Standard & Poor's Corp. (S&P):
　advisory newsletter *The Outlook,* 197, 220
　Industry Groups, 121, 122
　S&P Bond Guide, 220
　S&P Industry Reports, 95, 220
　S&P Register of Corporations, Directors, and Executives, 221
　S&P Stock Guide, 220
　S&P Stock Market Encyclopedia, 220
　S&P Stock Reports, 102, 178, 185, 205, 209, 219
　S&P 400 Midcap Index, 171
　S&P 500 Index, 171, 184
　Web site, 225
Standifer, Eric, 188
Statement of consolidated earnings (Figure 11.3), 189
St. George's Investment Club (SGIC) (Washington DC), 75, 77, 176–178
St. George's Junior Investment Club (SGJIC) (Washington, DC), 250, 251, 252
Stock(s):
　certificates, 137
　common/preferred, 172–173
　confirmation statement, 137
　how many to own, 99–101
　investing in (part of overall financial planning), 266–268
　listed/unlisted, 136, 173–174
　lots, 136
　orders, kinds of, 135–137
　over-the-counter (OTC) market, 136
　rapidly growing economy can be bad for, 169
　splits, 198, 226
　transactions, 135–137
Stock exchanges:
　American Stock Exchange (AMEX), 136, 171, 174

New York Stock Exchange (NYSE), 136, 138, 170, 171, 174, 175, 254
　regional, 174
　specialist, 136
Stock market, 153–175
　bullish/bearish (defined), 171–172
　crashes, 155–156, 168, 182
　Dow Jones Industrial Average, 30 stocks in (Figure 10.1), 154
　games, 254–256
　indexes, 170–171
　literature, 217–224
　market order, 135
　performance of, and club performance, 167–168
Stock picking:
　blue chips (defined), 164–165
　considering industries you work in, 162–164
　considering products you consume, 157–160
　member responsibility, 79
　paying attention to your surroundings, 160–161
　portfolio, four segments, 266 (*see also* Asset allocation)
　schools of thought (growth *vs.* value), 183
　growth, 32, 95, 163, 183, 266, 268
　value, 183–184, 198, 266, 268
Stock picking: research, 79, 86, 95, 102, 149, 176–202, 203–227
　art *vs.* science, 178–179
　Challenge Tree methodology, 191–194
　clues/tip-offs, 194–199, 203–204
　corporate annual reports, 185–189
　Internet as resource, 224–227
　literature, stock market, 217–224
　NAIC stock selection tools, 206–217
　professional techniques, 182–185
　reading stock tables, 179–182
　SEC-required reports, 10-K and 10-Q, 190–194
Stock picking: tip-offs (legal), 194–199
　corporate buybacks, 199
　dividends, 196–198

insider buying/selling, 195–196
stock splits, 198
Stock Research Group (Web site), 226
Stock screens, 226–227
Stocksmart (Web site)-226
Stock splits, 198
Stock tables, reading, 178, 179–182
Stock transactions. *See* Securities, buying/selling
Stop order, 136
Strange Register, 235
Street, The (Web site), 226
Street name, 74, 137
Study teams, 96–97
Subchapter S-corporation. *See* S-corporation, operating club as

Talley, Barbara, 166
TAP investment club, 199–201
Tax(es), 28, 41, 52, 53, 56, 62, 70, 107–120, 231, 235
    filing partnership and individual tax returns, 28, 108–117
    filing as S-corporation, 62–66
    and legal structure, 41, 56, 108
    real estate, advantages, 231
    selling off stocks at end of year, 118–120
Tax-deferred/tax-free investments, 269
Tax/estate plan, 261
Tax-exempt organizations (501C.3), 70
Tax forms:
    Form SS-4 (application for tax identification number) (Figure 4.2), 53
    Form 1065 (partnership tax) (Figure 8.2), 109–110
    Form 1065 Schedule D (capital gains/losses) (Figure 8.5), 116
    Form 1065 Schedule K partnership profit/loss (Figure 8.3), 112–113
    Form 1065 Schedule K-1 partner's share of income, credits, deductions, etc. (Schedule K-1) (Figure 8.4), 114–115
    Form 1120S (S-corporation) (Figure 4.4), 63–66

Tax identification number, 52, 53, 117
TD Waterhouse (deep discounter), 130
Technical analysis, 184–185
Teenage Research Unlimited, 248
Teenagers. *See* Youth/teenagers
Television programs, 205, 247
Templeton Developing Markets Fund, 236
Thompson, Simone A., 96, 121, 259
TIF (tap into the future) Investment Club (New York), 105, 106, 199–201
Tigue, Joseph, 197
Tobacco companies, 182, 236
Training/workshops, 8, 28, 77, 88, 96, 102–103. *See also* Games, stock market
Transaction(s). *See* Securities, buying/selling
Transaction costs. *See* Cost(s)/fees
Transfer of securities, 41, 52, 118. *See also* Securities, buying/selling
Treasuries, 32, 34, 169, 259, 270

Undervalued stocks. *See* Value stocks/investing (undervalued stocks)
Unit investment trust (UIT), 271
Unity Investment Partnership (New York), 155, 156, 165
Unlimited Investment Club (for youth) (Beaumont, Texas), 18
Upside-down ratio, 191, 193

Valuation statement, 106, 107
Valuation units, 108
Value Line Investment Surveys, 95, 102, 123, 126, 148, 178, 185, 193, 205, 209, 212, 217–219
Value stocks/investing (undervalued stocks), 183–184, 198, 266, 268
Vanguard, 264
Vickers Weekly Insider Report, 196, 222
Volatility, 184
Volume (in stock tables), 181

Waiting list (replacements for member leaving group), 87
Wallace, Perry, 52–54

Wall Street Journal, 205, 222
Wall-Streetwise, 90
Washington Metropolitan
    Investment Club, 94–95, 96, 98,
    99, 123
Washington Women's Investment
    Club (WWIC), 134, 229, 230, 231,
    238, 239, 240, 242
Watson, Nate, 55, 71, 80, 128
Williams, Saundra Wall, 88, 89, 90
Williams-Robinson, Carolyn, 157,
    160
Wilshire indexes, 171
Wilson, Chris, 90, 162
Windy City Investment Club
    (Chicago), 71, 118, 209, 212, 217
Withdrawals. *See* Investment club(s):
    member withdrawals/
    terminations
Women of the Millennium
    Investment Club (New York),
    146–149
Women's Investment Growth Club,
    15
Workshops. *See* Training/workshops
WWIC. *See* Washington Women's
    Investment Club (WWIC)
Wynn, Robert, 7–8, 95, 96, 255

Yahoo!, 178, 226
Yield, dividend, 180, 184

Youth/teenagers, 18, 244–256, 259,
    260
    asset allocation model for, 260
    Black Enterprise for Teens News, 247
    consumerism, intelligent,
        247–248
    early investing start, impact on, 4
    economic impact of spending by,
        248
    forming investment clubs,
        251–254
    investing from consumer
        perspective, 249–254
    reaping benefits of investing,
        248–249
    stock market games, 254–256
Youth/teenagers: investment clubs:
    Beaumont, Texas: Unlimited
        Investment Club, 18
    Detroit: Young Investors
        Investment Club, 244, 245,
        249
    St. George's Junior Investment
        Club, 250–252
Youth/teenagers: money
    management training, 246–247

Zacks Analyst Watch, 223
Zacks Investment Research (Web
    site), 184
Zweig, Martin, 205

SUBSCRIBE TO YOUR GUIDE TO FINANCIAL EMPOWERMENT